BOYS OF THE BRULE

Centuries of Comradery on
Wisconsin's River of Presidents

The day's catch, left to right, Ward Ames, Guide Dave Sample, Donald McLennan

BOYS OF THE BRULE

Centuries of Comradery on Wisconsin's River of Presidents

ROSS FRUEN

Brule, Wisconsin

BOYS OF THE BRULE
Centuries of Comradery on Wisconsin's River of Presidents

First Edition

Published by:
Cable Publishing, Inc.
14090 E Keinenen Rd
Brule, WI 54820
Website: cablepublishing.com
E-mail: nan@cablepublishing.com

Soft cover: ISBN 9780979949425

Library of Congress Control Number: 2018951126

Front cover Photo: Gitche Gumee Camping members in front of first lodge, 1890s. Judge George H. Noyes, far left with gun in lap. Photo by Truman Ingersoll
Back cover Photos: Clock-wise from upper left, Rob Pearson (L) and Ross Fruen (R) in front of Noyes Camp, 1966
Calvin Coolidge (L) and Herbert Hoover (R) at Cedar Island, Brule River, 1928
Billy Dalrymple's (second from right) May fishing group, thigh deep in snow at Noyes Camp

Cover design by larry@lvmultimedia.com
Layout by BareBonz Design

Printed in the United States of America

DEDICATION

"…Even in August you need a fire in these north woods.

I see the wicker rocking chair, a lamp that needs rewiring.

Bats hang upside down from curtain folds, suspended until night.

They look like withered figs.

On the wall, rubber waders nudge each other

when the kitchen door bangs shut.

They're split like the bamboo rods that flicked

and bent above the Falls at midnight.

Like the post along the fence that made me call your name

one evening after sunset…"

CICELY D'AUTREMONT ANGLETON, *"Brule in August"*

The mouth of the Brule, Lake Superior *Courtesy of Amy Kenner*

TABLE OF CONTENTS

Canoe in the rain, Noyes Camp, *Courtesy of David Hyde*

GLOSSARY

OJIBWE is the name given to the Native Americans associated with the Brule River region for the past few centuries. CHIPPEWA is how the word was heard by Anglos. The Ojibwe refer to themselves as ANISHINAABE, the "First" or "Original People." The Ojibwe are a branch of the Native American sub-family of ALGONQUINS.

The Ojibwe language was passed down orally so there are a variety of spellings for words. Wherever possible the "double vowel" system is used here which is gaining in popularity and helps illustrate subtle sound inflections in pronunciation.

There are many separate bands of the Ojibwe, each with their own slightly different spellings and versions of cultural stories. Lake Superior Ojibwe seldom acted as a single entity. Different bands with different chiefs operated autonomously, joining together on occasion to support a common cause. Wherever possible, I have used information from the south shore bands closest to the Brule River.

The name of LAKE SUPERIOR comes from the French *"lac superieur"* or the uppermost lake. The Jesuits called it Lac Tracy for a while but the name did not stick. The Ojibwe call it *gitchi-gami* which Henry Wadsworth Longfellow wrote as Gitche Gumee. Superior has also been called "The Great Unsalted" or the "Freshwater Sea." During the last Ice Age it was known as Glacial Lake Duluth.

The Brule River has had a succession of names as described in the chapter, *The Name Game*. The clubs central to *The Boys of the Brule* are:

WINNEBOUJOU or the "St. Paul Club." WINNEBOUJOU is the name for the Ojibwe Trickster in folklore. Another spelling for the Trickster is "NANABUSH."

GITCHE GUMEE CAMPING CLUB (GGCC) or the "Milwaukee Club." The home of Noyes Camp, Gitche Gumee Lodge and Au Sable.

GGCC original member nicknames: Colonel (Markham), Doctor (Holbrook), Commodore (Titsworth), Judge (Noyes).

NOYES CAMP: my extended family's 7 generation home on the Brule River.

There is a subtle distinction between "Brule," the town, and, "The Brule," the river. Year round residents understand this difference. The title of the book says "The Brule" to be inclusive of the various groups of people who have occupied the river over the eons. "The Boys of Brule" (BOB) is the appellation used by my friends who visit every May.

THE BOYS OF BRULE nicknames:
Robert Pearson: BOBBO
Charlie Hullsiek: CHUCK
C, Martin Schuster: TALL PAUL
Jim Hurd: LUMBER, MR. JIMMY, THE FIDDLER
Mike Melander: MICKEY, MIKEY, ZIPPY
Tom Melander: BIG "T"
Walter M. Chambers III: DR. BUD THE FISH SURGEON
Scott Shorten: OLD DOC SHORTEN
Charles J. Michel Jr.: CHIP
Bill Lorntson: LORNY, TWO SYLABLES
Joel Hartelt: GLENCOE
Steve Duea: DU, DEWEY
Bill Wilson: WILS, DR. BEVO
Dana Fitts: DANA
Rus Emerick: RUS
Ross Fruen: ROSCOE

WENDIGO is the name of the Saunders/Lindeke lodge. This creature from Ojibwe folklore had other spellings, too.

HOLBROOK: The name Dr. Arthur Holbrook is that of the original Gitche Gumee Camping Club member and is found almost exclusively in the chapters, *The Honeymoon and the Breakup* and *North Wood Characters with Character and Dastardly Deeds*. He was a dentist. His son, Dr. Arthur T. Holbrook, was a medical Dr. and the author of *From the Log of a Trout Fisherman*. As children we called him "Dr. Chipmunk."

BRULE RIVER LEXICON
LANDING, not a Dock
COUNCIL ROOM, not a living room
They are PADDLES not oars.
It is a CANOE not a boat.

INTRODUCTION

"The Great Out of Doors Snob…talks of himself as a 'man's man' because he insists that men can only be men in the presence of their own kind and a long way from home. To him…nothing so entrances the palate as a trout he has caught on a dry fly. To him all country that is four hours' drive from home is 'God's country.' It is not surprising that the most snobbish Great Out of Doors Snob earn their livings and spend the greatest part of their lives in cities as far removed from nature as possible."

RUSSELL LYNES, *Snobs*

IT IS POSSIBLE THAT 300,000 years ago Homo Erectus males sat around the fire and shot the breeze. They had an anatomical make-up that allowed for simple primate verbalization, archaeological evidence of using fire in cultural settings and the motivation for stress release after a long day of trying to survive in a Paleolithic world. One could say, in that respect, the Boys of Brule have not evolved much as we warm ourselves in front of the massive granite Noyes Camp fireplace on a cold, early May evening.

My circle of friends, the self-anointed "Boys of Brule," may not have invented male bonding, but we certainly have perfected it. After 33 years of gathering in northwestern Wisconsin, often before ice-encrusted piles of snow in the forest have melted, our group has the rituals and duties of a long weekend on the Brule River down to a science.

With the exception of seasonal native camps, the Brule River Valley was frequented primarily by men beginning perhaps over 10,000 years ago when nomadic bands hunted the mega-mammals along the fringes of the retreating glacier. This continued up to the last quarter of the 19th Century when the sportsmen's era began. Paleo Indians were followed by a variety of native cultures becoming more sophisticated in their technology; improving tools, weapons, storage, dwellings. As Old World traders and trappers pushed west, it created competition for

Wisconsin aboriginals as they fought over territory. The Dakota and Ojibwe were present when the French and British arrived to feed the beaver-fur hat frenzy in Europe by trapping the animal to near extinction.

The Brule River provided a variety of attractions over the eons: a cornucopia for subsistence and convenience as a route to the Mississippi from Lake Superior, the wild rice stands and a path to war. Its wildlife and timber were plundered by rapacious interlopers. Voyageurs, explorers and missionaries paddled its waters. Men have used the river for proselytizing, political cronyism, to line their pockets and explore its resources and geography. Immigrants came to the region for a fresh start and the opportunity to own land. More recently, the Brule has been savored for its beauty and solitude: as an escape from technology and the constant buzz of the modern world.

My Great-grandfather George Noyes and some Milwaukee friends, Arthur Holbrook, George Markham and Judson Titsworth, began visiting the stream together in the 1880s, and the tradition of early May forays to the north woods continue unbroken to this day. The pages that follow detail, and pay homage to, those who paved the way and continue to enjoy, revere and protect the fragility and beauty of the Brule River Valley. The common strand in the essays of this book strives to illuminate the history, magic and complexity of character of the 44-mile-long Brule River, its habitués and the boreal forest that surrounds.

I wrote this book because the past matters. If we ignore or forget it, we are prone to repeat mistakes. If we fail to revel in it, we lose the inherent joy it holds. These essays are intended not only to honor my ancestors, fellow travelers and the beautiful Brule, but also to celebrate the bonding that shared experiences create.

Rivers age, as do humans, and while their waters may spill over rocks and veer off into different channels, as do the stories here, the stream shows the way to paddle with the trough of an upside down "V" holding the most water, always progressing downstream. The Boys of the Brule, from countless generations, haunt the river, and their voices continue to reverberate throughout the stately pines.

[1]

THE SIGNIFICANCE OF PLACE

"…a place is not a place until people have been born in it, have grown up in it, lived in it, known it, died in it—have both experienced it and shaped it, as individuals, families, neighborhoods, and communities, over more than one generation. Some are born in their place, some find it, some realize after long searching that the place they left is the one they have been searching for. But whatever their relation to it, it is made a place only by slow accrual, like a coral reef."

WALLACE STEGNER, *The Sense of Place*

ANCESTOR NICHOLAS NOYES LEAPT from his boat in 1635 to the shore of what would become Newbury, Massachusetts; the first Puritan to set foot on the Quascacunquen River bank where a rock commemorates the occasion with an etched "Landing Place of the First Settlers." This was the site the expatriates chose to realize their dream of independence from the Church of England.

On an autumn afternoon, my parents and sister picked me up from school in the station wagon and we headed north, roughly following the St. Croix River into Wisconsin. We only had two hours of daylight, but the fall foliage was at its brilliant peak.

After what seemed an eternity, we left Highway 27, entering a long, rutted dirt driveway lined by old-growth pines splashing through rain puddles, until reaching the end where Noyes Camp stands on a point of land created by a horseshoe bend in Wisconsin's Brule River. We exited the car and inhaled traces of cedar, firewood smoke and the scent of a crisp, clean pine forest. It was as if our family had entered a wardrobe and emerged into a Narnia-like world: magical and a bit scary. In the morning we awoke to the sights and the sounds of the stream and the woods.

A landscape becomes a place when it is infused with emotions and memories. Multi-generational locations like the Brule are anchors for my family and focal points as part of my identity, and references for comparison as my life progresses. They have a primal effect so strong as I return: almost a spatial overload that pulls me to the past. Seven generations of my family have occupied the site.

When I was in my thirties we moved to Connecticut for three years, and I suffered a palpable case of dislocation. We lived in a wonderful community, but I was homesick, missing not only family and friends but my places. The bond with my environment was much stronger than I realized.

One is tethered to a location by history, rituals, stories, the senses and experience. A place can be physical such as a home, mountain, desert, lake or river. John Winthrop's "city upon a hill" quote, written in 1630, was conceptual, as are the Pastoral Ideal and the American Dream. My ancestors believed in the essence of America before they reached its shores.

A place is fragile, as Gertrude Stein suggested when she visited her childhood neighborhood in Oakland: "There is no there, there," lamenting the destruction of her home and stable community, victims of urbanization. Disassociation occurs when the intrinsic nature of place is gone, replaced by strip malls—fast food, seasonal stores and tax accountants, coffee and yogurt shops. Placeless: they could be anywhere.

A place can be primal, ground zero as a point of comparison. Native Americans value the spirit of place. When a place of importance is altered or removed the genius loci, or protective spirit of place, is damaged. When our home at Brule burned to the ground, the pain was greater than the loss of a building. We are bound to places that form and stabilize us. A legacy is constructed on layers of events and memories and the people who shared them.

People deal with disconnection in different ways. When Aunt Patty moved to the desert near Phoenix in 1947, she built a log cabin in the White Mountains of Arizona, creating a replica of Noyes Camp nestled in the pines, with many of the original's distinctive features. Her children were able to experience a version of her ancestral summer haven.

Great-great-grandmother Hannah Cole Haskell was raised in the greenery of Vermont and married in Wisconsin. She moved first to Sierra City, California, high on the western slope of the Sierra Nevada mountain range with her husband George, and then Washoe City, Nevada, on the eastern side, to support her husband George's get-rich-quick dream of capitalizing on the gold and silver discoveries in the rough-and-tumble West. She suffered an anxiety causing unhinging.

When visiting family in Wisconsin she wrote home in a July 14, 1863, letter: *"…these green fields and trees and beautiful yards and gardens look very pleasant to me and contrast with the sage and brush of Washoe…I feel if you all were here and we were pleasantly situated, I could very well content myself…"*

Place can provoke a flood of feelings. When the members of the Gitche Gumee Camping Club at Brule argued about seemingly petty issues in 1912 like outhouses and garbage pits, the contentiousness reached a fever pitch. Neighbor Dr. Arthur T. Holbrook wrote a letter to my Great-grandfather George Noyes on behalf of his father. There had been a meeting which ended unpleasantly: *"…no one could regret more than he, his loss of self-control and the unfriendly accusations… he realizes that the matters may be of small consequence to others…but they mean so much to him in a life that is now so limited that his comfort on the Brule practically constitutes his sole pleasure…."*

Amerindians value the spirit of place. The Lake Superior Ojibwe cherish Madeline Island as their spiritual home. They call it *Monningwanekaaning*, "the place of the golden-breasted woodpecker." They had traveled far and endured much before reaching the island in Chequmegon Bay. It is thought that the Ojibwe were first pushed westward by the Black Death brought from Europe in 1350 by Europeans fishing on the Grand Banks of Newfoundland.

They were evicted from the mouth of the St. Lawrence River to the eastern edge of the Great Lakes as the bellicose Iroquois had acquired firearms from the Dutch. The European avarice for the fur trade continued to displace the Ojibwe, who found more adversaries such as the Fox tribe and later the Dakota with whom they fought for 100 years, clashing over hunting territory and wild rice beds in Wisconsin.

It is easy to understand the Ojibwe veneration of Madeline Island where they lived in peace for scores of years with all their needs, physical and spiritual, fulfilled.

"In a tribal view of the world, where one place has been inhabited for generations, the landscape becomes enlivened by a sense of group and family history. People and place are inseparable…once we no longer live beneath our mother's heart, it is the earth with which we form the same dependent relationship, relying completely on its cycles and elements, helpless without its protective embrace."

LOUISE ERDICH, OJIBWE AUTHOR,
Where I Ought to Be: A Writer's Sense of Place

The Ojibwe are returning to Madeline Island incrementally. A wiigwaam was built for the first time in many generations. It is called *Giiwedining*, the place we come home to. They have planted gardens and held ceremonies. New signs on the island are bi-lingual: both English and Ojibwe. Winona LaDuke, Ojibwe leader and author, articulates the significance of the rededication to the island: *"Denied a homeland we are without a compass. Where we were forced to live is not the place the Creator has instructed us to live. And that is why niwii giiwemin [we are coming home]. The wood pecker waits. She remains there, watching, centuries of humans come and go, and she remains. Each time I am present on the Island, I look up and see the golden-breasted woodpecker and I know I am home."*

It is common for us to appreciate the grandeur of America while thumbing through coffee table books and gazing at picture-perfect postcards, but the spirit of nature is revealed when a metaphysical bond is forged between people and landscape. This explains the veneration the Ojibwe give Madeline Island and generations of families accord the Brule River, a place where the Boys of Brule return every May.

In a world where slap-dash expansion and materialism are eradicating the uniqueness of America, it is natural to revere place. For me, Noyes Camp on the Brule River represents a mooring, a centering influence when the world knocks me off kilter. I am bound to the river.

★ ★ ★ ★ ★

"We shall not cease from exploration
and the end of all our exploring will
be to arrive where we started and
know the place for the first time."

"The Little Gidding." T.S. ELIOT

The Noyes/Holbrook Boathouse *Courtesy of Amy Kenner*

The steps to the lodge *Courtesy of Bill Weihr*

[2]

HUMAN HISTORY ON THE BRULE

"In June, 1680, not being satisfied with having made my discovery [of the Mississippi] *by land, took two canoes, with an Indian who was my interpreter, and four Frenchmen, to seek means to make it by water. With this view, I entered a river* [the Brule] *which empties eight leagues from the extremity of Lake Superior on the south side, where having cut some trees and broken about a hundred beaver dams, I reached the upper waters of said river, and then I made a portage of half a league to reach a lake* [Lake St. Croix], *the outlet of which fell into a very fine river, which took me down to the Mississippi."*

Daniel Greysolon, Sieur du Lhut, *Journal*

WHILE THE BRULE RIVER was not mentioned by name, this was the first recorded description by a European. The journal entry provides a clue why there was no mention of trout during the early accounts of the river. Trees and beavers stopped the flow and prevented habitat for fish to spawn, feed and migrate.

Daniel Greysolon du Lhut was a French soldier who came to the New World and developed a strategy for securing exclusive rights to the lucrative fur trade in the western Great Lakes region. He led a secret, unsanctioned and dangerous expedition up the St. Lawrence River and through the easternmost Great Lakes until he reached Sault Ste. Marie and the home of the Saulteurs Ojibwe, the "People of the Rapids," with whom he forged an agreement.

Du Lhut portrayed himself as a master diplomat in his journals but in actuality, he tagged along with the Ojibwe to attend the famous meeting in 1679 with the Dakota south of the western tip of Lake Superior.

"In reality, the Ojibwe and Dakotas were in charge of the events that transpired at that historic council. They effected an alliance that benefited both sides. The Dakota were eager to participate in trade, especially anxious to acquired firearms; the Ojibwe gained hunting rights in Dakota territory... They smoked the calumet together, the traditional ceremony signifying peace, and finally, creating the most compelling of kinship ties, Dakota warriors married Ojibwe women—a pact that carried more authority and social enforcement than any written treaty."

Mary Lethert Wingerd, *North Country*

It is often believed that the Ojibwe and Dakota had always been at odds. Until 1737, the two tribes, except for the occasional minor skirmish, had been allies rather than enemies. In addition to their trading relationship the two joined together to fend off attacks from raiding bands from the northwest, east and south including the Fox and Mascoutins.

An ugly incident broke the peace and the two tribes began a long period of conflict. French explorer Pierre Gaultier de Verennes, the Sieur de La Verendrye, had established the northern and westernmost European outpost, Fort Charles, on the shores of Lake of the Woods. After a severe winter, an expedition of 21 Frenchmen, including missionary Father Aineau, was dispatched to Michillimackinac to procure emergency rations. They made it fifteen miles before all 21 were slaughtered, beheaded and desecrated by a band of Dakota warriors. The Ojibwe were forced to align with their trading partners, the French, and the peace between the natives was shattered.

The transportation advantages afforded by the waterways of the Brule territory and the abundant natural resources led to a variety of tribes who came and went including Mascoutins, Potowatomi, Huron and Ottawa. As the European fur traders pushed west, a domino effect existed with the Dakota and the Ojibwe being the final natives to occupy the region.

After the fur trading era ended, a series of events conspired to attract economic activity in the Brule region once again. Wisconsin gained statehood in 1848, making the northwestern region safer for exploration and habitation. The Ojibwe signed what came to be known as the Copper Treaty in 1854. Miners rushed to the Brule-Lake Superior region, a vein of the metal was located near the river and a mining operation was started by the Percival Company. Exploratory shafts and pits revealed too little of the commodity to continue.

Many of the early Anglo movers and shakers of the Brule River Valley were not to the manor born. They were in the right place at the right time and seized opportunity when they found it. Frederick Weyerhaeuser is an excellent example. Born in 1834 in Niedersaulheim, Germany, he immigrated to the United States during a time of great turmoil and revolution in Europe. He arrived in Pennsylvania still a teenager, seeking a German community for support as he had no real skills or education nor even a rudimentary command of the English language. Frederick worked in a brewery, but as a strict Lutheran and straight arrow he was dismayed by *"how often brewers became their best customers."*

After two years brewing beer Frederick worked on a farm for $13 a month. This did not create enough capital to buy farmland in Pennsylvania and he moved to Rock Island, Illinois on the recommendation of a cousin. When he discovered the scarcity of available farmland in the area he worked building a railroad and once again in a brewery. He met and married another German, Sarah Bloedel, and his big break came when he went to work at the Mead, Smith and Marsh sawmill. His position consisted of counting logs and separating them into four different quality grades. The financial panic of 1857 drove prices down and the sawmill went bankrupt. Weyerhauser and his brother-in-law, F. C. A. Denkmann, scraped together $6,200 and bought the business at auction.

Frederick was drafted into the Union Army during the Civil War but hired a substitute to serve in his place. After the conflict ended Weyerhaeuser and Denkman expanded quickly, supplying St. Louis home builders and the Union Pacific Railway. The demand for white pine seemed infinite but the availability of prime woodlands was not. Weyerhaeuser set his sights on Wisconsin and Minnesota, a lumberman's dream: thinly populated and heavily forested.

"...the lumber industry was already almost entirely committed to working with white pine for several reasons: white pine was light and easier to float downriver than hardwoods like oak; sawmill operators preferred white pine because it was strong, durable and the grain often went in one direction; and manufacturers and salesmen desired white pine because once processed it had a shiny and attractive finish."

Luke Ritter, *Immigrant Entrepreneurship*

When Frederick first gazed at the forest surrounding Wisconsin's Chippewa River he realized that as much as he wanted to keep it all to himself, he needed help. This was the genesis of the "Weyerhaeuser Syndicate," a coalition of lumber companies, transportation entities, sawmills and other operations. The goal was to make the industry more cost effective and forward thinking. Up to this point lumber companies would flatten a region and move on to the next with no thought of the future.

Weyerhaeuser owned the Nebagamon Lumber Company which was responsible for logging in the Brule River watershed. Once an area was logged his American Immigrant Company would sell the cut-over land to farmers not only producing income from property no longer of use for timber, but also avoiding the onus of property taxes. While Frederick did deplete the regions natural resources, he spearheaded efforts for sustainability and donated 4,320 acres to jumpstart the Brule River National Forest which has grown to over 43,000 acres. Much of the additional acreage was seized due to delinquent property tax payments. The humble German immigrant tried to keep a low profile, but in his time he was America's largest landowner and one of its wealthiest citizens.

"After his wife's death in 1911, Weyerhauser spent the remainder of his days quietly tending to the garden of one of his Pasadena homes. He once told two of his children how amused he was when tour busses stopped outside his mansion and announced 'Frederick Weyerhauser, the richest man in the world, lived there…' 'If they had only realized,' son Frederick and daughter Louise Weyerhauser recounted, 'that the man spading his poppies, dressed in gardening clothes, topped most of the time with a rather worn gray sweater, was the man they were trying so hard to meet, they would have been surprised indeed.'"

LOUISE WEYERHAEUSER,
Frederick Weyerhaeuser, Pioneer Lumberman, PRIVATE PRINTING

Col. John H. Knight was born on a Delaware farm in 1836 and he went to school during the winter as the other months were devoted to manual labor on the family's land. He had his sights set on a life away from the farm. John graduated from the Albany Law School where one of his classmates was William Vilas, another important figure in Brule River history.

Soon after starting his law practice in Dover, Fort Sumter was attacked and Knight answered President Lincoln's request for 3 month volunteers. He was named 1st Lieutenant of Company H of the First Delaware Infantry Regiment stationed near Baltimore when his unit was engaged in the First Battle of Bull Run. When his 90 days were through he was promoted to Captain in the 18th United States Infantry. He participated in the Battle of Perryville, Kentucky, even though he was exhibiting symptoms of typhoid. An exploding shell rattled his spinal nerve roots, rendering him incapable of walking for 3 months. While his constitution was never the same, Knight persevered.

The Captain rejoined his unit in Chattanooga in time for the battles of Missionary Ridge and Lookout Mountain. At this point, word of his health issues reached the top brass and Knight was assigned to Detroit to be in charge of mustering, recruiting, disbursing and the handling of veterans for the state of Michigan. The Governor of Delaware then honored him with a promotion to Colonel of the First Delaware Cavalry. Knight remained in the army until 1869 when, during a visit to Washington D.C., President Ulysses S. Grant convinced him to be in charge of the Indian Agency for the Lake Superior Ojibwe, believing that the change in climate would have a beneficial effect on his well-being.

The Colonel's interest in the move was piqued when he heard of the Northern Pacific Railroad's plan to build a line from Wisconsin to the west coast. He had witnessed the effect of railroads on the Union's victory in the Civil War and, after the cessation of hostilities; he imagined the economic impact of such transportation in the untapped region of northern Wisconsin. He assumed the role of Indian Agent in Bayfield, Wisconsin, on June 30, 1869, and from that point on, concentrated his efforts in the development of the region.

After a short stint at the agency, Knight put his law degree to work and invested in real estate, moving a short distance down the peninsula to Ashland in 1880 when he started the Superior Lumber Company.

"John H. Knight was the first person to build a summer home on the Brule River, and he played a strong political role in the Chequamegon Bay Region… Knight's interests were not strictly relegated to conservation since he also made his fortune as the founder of the Superior Lumber Company. One newspaper credited Knight with establishing the Brule River as a vacation area, reporting ironically that 'it was on the Brule that Colonel John H. Knight planned and carried out a greater Ashland,

cleared the forest and made northern Wisconsin not only a playground, but a rich and prosperous country.' Knight invited a number of politicians to visit him in northern Wisconsin to enjoy this 'wonderland.' These men included...Senator William Vilas of Wisconsin.... According to the paper, it was around the campfire that these men planned the economic development of Wisconsin and Minnesota. This was, of course, the same economic development that transformed the landscape into cutover."

CHANTAL NORRGARD, *Seasons of Change:*
Labor, Treaty Rights and Ojibwe Nationhood

★ ★ ★ ★ ★

There was comradery and cronyism around the campfire, and not a little money to be made. Knight's first wife, Susan Clark, died in 1867. He then married her sister, Ella. The Colonel had a total of 7 children and spent the rest of his life in Ashland, and on the Brule, dying in 1903.

Wisconsin Senator William Vilas had a head start in life. His Grandfather Moses was a pioneer Vermont farmer and his father, Levi, expanded the family fortune with real estate investments. After his graduation from law school, the Civil War beckoned and William rose to the rank of Lt. Colonel. He served under General Grant at Vicksburg and a bronze statue depicting Vilas in a gallant pose, commissioned by his widow, Anna, stands at the battle site. After Appomattox, Vilas was a professor at the University of Wisconsin Law School and his holdings grew exponentially. Vilas owned a sawmill, a cranberry bog, real estate and timber lands.

The Senator had joined forces with his Albany Law School classmate, Knight, who wore many hats in northern Wisconsin, including the part time position of Bayfield Land Office agent. Knight had insight into the most valuable tracts of land in the region. This was an unstoppable combination: Knight's inside information and Vilas' access to capital. They partnered in the Superior Lumber Company. An example of their shrewd business acumen was the sale of a parcel of land to Frederick Weyerhaeuser for $15.62 an acre. They had paid $1.99. The two men expanded their empire by operating a stone quarry business in the Chequamegon Bay region.

By the time Vilas became Postmaster General in President Cleveland's cabinet, his net worth was estimated at $300,000. As Secretary of the Interior he was a proponent of logging, dam building and the policy of Indian Land Allotment.

He was vilified regarding his removal of Republican postmasters throughout the nation and replacing them with Democrats. Upon leaving the Senate in 1897, William practiced law in Madison and grew his investments.

Once the timber was removed, the denuded forest land was worth little. Knight and Vilas sold the cut-over land mostly to immigrants realizing their dreams of land ownership and farming. They saved themselves some original growth forest land along the Brule River to use for their own enjoyment, building the Knight-Vilas, or Nississhin lodge, just north of Ashland Lake and close to what would become the Gitche Gumee Camping Club property.

"Henry Clay Pierce lived large in the Gay Nineties. His Vandeventer Place mansion stood out for its gaudiness on the city's [St. Louis] *most fashionable street, where extravagance reigned. He entertained regally in a ballroom large enough to hold one hundred people, with an elevator that carried up iced champagne from the hotel sized kitchen. To build his manse, he spent $500,000 (some even say $800,000), a sum almost inconceivable at the time* [more than $12.5 million in 2018 dollars]. *It boasted nothing as common as wallpaper: only silk tapestries and wood paneling covered its walls. His life practically defines the term 'robber baron.'"*

Carol Fenning Shepley, *Movers and Shakers,*
Scalawags and Suffragettes: Tales from Bellefontaine

During the Gilded Age, the American Dream took a beating. Increased industrialization, poverty and the increasing visibility of concentrated wealth began to cause discontent in the working class. Long hours and low pay dimmed the optimism the founding fathers of the U.S. engendered. Inspirational, rags to riches Horatio Alger stories became very popular. The common theme suggested that hard work and high moral standards paved the road to success. Some biographers tried to equate Henry Clay Pierce's road to wealth with these feel good stories, but it really wasn't accurate. He was born in St. Lawrence, New York, to Dr. Dyer and Mary Pierce. It is true that as a 16 year-old Pierce left home and traveled the St. Lawrence River to Chicago, where he proceeded to St. Louis and took a job as messenger in a bank.

Pierce forged his fortune the old fashioned way, he married well. His wife was Minnie Finlay, daughter of the Scottish owner of Waters Oil Company. Her father, John, took a liking to Henry and made him a partner in the Waters-Pierce Oil

Company. Pierce had a knack for the oil business, developing a virtual monopoly in the nascent Mexican petroleum market while profiting from railroad and shipping concerns. At one point in the early 1900s his wealth was estimated at $60,000,000 but it dissipated through lawsuits and business reversals. He heard about the Brule River from St. Louis associates and purchased slightly over 4,000 upriver acres. Pierce spent millions sculpting his personal paradise. He had homes in St. Louis and New York, but his passion was for his Brule River sanctuary. He was more of a recluse than a swashbuckler like his Cedar Island predecessor, Frank Bowman. Fences and "No Trespassing" signs were strategically placed.

Knight, Vilas and Pierce were on a collision course. The lumber men logged the upper Brule and sent the timber downstream right through Pierce's Cedar Island holdings. Henry was incensed and took the two partners to court: *The log drive, argued Pierce, represented an act of trespass that prevented the 'actual, peaceable, and undisputed possession and enjoyment' of his land. Pierce lost his suit, for state law allowed log drives along all navigable watercourses. But the case demonstrates how men like Pierce viewed their wilderness property and the extent to which they would go to protect their ability to retreat into nature."*

JAMES W. FELDMAN, *A Storied Wilderness*

Henry Clay Pierce died in 1927, the year before the Coolidges and their entourage used his estate as a Summer White House. It was just as well. He would have hated the disruption.

No name looms larger in the history of the Brule River than that of Joe Lucius. He was a master of all trades: builder, hotelier, caretaker, guide and canoe builder. Born in Kirby, Ohio, on February 3, 1871 to parents of Belgian ancestry, the family relocated and homesteaded in Solon Springs, Wisconsin near the sources of both the St. Croix and Brule Rivers. Lucius headed to Lake Superior and worked off and on in Captain Alexander McDougall's shipyards until 1895 when he moved with his wife, Helen, to the Brule where he began to build his cedar home on the high western bank on the downstream end of what is called Joe's or Lucius Lake in his honor. Some extra cabins were erected as Joe and Helen ran a fishing and hunting camp for 3 years.

Lucius was instrumental to the Gitche Gumee Camping Club, and Noyes Camp in particular, as a builder and a man with knowledge of the river and its valley. Arthur T. Holbrook, son of the GGCC founder, and 2 friends visited Joe and Helen's camp to hunt deer one autumn. One evening, exhausted from a long day, they hit the sheets around 7 PM. They fell asleep immediately and later Holbrook heard the stove door slam shut and saw the lantern light in the Lucius' cabin and proceeded to wake his buddies to prepare for the morning hunt: *"….[I] gave the signal, 'All up!'…We splashed ourselves with the cold water from the granite ware basins, chattered our teeth as we pulled on half-dried socks and heavy high-cut boots, bundled up, and stepped into the pitch black and cold morning for a quick rush to Joe's door and breakfast. You have probably guessed it right: Joe was in his heavy woolen night shirt, Helen was just disappearing into her bedroom, and the clock on the shelf registered 10:30* [PM]."

Dr. Arthur T. Holbrook, *From the Log of a Trout Fisherman*

Lucius constructed many lodges on the upper river and his meticulous craftsmanship is evident at Noyes Camp where he supervised the replacement lodge for the one destroyed by fire. Lucius added special touches to every project whether it was a summer home, a canoe or even the cribbage board he made for our family. A note accompanied the gift: *"My compliments to Gitche Gumee Lodge on the Brule. This cribbage board is made of woods of many countries. The black dot in the middle is from the first passenger and freight boat on Lake Superior. Built on Lake Erie in 1834, came to Lake Superior before the locks were built. It was hauled around the falls with oxen.*

Joe Lucius"

Joe and Helen were so devoted to the river and its residents that they named their two children after Dr. Arthur Holbrook and his wife: a son, Holbrook, known as "Holly," and a daughter, Josephine. Joe's imprint, even when Helen and he eventually moved back to Solon Springs, is indelibly stamped in the annals of Brule lore.

In 1885, a rail line stretching from Superior to Ashland stopped in the town of Brule. From there the campers could reach their destination via native canoes or a bumpy wagon ride on an ill-defined trail through the woods. Some preferred to walk the five miles.

Within a few years, the Duluth, South Shore and Atlantic Railroad Service brought the vacationers even closer to their camps. The trestle was just below the

Winneboujou Club and whistle stops could be arranged. Even if the train didn't stop at the river, a newspaper was often flung by a conductor for the campers to catch up on the news.

The early 1890s were boom times for the town of Brule, and many of its business people optimistically predicted an economy to rival Superior. The area was home to ten logging camps and a sawmill. The fertile ground in the Superior Lowlands, albeit with a short growing season, seemed perfect for farming. In 1892 the *Superior Citizen* reported the opening of many new businesses. Hotels included the York House, the Brule Hotel and the Krause House, heralded as the area's finest hostelry. Frank Porter was the first proprietor of the Brule Railroad Depot, which included some beds and a small eatery. A moose head adorned one of the walls, purportedly the last such hooved mammal killed in the region.

There were nine saloons, although the decibel level was said to reach that of twice as many. Delmonico's Restaurant and Saloon and J.N. Christie's on Main Street were popular, with the latter consisting of a saloon on the first floor and a music hall on the second. Two boardinghouses were available for lumbermen. Three general stores were in operation offering groceries, furniture, hardware, logging supplies, hay, flour and home furnishings. The town butcher was Lansworth and Son.

The Homestead Act of 1862, expansion of the railroad system, treaties with the Ojibwe and marketing drove an influx of people to the north woods. The Brule River Land and River Improvement Company was champing at the bit to sell lots in the region. The advertising in May 1892's *Inland Ocean* read, "Brule will be the Largest Town Between Superior and Ashland." Many Finnish-speaking immigrants came to eke out a living by farming. Potatoes and other produce were staples sold to logging camps.

Brule area homesteaders depended on supplies delivered by boat from the Twin Ports of Duluth and Superior. Those needing to travel to Ashland or Superior waited at the mouth of the Brule and hitched a ride. An improvement in the quality of life occurred when roads were carved through the forest and cows could be driven to Brule.

In the winter many Finns moonlighted by working in logging camps after their harvests were stored underground in root cellars lined with logs chinked with moss. Lack of money prevented many of the farmers from owning guns, ammunition and horses, making protein difficult to obtain. Winter was even harder as blizzards immobilized the communities for days. The farmers sometimes competed with predators for survival as Oscar Ekstrom wrote in his memoirs: *"One day I was hauling hay for a neighbor with an ox, when I came face to face with several timber wolves. I kept a tight grip on my pitchfork, the ox stared sullenly, and when the wolves finally slunk away, my cap settled down on my head as my hair returned to normal from an upright position."*

★ ★ ★ ★ ★

Boys brought their guns to school in the morning, placed them in the gun rack and hunted for dinner on the way home. A depression in 1893 brought economic development in the Brule region to a screeching halt as it did in most of the United States. Fifteen-thousand businesses and 500 banks closed and unemployment surged to 18% nationwide and much higher in Wisconsin.

The summer people who congregated on the banks of the Brule formalized their previously loose arrangements in the 1890s and soon occupied most of the land on the upper river. In addition to Winneboujou and Gitche Gumee came Cedar Island, Nississhin, McDougall, Kline's, White Birch and others. In 1906 the Club People fended off an attempt to create a mile-long public access on each side of the stream, fearing that marauding "meat" fishermen would drain the Brule of its last trout.

The Noyes family's long history of conservation efforts began with my great uncle, Haskell Noyes Sr., whose name was spoken in the same breath as people like Aldo Leopold. He was an ardent champion of the Brule River fishery and had a special affinity for Wisconsin's game wardens. In 1927, when there was no money in the coffers, he purchased new uniforms for them. They featured a blouse-style jacket with badger lapel pins, and the breeches were tucked into 10" rise boots.

Neighbor Dr. Arthur T. Holbrook paid Haskell Noyes the ultimate compliment. *"I can think of no man in my acquaintance who has put as much time, energy—and money, too—into any similar crusade as has Haskell Noyes for what he deemed important and best for the welfare of the Brule River."*

For over 85 years the "Watch," a gold pocket style, has been awarded by the Noyes family to the winner of the Haskell Noyes Efficiency Award. It is a highly coveted honor presented to the year's top Wisconsin game warden. Cousin Bob Banks continues the family's heritage of conservation as long-time President of the Brule River Preservation Society. Cousin Chris Noyes is on the board of the Nature Conservancy.

Dr. Arthur T. Holbrook continued his father's tradition of May comradery on the Brule, naming the group "The Boys Busy Life Club: perennials who braved May frosts and snows." His stories of their activities closely precurse our annual outing: *"After a grand day all came back for the cocktail hour, when the yarns of the day's experiences were related…before we sat down to dinner, enlivened by jokes, gags, impromptu speeches, and songs galore."*

For much of its history the Brule River was decidedly a male dominated stream. The south shore rivers of Lake Superior were known to the Ojibwe as "the roads to war." The voyageur and logging eras were populated by rough and rowdy men. The camping influx of the late 1800s introduced women and children to the stream in summer. The wives of the Milwaukee Club first visited in 1887 and in the early years the families occupied the campsite in August. Early May at Noyes Camp, however, remains the domain of "The Boys of Brule," who still gather on the banks of the crystalline stream.

Northwestern Wisconsin Ojibwe camp

Douglas County lumber camp

[3]

THE BRULE A JEWEL, WITH TROUT NO DOUBT

"There is a little valley, or rather lap of land, which is one of the quietest places in the whole world. A small brook glides through it, with just murmur enough to lull one to repose and the occasional whistle of a quail, or tapping of a woodpecker, is almost the only sound that ever breaks in upon the uniform tranquility... If ever I should visit for a retreat whither I might steal from the world and its destruction, and dream quietly away the remnant of a troubled life, I know of none more promising than this little valley."

WASHINGTON IRVING, *The Legend of Sleepy Hollow*

★ ★ ★ ★ ★

TODAY'S RESIDENTS OF THE Brule River are reverential to the point of religious fervor. The stream is a refuge from the increasing noise and static of the modern world. It was not always seen as a beautiful sanctuary, however, but rather a means of survival, a highway to the Mississippi, Lake Superior or the (Folle Avoine) wild rice beds, an asset to plunder, a place to proselytize, a path to war or a damn nuisance depending on the period and the nationality of the visitant.

Paleo Indian men banded together to hunt the mega-mammals such as mastodon, bison and mammoths as the retreating ice sheet of the Wisconsin Glacial Episode opened up land where vegetation grew about 11,000 years ago. At one stage Glacial Lake Brule existed in the current river valley with its head near Winneboujou.

The waters of Glacial Lake Duluth, eventually receding to form Lake Superior, left large amounts of clay along the river bottom of what would eventually become the Brule north of the Copper Range while the retreating ice sheet dumped rock, sand and gravel to the south, prompting the stream's two distinct personalities.

Initially the Brule River was a much larger stream flowing swiftly southward to the Mississippi. When a continental divide was formed, the smaller Brule flowed north and the St.Croix south, creating a thoroughfare for migrating caribou. The herds could total well over one-hundred animals. The high banks of the valley were perfect vantage points for aboriginal hunters.

"In the sandy wastes of the Upper Brule, the stream is mostly placid and runs through a broad valley…Adjacent to this valley there are many square miles of land without any streams or watercourses. Rain and snow that fall on the gently rolling barrens sink into the sandy soil and find an outlet at the bottom of the Brule Valley in the form of springs, thousands of springs of clear, cold water.

LEIGH AND RICHARD GERRARD, *The Brule River of Wisconsin*

For some men, the experience of traveling via the Brule was downright miserable. Reverend William Boutwell complained bitterly of the experience in 1832 when he was accompanied by an attachment of U.S. soldiers. And they were paddling downstream! The military escorts were landlubbers and by the time the flotilla limped into "The Great Unsalted" they were bruised, battered, cut and sprained. The remnants of their canoes were even worse. Boutwell ranted, *"Never was I in a much worse hole than here… But what is a matter of no little surprise to me is that this is the highway to two or three posts, and yet you would hardly suppose a rat could even pass…Our canoe was filled with sticks, leaves, bugs, worms and spiders of every kind… Of all the streams I have seen this is the most dismal for ten to fifteen miles from its head."*

Not long after Wisconsin gained statehood in 1848, Geologist David Dale Owen disparaged the Brule region, calling it *"hopelessly arid"* and not worth the time to survey. He continued, *"Fish, frogs and waterfowl, in our day at least, be the only inhabitants. The prevalence of venomous insects in such insufferable quantities destroy all comfort or quiet by day or night…myriads of gigantic musquitoes carry on incessant war against the equanimity of the unfortunate traveler."*

★ ★ ★ ★ ★

It didn't take long for the American mercenaries to see the Brule River Valley as an economic windfall, not long after the region had been stripped of virtually all its fur-bearing animals. Logging camps and the railroads polluted and gouged the stream, destroying trout habitat and raising the water temperatures. Commercial fisherman stripped the river of much of its native brook trout population. Still, some naively believed nature and commerce could coexist effortlessly along the stream.

"BRULE—There is timber galore and Every Necessary Element to Make a Great Metropolis Sinuous and straight, now rapid and now slow, now murmuring soft, now roaring in cascades, there art the same romantic stream which charms today and charmed a hundred years ago. It is in this sparkling river that the finest trout in all the north is caught and along the banks the modern Isaak Walton has built cozy cabins and inviting retreats. In the depths of forest primeval the axe of the pioneer, though still ringing, has reared the city—one of those wonderful developments of advancing west— where a few years ago none but the red man and the wild beast had found a home are the dwelling places of a happy and prosperous people. If one could look forward two or more decades what changes he could foretell in the development of this great section of the country. He would see a mighty metropolis where now the modest city stands, and myriads of finely cultivated farms would mark the spot now covered by dense forests. The trains of today will become great highways and instead of two there will be dozens of railroads."

Superior Evening Telegram, OCTOBER 14, 1893

★ ★ ★ ★ ★

Cedar Island Estate is a magical place. It was created by Henry Clay Pierce of St. Louis from his 4,160 acre parcel of land in the cedar and first growth white pine forest of the upper river. Pierce was an ardent wilderness camper and followed unfettered nature west when he heard of a wonderful trout stream, the Brule. The island itself is small, only 150' in diameter and formed by a momentary fork in the river.

An octagonal log residence, finished with weathered cedar bark, resembles a picturesque English cottage, particularly in the frequent light mist or fog, and sits on the island with the always beautifully groomed lawn sloping gently to the stream.

The building has a circular living room, eight bedrooms, four bathrooms, and the screened porch affords a view of the river and canoes lashed to cast bronze frogs holding rings, straining at their ropes and swaying in the current. The interior is constructed with polished red cedar walls and decorated with brass beds, oriental rugs, French wicker furniture, Italian oak paneling and a maple piano with gold inlay.

The bathrooms feature white marble with "no gray streaks" as mandated by Pierce. The living room walls were initially covered with tan colored burlap and the red leather chairs were painted with hand-painted wildlife scenes. Its chandelier is accented with small, hazy glass canoes and polished oak paddles.

A small footbridge arching over the water and lighted by bronze owl, squirrel and bear fixtures, provides access from the mainland where a similar bungalow houses the dining room, the marble-lined kitchen and servants' quarters. The mahogany dining room table, with clover-leaf accents, is 14 feet long and accommodates 30 diners. Originally a vault protected the silverware and there was a "dairy" room as well as one for "refrigerating." The library is fashioned from hand-carved Italian oak. The lamps in the room are made of deer legs with polished hooves. The overhead lighting consists of chandeliers made to resemble fish in netting. Pierce spared no expense. He brought Italian masons and Swedish cabinet makers to the wilderness to complete his extravagant get-away. It took 20 years and $1.25 million to turn the low lying marshland into an exquisite retreat.

The trunks of the white cedars lining the river banks lean and twist toward the water from each bank with their dense web-like foliage providing a low canopy while the pines tower over all the other trees. The shallow spring ponds of Cedar Island number over a dozen. Countless plumes of gravel and sand spurt from the bottom into the crystal-clear water. The various stocked lagoons, ponds, holes and sloughs on the east side of the river are home to a large trout population, and catching fish there is considered "dumb fishing," like shooting them in a barrel. The trout are placed in various locations depending on size and specie.

The fish are so tightly packed they can be caught in a net and are so used to being hand fed they have little fear of humans and strike almost anything from a piece of chewed gum to a pebble dropped in the water. On a warm summer day, the temperature seems to dip a few degrees when one paddles into the middle of the Cedar Island property. Perhaps it's the combination of the spring-fed ponds and the lattice work of the low hanging trees or maybe my imagination. Watercress floats on the water and Forget-Me-Nots grow on the fallen, partially submerged logs.

In 1905 Pierce fenced off the ponds, limiting them to personal use and laying the ground work for an eventual commercial hatchery. He hired "waterscaper" Fred Mather to design his private fishing paradise of connected spring ponds. Only fly fishing with barbless hooks was allowed. Signs were posted, gates installed and caretakers and watchmen assigned to stand guard. The changes were controversial, but had these precautions not been undertaken, the banks of the Brule would have been trampled and the trout decimated.

Pierce was proud of his trout propagation efforts in Hatchery Pond, also known as "Pierce Hatchery #7." In 1893 he detailed the operation, *"A chain of ponds or small lakes, really a series of springs, extends parallel with the river, opposite to [Cedar] Island…and is connected, at one end of, through screens the river. One of these lakes I have a trout hatchery of 3,000,000 eggs capacity, annually. The lakes are now filled with wild trout which weigh 1/3 to 3 pounds each. My hatchery is to keep up the supply, and I turn the surplus hatch into the Brule River, for the benefit of the brotherhood."*

★ ★ ★ ★ ★

Thirty-one structures were added to the property including a power plant, canoe repair shed, lumber mill, livestock barns and a zoo featuring black bears. When the estate was used as the Summer White House in 1928, soldiers appropriated one of the smaller buildings to house passenger pigeons used for communication.

Early in his presidency, Calvin Coolidge had dismissed fishing as the hobby of "old men and boys." Advised that he had potentially alienated millions of voters, he tried fishing for pike with worms in South Dakota. "Humdingers" or "Garden Hackle," as the bait was called in the Brule area, was anathema to local sportsmen and he was soon converted to a dry fly angler when he chose the river as his summer retreat.

"Col. Edward W. Starling, official summer White House inspector, had returned to Washington at last with a description that sounded like the land at the end of a rainbow: high altitude, cool nights, few flies, commodious quarters, beautiful trees, abundant game, and trout—500,000 of them, stocked bred, liver-fed for 30 years— brook trout, lake tout, steelhead trout—yes even, rainbow trout."

Time Magazine, Vol. XI, No. 24, June 11, 1928

★ ★ ★ ★ ★

Not everyone was impressed by Silent Cal's intrusion into their hidden haven. The Brule River Valley hadn't been so trampled and commercialized since the logging era. Despite Coolidge's desire for solitude, his entourage included 90 soldiers from Minneapolis' Fort Snelling's 3rd Infantry Regiment, 10 Secret Service agents, 14 servants and 75 members of the press. A cottage industry with a carnival-like atmosphere littered Wisconsin Highway 27 as peddlers hawked souvenirs. The spectacle was disturbing to long-time residents and some spent the entire summer elsewhere.

The local Ojibwe were divided in their thoughts about the presence of the President. The tribal council of the Lac Courte Oreilles *"....came up with the idea of giving the president a name at a tribal induction ceremony so that Coolidge would put in a 'good word' for the community. However, in order to give the president a name they had to seek the help of a person who had the ceremonial authority to do so. When they asked John Mink, a respected elder, for his assistance, Mink responded, 'You want me to dream up a name for some goddamn white man? I don't care what he is president of.'"*

Chantal Norgaard, Seasons of Change

Lillian Cocroft decided to honor the President with the traditional Winneboujou greeting: a salute from the club's tiny toy cannon. The kindly, diminutive English nanny pulled the cannon by its rope through the woods with her retinue of children trailing behind, holding hands. When the Coolidge cortege passed, she fired a blank, precipitating a flurry of activity as Secret Service agents materialized from behind massive pines and converged upon the equally startled Miss Cocroft and her small entourage.

In July 1928, a strained form of Presidential male bonding took place on the Brule River. Coolidge had decided not to seek re-election for a variety of reasons but mostly because his heart wasn't in it. His 16-year-old son Calvin Jr. had died in 1924 from a staph infection that had attacked a foot blister. The President still grieved. Herbert Hoover came to Wisconsin to seek the President's blessing after his nomination at the Republican convention. There was no love lost between the two men. Silent Cal took a swipe at his Secretary of Commerce, saying *"for six years that man has given me unsolicited advice—all of it bad."*

Hoover, probably the most proficient Presidential fly fisherman, responded in kind, *"Being a fundamentalist in religion, economics and fishing, [he] began his fishing career for common trout with worms. Ten million fly fisherman at once evidenced disturbed minds. Then Mr. Coolidge took to a fly. He gave the Secret Service guards great excitement in dodging his backcast and rescuing flies from trees."*

Although political comradery was nowhere to be found, the President gave Hoover his unenthusiastic, tacit approval. He was elected, and the country slid into the Great Depression. The River of Presidents came close to having a native son in the executive branch of the government. Wisconsin Senator Irving Lenroot had his own lodge on the Brule. During the 1920 Republican Convention, party leaders floated the progressive Lenroot for Vice President as the perfect balance to the conservative presidential candidate, Warren Harding. As the convention wound down and the Republican party bosses left Chicago, the delegates took over and the hero of the 1919 Boston Police Strike, Calvin Coolidge, beat out the candidate from the Badger State.

General Dwight D. Eisenhower found the solitude of Cedar Island restorative after World War II when he spent time there with his friend and comrade General Mark Clark as the guest of John Ordway who had purchased the Pierce estate. Ike's stated "number 1 plan" for rest and recuperation was simply "to sit on a bank and fish."

Ike was characteristically modest when interviewed by the Milwaukee Sentinel in Superior in 1947 referring to himself as a *"persistent if not skillful"* fisherman and when reminded Presidents Coolidge and Hoover had plied the waters of the Brule, he parried, *"and now you've got a lowly soldier."*

While he enjoyed the Brule's curative powers, he returned to public life for 15 more years as Army Chief of Staff, the military commander of NATO and President of Columbia University. Eisenhower returned to Brule in 1952 for some rumination and fishing at Cedar Island before accepting the nomination at a fractious Republican convention.

There are unsubstantiated reports from usually reliable sources that Eisenhower surreptitiously visited the Brule during his Presidency. Air Force One would land at the Cedar Island landing strip on a Friday and Ike was shuttled to the estate where he would fish and relax until Sunday when he returned to Washington. During the interim, the President's plane stopped at the Strategic Air Command base just west of Duluth for refueling and maintenance.

★ ★ ★ ★ ★

While Coolidge and Eisenhower were the most heralded visitors to the river, others preceded them. U.S. Grant fished the Brule in 1870 in between his service as Commanding General of the United States Army and President. He proclaimed, *"If I ever get some money I will buy some land here."*

Grover Cleveland visited the river in 1880 at the lodge of William Vilas and John Knight, owners of the Superior Lumber Company. They managed to save the portion of the forest that surrounded the location. Vilas was a close friend and a trusted advisor to the future President Cleveland who subsequently named him to his cabinet, first as Postmaster General and then Secretary of the Interior. The lumber baron later won election to the U.S. Senate. For Coolidge, Eisenhower and others the Brule provided freedom and escape from their stressful roles serving their country at the highest levels.

★ ★ ★ ★ ★

My mother Leslie's generation loved going to the Brule, playing outdoors with all the cousins and exploring the river and the forest. Noyes Camp at that time was run with an iron fist by my Great-grandmother Agnes Haskell Noyes. Vestiges of Victorian child-rearing were in evidence, and children were expected to be neither seen nor heard. Mom admitted to fearing her Grandmother Agnes more than loving her. They ran through the woods as Native Americans with headdresses as the Ojibwe presence was still strong in the valley. The children were sent on upstream boondoggles to fetch the lightly mineralized water from "The Spring." They were dispatched to the Pine Barrens to pick blueberries, hopefully returning with enough to make muffins or a pie. They carried their pails through the woods on pine-needle-carpeted trails, passing rotting, spongy lichen and moss-covered fallen timber, trailing pine and large patches of ferns. The cousins passed mushrooms and flowers such as Trillium, Indian Pipes and the occasional Lady's Slipper. While blueberries were the main objective, wintergreen, strawberries, thimble berries, raspberries and blackberries could sometimes be found.

"Ed Saunders was miserable the spring of 1884 when he met Chris O'Brien at the Minnesota Club [St. Paul]. Mr. O'Brien asked him to go fishing with him, saying he would take him to the prettiest spot on earth and to a river where the trout were

plentiful. So together they went in May of 1884. Ed returned so improved in health after ten days on the Brule River that he and Mr. O'Brien determined to spend ten days again in this most enchanted spot."

MEMOIRS OF MRS. E.N. SAUNDERS, *Winneboujou Chronicles*

★ ★ ★ ★ ★

The good old days weren't always so great. By the 1880s Judge George Noyes and his Milwaukee friends started heading to the Brule to camp, fish and hunt. Perhaps it served as an escape from the turbulent times in Milwaukee and other large U.S. cities. By 1890 the director of the U.S. Census Bureau declared the American settlement of California signaled the end of the frontier. Yankees were looking backwards with nostalgia to what they believed were simpler times. Immigrants were flooding to the cities in search of blue-collar jobs.

Milwaukee was not homogeneous anymore. Scandinavians and Germans came to town and Republicans pushed back, proposing legislation to ban Catholic and Lutheran schools. Some referred to Milwaukee as the "German Athens," and other ethnic groups brought socialist politics and railed against the excesses of big business. The population exploded from 9,500 in the mid-1840s to 200,000 by 1890 as laborers flocked to work in the steel, iron and other industries ranging from brewing to meat packing and flour milling. The days of a clubby, Yankee enclave were long gone in Wisconsin's largest city.

The Brule River became an oasis for Great-grandfather and his sportsmen friends who camped near an Ojibwe village. Already the urge to retreat from the complications, and the increasingly strident mechanized thrum of city life, was palpable. Judge Noyes and his Gitche Gumee Camping Club friends jealously guarded the stream. Their Promised Land was not to be promoted or praised in a public, cavalier manner. The Milwaukee newspapers employed a vague code by printing, *"Judge and Mrs. George H. Noyes have gone to northern Wisconsin"* or *"Mr. George C. Markham and Dr. Arthur Holbrook are on a fishing trip to the Lake Superior country."*

Great-grandfather and his friends arrived just in time to experience the end of the early halcyon days of the sportsmen. The Ojibwe were still present in numbers. Speckled trout ruled the river before competition arrived. The Brule has a split personality. The Club People settled on the relatively placid upper half: cold, spring-fed water; sandy bottomed with a diverse range of diet options for the native fish. The lower half races to Lake Superior, dropping almost 350 feet in the last twenty-some miles. The river there is warmer, rockier and often root-beer colored from the clay banks.

While the club people were guarding their space on the Upper Brule, an English social experiment was underway near the mouth of the stream. Three thousand three hundred and three acres were purchased and named Clevedon Colony. In 1880, thirty tradesmen and their families arrived to fish, farm and saw timber. Their Eden was a noble idea but the Garden bit back, and it was done in by the weather and the economy. The community began to fail as some residents died, some moved back to England and young people married and left for better prospects. As nature began to reclaim the abandoned Clevedon Colony, others found it very alluring, at least in the summer. In July 1897, the *New York Times* commented on the odd community that occupied the previous site, "*...in this town it is different. Nobody works, nobody grumbles, everybody is well fed, and there is no strife for the possession of worldly riches. It is the queerest little town on earth. It is the laziest town in the world without exception, yet it is the most prosperous, for prosperity in this place means rest, and there is more rest here to the square yard than there is to the square mile in the Land of Nod.*"

Some 55 "turnpikers" descended on the deserted town nicknamed "Hobohurst" or "Trampville" and found the empty buildings to be their version of paradise. An election was scheduled to name town officers and settle on a name. The front runners were "Electric Chock," "Deep Water Charlie," and "Murphy the Swede." Daily chores ranged from hunting for food in the woods, fishing in the lake and the river as well as appropriating produce from the root cellars of the nearby farms. Leisure time was spent playing cards, napping, playing the harmonica and telling stories. There is no record of the election results or the fate of the "soapless and sockless," but in the interim, according to the *Times,* the men enjoyed their comradery, "*In this desolate, wild and dreary spot, where the roar of the great lakes mingles with the constant murmur of the tall, waving pine tops; where the rippling River Brule mingles its crystal clear water with the turbulent, discolored breakers of* [Lake Superior]...."

The Brule River is redolent of history. One half expects to see an Ojibwe ricing party heading upstream under an August Wild Rice Moon, the *monoomini-ke-giizis.* or a canoe laden with packs of beaver pelts as the voyageurs clad in red toques and sashes paddle from the interior to the cadence of "C'est l'aviron," en route to the annual rendezvous in Grand Portage.

At Cedar Island one can envision President Calvin Coolidge making the transition from a spinning reel to a fly casting technique under the watchful eye of John LaRock, the Dean of French-Ojibwe fishing guides. The long strand of driveway into Noyes Camp resembles the center aisle of a great cathedral with a congregation of ramrod-straight pines worshiping on the sides.

Retroscapes abound of my parents, grandparents and even the great-grandparents I never met, images created with memories, stories, perspective and imagination. The exploits of May Boys of Brule excursions, 30+ years in the rear-view mirror, are still top of mind. In addition to all our north woods activities, we cherish the opportunity to be ourselves, without the strictures of everyday life. We take a deep breath; enjoy the pristine setting and each other's company.

The Cedar Island main lodge

May's Ledges *Courtesy of Diane Beuch*

[4]

NORTH WOODS CHARACTERS WITH CHARACTER AND DASTARDLY DEEDS

"The 93-year-old Chief Buffalo making the journey to Washington, D.C., paddling a quarter of the way in a canoe to defend tribal treaty rights, speaks volumes, and so eloquently, of the sacrifice, pain and determination many have gone through to defend our legal and human rights all the while envisioning a better world for our children."

GREAT LAKES INDIAN FISH AND WILDLIFE COMMISSION,
Ojibwe Journeys

★ ★ ★ ★ ★

KECHEWAAISHKE, CALLED CHIEF BUFFALO by Americans, was born on Madeline Island into the Loon clan. He was the leader of the Lake Superior band of Ojibwe for 50 years and one of the greatest champions of Native American rights ever known. In 1852 he embarked on a difficult expedition to the U.S. Capitol with his son-in-law Benjamin Armstrong and five other Ojibwe in an effort to halt the evacuation of his people from their ancestral homeland.

The "Trail of Tears" episode in American history is thoroughly chronicled as Andrew Jackson's "Indian Removal Treaty" was implemented in 1830. The "Big Sandy Lake Tragedy" is not so well known. In October 1850, thousands of Ojibwe from 19 Michigan, Wisconsin and Minnesota bands were lured to Big Sandy Lake, fifty some miles west of the tip of Lake Superior, under the guise of receiving their annual payments and provisions guaranteed by treaty. Usually the annuity compensation was paid on Madeline Island, but the U.S. government perpetrated this contemptible migration to remove the natives from their lands in order to pounce on the vast stands of timber and veins of copper on the south shore of Lake Superior.

Winter came early and no payments were made to the Ojibwe, who began dying from starvation, exposure and illness including measles and dysentery. By December 2nd, when a partial reimbursement was given, 150 natives lay dead. The next day the surviving Ojibwe left for home with three days' provisions, refusing to stay on the shores of Big Sandy. Lakes and rivers were frozen, making water travel impossible, so they trudged east through a foot of snow. 250 more perished before the ordeal was over. The 92 year-old Chief Buffalo was tired of the broken promises and treachery and determinedly planned his pilgrimage to Washington, D.C.

The contingent, including under-chief Oshaga, 4 Ojibwe braves and interpreter Armstrong, left Madeline Island the morning of April 5, 1852, in a 24-foot birch bark canoe and slept under the stars. They had departed with meager provisions and depended on fish and game caught en route for sustenance. As they traveled, signatures were added to their petition at various Ojibwe villages, intended for the politicians, as the canoe hugged the south shore of Lake Superior and the western edge of Lake Michigan.

Their trip was not sanctioned by the federal government and they were plagued by bad weather, scarcity of funds and bureaucracy every step of the way. Upon reaching New York Benjamin had 10 cents in his pocket and they were forced to raise money. After 10 weeks traveling by canoe, steamboat and train, the group reached their destination in June 1852. They were rebuffed by border agents, the Commissioner of Indian Affairs and the Secretary of the Interior, but persevered.

Just when things looked the bleakest and warfare, and the annihilation of the Lake Superior band seemed inevitable, a dejected Armstrong returned to the hotel to find a crowd clustered around the Ojibwe men, curious to learn the purpose of their visit. Whig Congressman George Briggs of New York was one of the interested parties and arranged a meeting with President Millard Fillmore at 3 PM the next day.

The President was cordial and all attendees smoked a peace pipe specially made for the occasion. Chief Buffalo's spokesman Oshaga spoke for an hour about the removal and other broken treaty issues with Armstrong acting as translator. Fillmore promised to render a decision soon and two days later rescinded the order of removal decreed by previous President Zachary Taylor. He also offered a new treaty to create reservations on their current homeland, fishing grounds and wild rice territory in addition to making the annuity payments on Madeline Island. The men triumphantly returned to Wisconsin by train.

In February 1855 Chief Buffalo made another difficult trek by train to Washington at the request of President Franklin Pierce to discuss a treaty for the Minnesota Ojibwe. Buffalo posed for an artist who made a clay model of the Chief's head. He was paid $5 for 3 days of posing for the sculptor. Today a marble version sits in the U.S. Senate building and a bronze bust is displayed in the House wing. Chief Buffalo, the strong and sage champion of the Lake Superior Ojibwe, died that autumn of heart disease. Recently the Senate declared, *"This formidable Native American was also called Great Buffalo and the adjective was clearly deserved....[he] was chief of the La Pointe band of Ojibwe, located on Lake Superior in Wisconsin, he also led all the Lake Superior and Wisconsin Ojibwa during much of this cultural transformation."*

George Bonga lived at the end of the Northland's fur trapping and trading era and was a sterling example of the pastiche of influences that shaped the region and country during the nineteenth century. He was born in 1802 somewhere near the western tip of Lake Superior, the son of Pierre Bonga, a black fur trader, and an Ojibwe woman named Ogibwayquay. His Bonga grandparents were slaves from Africa via Jamaica and the French West Indies who were brought to the fort on Michigan's Mackinac Island to serve British officer, Captain Daniel Robertson. They were emancipated after the Captain's death and started a hotel on the island.

Pierre made enough money in the fur trade to educate George in Montreal where he graduated speaking English, French and Ojibwe fluently. George inherited his father's aptitude for the fur trade and his size and strength, well over 6' and 200 pounds, made him a popular man in the forests of Wisconsin and Minnesota. He once portaged seven 90 pound packs of furs and supplies, weighing well over 600 pounds. He exercised more than his brawn, using his brains and personality as he operated comfortably in the various cultures of the area.

His skills attracted the attention of Lewis Cass, who hired Bonga to guide his sortie to locate the source of the Mississippi River. Subsequently, George acted as an interpreter, negotiator and signatory for the treaties of 1820 and 1867. He served as a champion of Ojibwe rights when they were mistreated by U.S. agents.

When the fur trade sputtered to an end in the 1840s, he married an Ojibwe named Ashwin and raised four children. They opened a lodge on Leech Lake in Minnesota, where he entertained guests with the songs and stories of the fur trading period while he continued to aid the natives by monitoring their annuity payments, ensuring their rights were protected. Upon his death in 1884, Reverend Henry Whipple, the first Episcopal Bishop of the state of Minnesota, honored him by saying, *"No word could be better trusted than that of George Bonga."*

★ ★ ★ ★ ★

The first members of the Gitche Gumee Camping Club, despite their common interests, certainly had different personal characteristics. George Markham was the most impish and jolly, and when excited, broke into an Irish jig. He was born in a settlement called "Markhams," later known as Wilmington, in upstate New York. Mr. Markham was a great storyteller and many of his tales harkened back to his earlier days in the Adirondacks. His Brule River lodge was named "Au Sable" after the trout stream that flowed from the mountains into the majestic High Falls Gorge on its way to Lake Champlain. He was a sharpshooter, the best hunter in the group and a member of the Milwaukee Rifle Club.

Mr. Markham was a maritime attorney in Milwaukee and a Great Lakes cargo ship, the *George C. Markham,* was christened in his honor. After a career in private practice he assumed the position of President of the Northwestern Mutual Life Insurance Company. His wife Rose died in 1893 after giving birth to 3 children, George Francis, Stuart and Susie. After retiring, he moved to Pasadena, California, to be with his brother Henry, the ex-Governor of the Golden State.

Rev. Judson Titsworth was Henry David Thoreau and St, Francis of Assisi combined, loving the wildlife and scenery of the Brule region. He was often spotted leaning against a tree, deep in thought, smoking his pipe and reading a book. The Reverend was no pacifist, however, when it came to defending his country. As a 16 year-old, the Shiloh, New Jersey, native enlisted as a private in Company D of the 11th New Jersey infantry in August, 1862.

During the Civil War he transferred to the Union Navy, served at the blockade of Galveston, Texas and observed the final Confederate surrender there on June 2, 1865. After he was honorably discharged, he concentrated on his first-rate education at Amherst College and then the prestigious Union Theological Seminary. He humbly turned down honorary Doctor of Divinity degrees from Beloit College and Amherst.

His ministerial career brought him first to Westfield, Massachusetts and then Chelsea in the same state. He assumed the pastorate of Plymouth Congregational Church in Milwaukee where he served for 25 years. He expanded his role to include community outreach and served on many boards of organizations such as the Wisconsin Home and Farm School for Boys. The Reverend was involved in the Congregational Church at the national level and was a pioneer in his goal of providing more than spiritual inspiration. Plymouth Church was described as: *"an active and outward-looking congregation, led by the able and imaginative Rev. Judson Titsworth. With extensive sewing and cooking schools, a gymnasium, a boys' club and other activities, Plymouth is providing a new kind of ministry in America, serving an urban community of a quarter of a million, half of them identifiably German and many of them newly-arrived immigrants."*

Christopher Redmond, *Welcome to America, Mr. Sherlock Holmes*

Dr. Arthur Holbrook was the leader of the club, which never would have been formed without his vision and guidance. He was an avid sportsman and steward of the Brule's resources. His disdain for fishing with anything but a fly was well-known. He was born in Madrid, New York, and studied dentistry with his father, and after moving to Waukesha, Wisconsin, with his uncle. The Dr.'s studies were interrupted by the Civil War, and he enlisted immediately upon President Lincoln's call for volunteers. He served at the front during the Potomac Campaign from July, 1862 until the autumn of 1862 with Company F of the Fifth Wisconsin Infantry and was promoted to 1st Lieutenant.

In the Spring of 1864, the Union Army called for "100 Day Men." The concept was to make a concerted effort to end the war in 100 days by having recruits relieve the regulars of their mundane duties to free them to fight. Arthur was commissioned the adjutant of the 39th Wisconsin Infantry and the men headed down the Mississippi River in a steamboat to Memphis, where they were short on rations and long on heat and mosquitoes.

On August 21, General Nathan Bedford Forrest led the Rebels in an attack on the city at 4 AM. The goal was not to capture the city but to create a nuisance and perhaps capture a Union general or two. Holbrook was an assistant adjutant general of the 4th Brigade during the skirmish. As Forrest and his men entered the city they encountered stiff resistance and retreated. It was actually more of a raid than a battle, but Forrest accomplished his goal of being a pest, capturing hundreds of prisoners and making off with a large quantity of supplies and horses.

Holbrook mustered out of the Army on September 22, 1864, and resumed his dental training. He graduated from the Philadelphia Dental College in 1867, moved back to Wisconsin and was one of only two formally educated dentists in the state in 1868. The Dr. married Josephine Tenney who became an integral member of the Gitche Gumee Camping Club. They had four children: Florence (Floy), Arthur T., Hortense and Harold. Dr. Holbrook was honored at a banquet in Milwaukee on January 21, 1914 and the editor of *The Dental Review* praised him: *"When the name of Dr. Arthur Holbrook is mentioned in any gathering of dentists in Wisconsin there is not a man who does not instinctively feel like taking off his hat. Never was a man so universally beloved and never did a man more richly deserve it.... Arthur Holbrook could never think a mean thought, or do a wrong act. He makes no compromise with himself, while with others he is charity and grace, and forgiveness...."*

My great-grandfather, George Henry Noyes, came from humble beginnings. He was born in McClean, New York, and moved with his family to Delafield, Wisconsin. He worked his way through the University of Wisconsin as a tutor, teacher and librarian. During the summer, he worked on the family farm. Chief Justice John B. Winslow of the Wisconsin Supreme Court recognized his diligence and said, *"he won his education in a hand-to-hand conflict with poverty..."* He graduated Phi Beta Kappa and, after law school, entered private practice, eventually becoming a partner with his friend in the firm Markham and Noyes.

In 1888, Great-grandfather was elected the first judge of the newly formed Superior Court of Milwaukee County. Judge Noyes served for two years and, although it was a great honor, he chose family over prestige and went back into private practice as he *"desired to provide more liberally for the education of his children than the salary of this office would permit."* Great-grandfather joined the firm of Miller, Noyes and Miller. He sent the children east to boarding schools. Two daughters, Emily and Katherine, went to Smith for college and the other two, Margaret and Helen, to Vassar. Son Haskell attended Yale. At the time of his death, the Judge held the position of general counsel of the Northwestern Mutual Life Insurance Company, where his friend George Markham was president.

The concept of education for George and wife Agnes also meant learning other cultures and traveling both domestically and abroad. Much was expected of the children, and their parents set a good example. George Noyes was a founder of the Associated Charities of Milwaukee and a trustee of the Milwaukee Emergency Hospital. He served on the University of Wisconsin Board of Regents for 12 years, 2 of them as president.

Great-grandfather, in addition to his penchant for details, was an entertainer on the river. He played the Spanish Fandango on his guitar accompanying the singers in the group. His dramatic readings were also a campfire favorite.

On the occasion of the Judge's death, the Milwaukee Bar Association offered this memorial: *"This brief recital of the life and career of Judge Noyes is in itself the highest testimony of his character. It evidences his sterling qualities, inherited from a race of sturdy ancestors, his courage of strength and will, his successful struggle against adverse circumstances, his superior scholarly attainments, his great legal learning and skill, his professional success, his high conception and faithful performance of its duties as judge, lawyer and citizen, his perfect integrity, and the esteem in which he was held by his fellow men…. Judge Noyes, while at all times dignified, and somewhat reserved in manner, was a man of most gentle and kindly nature and of a singularly pure nature."*

★ ★ ★ ★ ★

C.D. O'Brien was not a man to let grass grow under his feet. By the age of 18 he had immigrated to Lake Superior's Madeline Island from Ireland with his family, walked most of the way to St. Anthony, Minnesota (now part of Minneapolis), worked in a general store, drove a mule team for Major Alfred Brackett in his campaign against the Dakota Indians in North Dakota and moved to St. Paul to begin his legal studies.

O'Brien became a prominent St. Paul attorney and in 1883, he was elected mayor. He maintained a "closed administration." Vice and bribery were not tolerated. From 1865-1883, the city had a corrupt reputation and police herded all of society's ills, the bright light district, into one area where it could be monitored. On a monthly basis the madams came to court and paid their brothels' fines. It was actually taxation. Chris did not accept that arrangement. He ordered the closing of all brothels and was reviled by many businessmen for his action as they felt it was detrimental to their interests. In 1888 he was a delegate to, and a speaker at, the Democratic National Convention.

O'Brien was the architect of the formation of the Winneboujou Club, our congenial Brule River next door neighbors. He had prior knowledge of the beauty of the valley as his parents, Dillon and Elizabeth, moved the family to America from County Galway in 1857 during the Great Famine when Christopher was 9. They taught the Ojibwe at the Madeline Island missionary school. Dillon was a noted novelist, scholar, speaker and educator. He was considered a great "Famine Generation" writer and penned *The Dalys of Dalystown* on the island. The family moved to St. Paul in 1863 and Dillon worked with Archbishop John Ireland to relocate impoverished Irish to Minnesota. They developed communities to establish a support system for the immigrants.

Christopher, as evidenced in his *Brule Chronicles*, inherited his gift for prose from his father and his lyrical descriptions of the Brule River enticed his St. Paul friends to form a club. Joseph Cullon, in his *Landscapes of Labor and Leisure*, said O'Brien *"literally transported St. Paul social elite to the banks of the Brule in the summer. Christopher was instantly recognizable on the river in his trademark tam-o-shanter and knickerbockers."*

Logging was an exhausting and dangerous occupation in the North Woods. At night the men enjoyed telling stories: some with a kernel of truth embedded within but greatly embellished. Paul Bunyan was a popular subject; six axe handles tall, with many accomplishments. It was said his ability to clear forests was responsible for turning the woodlands of the Dakota Territory into prairie. Once the giant sneezed so hard trees were toppled for miles around. Paul dug the Great Lakes as a drinking trough for his companion, Babe the Blue Ox. When he called his men for dinner, boughs cracked and fell from the trunks of pines.

Red Bob Cochran was not a myth but a logging foreman in the camps around Lake Superior's south shore. He was an imposing physical specimen whose red hair, beard and moustache matched his volatile temper. Many Red Bob tales came from Clifford McNeil and his parents, long-time Brule River residents. In the days before logging stripped the area of most of its virgin pine stands, the trees grew as close together as nature allowed. Once Red Bob bet he could travel 10 miles without touching the ground, jumping from stump to stump. He accomplished the feat, but was disqualified when one tree was toppled to aid his progress.

No one is sure of Red Bob's fate, but a local Brule timber cruiser, Sam Redding, said his chest was cleaved by the axe of an equally mean-spirited local Brule logger named Matt Nevala. Cochran purportedly removed the weapon and walked away, carrying it on his shoulder and leaving drops of blood in his wake.

"We were close, you see, and we knew when they (the Noyes clan) were there. They had boys somewhat older than us and we could always tell when they got new company especially. Whoever it was would arrive and the boys would dash them down and dump them in the river. Such screaming you could not imagine. Such screams gave way to the slam of car doors. And they, in turn, were augmented by the drumbeat of rock and roll leaking from the 'Peppermint Lounge' [old Noyes Camp Guide House].... Had Marshall intelligence gatherers sought to keep it, a fever chart depicting the growth of each generation would probably reflect the gradual rise and fall of the general decibel level as well."

Caroline Marshall, *Winneboujou Chroincles*

It is true that Noyes Camp has been called "Noisy Camp" on occasion and I am sure the Boys of Brule have contributed to that moniker. We have raucous ping pong tournaments, and sound is funneled up and down the river valley. Our language at Brule is also somewhat saltier than in our regular environment. While the Marshalls had a legitimate gripe, Uncle Ralph once chalked up the others' more picky complaints to jealousy, theorizing that our family "has more fun."

The Peppermint Lounge was a place where teenagers could blow off steam and escape the watchful eyes of the adults whose philosophy was a Victorian vestige when Noyes Camp children were expected to be mostly neither seen nor heard. The booming bass apparently throbbed down river as the Noyes Camp adults never complained. The old Guide House was also the perfect spot for a romantic interlude far from parental chaperones.

No matter the indiscretions perpetrated by the Boys of Brule, and we have had some cabin fever during long winters that kept us homebound, we can never match the horror of 1904. Johnny Govan, part Dakota, lived in a cabin with Bo Ka Dos, a woman with whom he tanned hides for hunters. During the winter in question, he was employed cutting ice for summer use from not much more than a pond just east of the Brule River. He worked with Alex Sevalia and spent that season in a shanty on the lakeshore.

The morning after a night of heavy drinking, Govan staggered back to the bar and blurted, *"Alex is dead. Killed up at my shack."* The bartender, noticing blood spatters on Johnny's clothing, provided wise counsel, suggesting he retain a lawyer and button his lip. The Douglas County Court could not determine whether Sevalia had died from blunt force trauma from a weapon or if he fell on a sled runner. Govan did not tarry long after the verdict and took off for parts unknown, never to be seen in the Brule River Valley again.

The majority of the sportsmen who first sought the Brule River after its beauty and bounty were identified, were gentlemen. They may not have been cognizant of all the implications of their fishing and hunting approaches, but their hearts were in the right place. Some were not as protective of the Brule River Valley. Dr. Arthur T. Holbrook excoriated game hogs like Frank Bowman, who epitomized the raping of the stream in the 1880s. He was one of the first owners of the Cedar Island estate and viewed the river as his personal domain. Dr. Holbrook writes, *"I myself have seen the carcasses of several deer...on the Brule River, which* [he] *had left on the bank to rot. Frank Bowman kept a loaded .22, silver mounted, beautiful sporting rifle constantly in hand, at shot right and left at squirrels, song birds, and any wild object that caught his fancy. He killed the first fox I had ever seen, and did not even bother to examine, but merely indulged his conceit in his marksmanship. Fish received the same treatment at* [his] *hands."*

Bowman built a chute bordered by drift fences for his dogs to drive deer into a pit, where they were summarily executed. Frank indulged in other extracurricular activities, which caught the attention of his wife. One summer day Mrs. Bowman and her guide paddled upriver and hid on the banks of the Cedar Island property. When her cheating husband and his "niece" appeared, the enraged Mrs. B. took several shots at the playboy, who high-tailed it into the woods with his mistress. Bowman was not as fortunate in 1927 when a Missouri farmer unloaded both barrels of buckshot into his torso at close range. Frank had come to collect a debt and left in a horse-drawn meat wagon en route to marble town.

Oliver "Old Man" Hart was Frank Bowman's kindred spirit and part of the St. Louis cadre of early proprietors of the Cedar Island property. He shared Frank's predilection for killing for pleasure. Ironically, one of Hart's specialties as an architect was designing churches. He viewed the bounty of nature as a commodity, gating and padlocking a cedar swamp pond full of brook trout known as Hart's Lake. Oliver was a business force in St. Louis. In addition to architecture, he was a banker, railroad man and President of the St. Louis Gas Company and the Western Mutual Fire and Marine Insurance Company. "Old Man" started and ran the Jupiter Works, the St. Louis Ore and Steel Company and the Vulcan Iron Works. One wonders if he ever slept. When Hart, Bowman and the other owners died or dropped out of the Brule holdings, Henry Clay Pierce was the last man standing. After Pierce's death the Cedar Island estate landed on the Douglas County delinquent tax rolls until John Ordway Sr. bought the property, which still remains in the family's care.

The characters comprising the Boys of Brule generally fall into one of two categories based on personality traits: "the high profile" or the "under the radar." Marty "Tall Paul" Schuster fits the former category. We met at summer camp between first and second grade and were classmates from that point through college. He marches to the beat of his own drum. Some of his most memorable Brule moments revolve around food. Marty once tried to order a Gorgonzola cheese pizza at a local, rural Wisconsin joint. One year he was assigned Saturday night dinner duty. Around 5 PM he asked, to no one in particular, "Where can I get some trout around here?"

It was obvious that little planning had occurred. He prepared some wild rice, which had the consistency of pine needles. The most edible part of the meal turned out to be leftover rolls from Friday. Rob "Bobbo"Pearson made the perfect statement by emphatically placing a bottle of ketchup in the center of the table. We retaliated by stashing the leftover wild rice, a large amount, in Marty's backpack to take home. In fairness, Tall Paul has redeemed himself many times over including an excellent trout dinner in 2005 and more recently, some Jambalaya.

When Schuster cooks he considers himself an artiste. He uses every contrivance, device, appliance, implement, utensil, pot, pan and dish in the house (and outdoors) and eschews nonstick cooking sprays as, in his estimation, they affect the taste of his creations. We periodically check on his progress, worried that we may be responsible for post meal clean-up. The kitchen resembles a war zone.

Marty is the chairman of a high tech company that manufactures products I can't even begin to understand. Sometimes his bossiness extends to his fellow Boys of Brule compatriots and, if you're not careful, he can talk you into things you really don't want to, and shouldn't, do. It just wouldn't be the same without Marty "Tall Paul" Schuster in residence. He bursts like a super nova and there is rarely a dull moment.

I met Chip Michel through business and he has become an integral part of the BOB fabric. He is our Tasmanian Devil who thinks nothing of driving home during our long weekend to attend a wedding and zipping right back when the bride and groom finish their vows. He is a perpetual motion machine, always involved in a project. Charles Michel Jr. is one of our best cooks and comes to Brule with trays of Shrimp Num Nums. One cocktail hour he brought a tray of Num Nums to town and had the waitress stick them in the oven to heat for us. He is fearless and has to be watched. Chip may be the most loveable Boy of Brule.

Chip and his co-conspirator, Jim "Lumber" Hurd, once spent hours trying to make the meat smoker work. One year he disassembled the gas grill to make it operate more efficiently and, when he discovered the problem, he reassembled the various parts and then trotted over to the neighbor's with the grates to have the caretaker power-wash them. He acts as Hurd's Hearts advisor, suggesting strategy best left ignored. Chip at times adopts a Scandinavian accent to deliver jokes only understood regionally. He owns a manufacturing company that sells consumer products across the U.S. including the drink holders that adorn our horseshoe pit.

Hurd is another college friend and the retired chairman of a lumber company. He is very methodical and diligent in every endeavor. (Check the "Pranks" chapter to capture his Brule essence.) Rus Emerick is a colleague of Marty's, and our technology guru. He is one of our best golfers and a veteran of the sex, drugs and rock 'n' roll world. (Refer to the "Music" chapter to learn about his war stories.)

Scott Shorten and I met on move-in day, as we settled into our fifth floor college dorm rooms on top of a hill in Vermont in 1969. He returned to the Boys of Brule fold after a 21 year absence during which he concentrated on balancing his medical career and family. Now retired, Old Doc Shorten brings his sardonic wit and strong card-playing skills from Ohio. Our political philosophies dovetail and we both speak our minds. Scott is a voracious reader, one of our finest ping pong players and the chief BOB medical officer. Doc is our most accomplished long distance runner and mountain climber. Like me, he does not perceive patience to be a virtue.

Mike "Mickey" and Tom "Big T" Melander are also known as the Klomper Brothers for their heavy-footed treks to the bathroom in the middle of the night. I met them when Mike was in my fourth grade class and T was in sixth. Tom is a kindly curmudgeon, easily baited and flummoxed by modern technology and political correctness. He had the texting function removed from his cell phone in a protest to the modern world. The man is an American original and belongs in a living museum. He is semi-retired from his commercial real estate business and always talks about "chasing the money." He has been known to kvetch, *"just one time I'd like to come home from vacation and have a check waiting for me."*

When annoyed, T has physiological responses including bug eyes, nostril flares and pursed lips. I periodically torture him by hiding his favorite golf club, a 5 wood. He is a champion of the English language and a woodworking savant. T is a raconteur and joke teller. His old chestnuts take twice as long to finish as he interrupts them often with his own laughter, tickled pink by his drollery. Brother Mike and he frequently quarrel over "false memories" from their earlier days, contesting the veracity of each other's versions. It is fun to bait them and sit back and watch.

Mike is a simply fun to be around. We have shared many escapades throughout the years. He is in the middle of every activity: fishing, canoeing, horseshoes, golf, cards and ping pong. Sometimes he peaks a bit early. One night at dinner he whispered, "I'm going to lay down for a little bit." Apparently "a little bit" was code for twelve hours, because we next saw his smiling face at 8 AM. Another night after a long day, Mike went missing. We searched for him high and low. We called for him outside and went down to the landing, but he was nowhere to be found. We were starting to panic until someone checked his room. He was fast asleep.

Mike is one of our golfing gurus. He won the Minnesota State Independent School Championship two years in a row. Mike is a great confidante and conversationalist with an upbeat attitude. He is a fixture at the card table when a game of Hearts is underway. He is a savvy player and must be carefully observed. Mick is retired from the electronics and software business. He is so pleasant and appealing; he could sell refrigerators in the Arctic.

There are Boys of Brule characters who effortlessly navigate the May weekend. Dr. Bud the Fish Surgeon, aka Walter Maurice Chambers III, is a college friend, ex-defensive back and a southern gentleman. Bud is retired from the financial sector. He understands the rhythms of Noyes Camp, the river and the forest.

He fills the wood box and straightens the boathouse and whips up a sumptuous dinner of ribs on occasion. Bud is our Kentucky Derby expert, which occurs every Saturday of our annual get-together. He has attended the Derby many times and experienced the shenanigans that occur on the track's infield along with 79,999 others. I appreciate his ability to stay up past 10 PM to keep me company.

Dana Fitts is perhaps our most disciplined and determined member: from cards to golf to horseshoes. Unfortunately his stays at Brule are usually truncated due to an annual stockholder's meeting he must attend in Omaha. He makes the effort to show up at for at least a few days. Dana is a friend from elementary school and one of the BOB hockey alumni. He is in the furniture business and often has to deal with work-related issues at the Brule, which is generally verboten, but he gets a pass because he works so hard. Dana was a member of the seminal Boys of Brule outing in 1975 when we camped in the dooryard, 1890s style. He is an example of a lower profile Boy of Brule, navigating his stay effortlessly, without incident.

People often say they have known each other "their whole lives," which translates to "a longtime." Rob "Bobbo" Pearson and I could say we knew each other from day one. Our mothers attended first grade together, and, so did Bobbo and I. He was the first friend I brought to Brule and he loved the place as much as I. Rob was our Renaissance man: well-educated and well read, an accomplished musician, artist, humorist and hockey player as well as a first-rate construction guru who troubleshot and solved the most perplexing issues facing the aging Noyes Camp. He was also an Eagle Scout, equally at home in the forest or a Vienna opera house. Bobbo and I shared countless memories.

Rob was fascinated by the meticulous craftsmanship employed in the construction of the Camp and not only advised us but often solved problems on his own. One day some of us returned to the house after a canoe trip to find one of the doors off its hinges and lying on makeshift sawhorses.

Bobbo had called Dana and asked him to stop by his house on the way north and pick up his power sander. The door had been sticking on the threshold so Bobbo and his brother-in-law, Joel, removed it, sanded it and rehung it. Rob's skills and creativity were abundant, exemplified by the day he made a detailed architectural drawing of Noyes Camp by hand, using only a tape measure, a straight edge and a pencil. He was driven by intellectual curiosity and his devotion to Brule. He succumbed to dementia on December 7, 2017, and the world is a colder, sadder place without him.

Joel "Glencoe" Hartelt first came to the Brule with Rob. He has become a fixture and his exploits can be found in the "Pranks" chapter. He is an inventor and manufacturer. Joel introduced us to Steve "The New Guy" Duea. Steve tries to retire from Polaris, where he is the quality control guru, but they won't allow it and pry him away from Florida. Because of his newcomer status, The New Guy is on double secret probation.

Bill "Two Syllables" "Lorny" Lorntson is our resident maniac and an ex-neighbor of mine. He hops in his car at 5:00 AM from Minneapolis and arrives at Noyes Camp in time for breakfast. He is game for anything and thinks nothing of jumping out of his car after beating Twin Cities traffic and boarding a canoe for another 4-hour trip, albeit on water rather than pavement. Perhaps his involvement in the transportation business explains it. He is a dedicated sports rube and a haunter of the Twittersphere. Bill is a native of the Northland, growing up in Beaver Bay, Minnesota, on the north shore of Lake Superior.

We lost Charlie "Chuck" Hullsiek to cancer in 2008 after a ten-year battle. He was brash, lippy and cocky, and we loved him for it. An enduring image is Charlie grinning broadly at the card table after a good hand, blowing cigar smoke in our faces, looking strikingly like the Penguin from Batman. Chuck insisted on teaching us a game, which we never understood as he made up the rules along the way, always to his benefit. He invented the "Flying Hullsiek" one year when perturbed by our barbs. It consisted of two middle fingers rotating rapidly like windmills. He loved to stir the pot.

His health was failing when he made his last trip to Brule. We gave Charlie the master bedroom with its own bathroom in deference to his condition. An intense thunderstorm struck the first night, knocking out the power and causing leaks in the room's ceiling, which were captured by a series of strategically placed waste baskets. Our good deed went bad, but Chuck took it in stride with his trademark sense of humor. He died a few months later.

I am the organizer and Den Mother of the Boys of Brule. I am the butt of many jokes, which is fair since if you dish it out you better be able to take it. I am a jack-of-all-trades and master of none, joining in most every activity-guitars, cards, canoeing, golf and ping-pong. Our group is a well-oiled machine and needs little direction and, after decades of early May experience, I am able to relinquish any control-freak tendencies and can sit back and enjoy the show.

Chief Buffalo's Washington D. C. delegation

Ojibwe Treaty with different clans represented

[5]

THE HONEYMOON AND THE BREAK-UP

"In conclusion, I cannot help saying that the association of our families on the old Brule River, has been one of the greatest pleasures in my whole life, and that this association has made a bond and an affection which I am sure cannot even be shaken by the arrangements we may make to meet the new conditions—arrangements which I trust may be completed that you and I and our entire families and our good friends may continue to enjoy the woods and river we love so well."

DR. ARTHUR HOLBROOK (THE ELDER), AUGUST 8, 1905,
LETTER TO JUDGE GEORGE H. NOYES

A PHYSICIAN'S ADVICE SET it all in motion. Dr. Arthur Holbrook, a Milwaukee dentist, suffered from hay fever in addition to other pulmonary issues stemming from his service in the Civil War. The prescription was the pine-scented fresh air of heavily forested northern Wisconsin on the southern shore of Lake Superior. Ashland had been the home to eight different native tribes as well as a destination for explorers, traders and missionaries. By the 1870s it was the largest town in the area, consisting of one main street of thick mud, or dust, depending on the weather, lined with wood buildings. The Holbrook family took the train to Ashland and used the Chequamegon Hotel as their base of operations. Fishing, camping and sightseeing were the activities that took them to locations such as the Marengo River and the Apostle Islands just off the town of Bayfield on the uppermost Great Lake. They visited Madeline Island to see the ancient home and burial grounds of the Ojibwe.

By 1878, the Dr. had mostly exhausted places of interest in the Ashland vicinity. In August of that year, his friend Dr. Carpenter of Chicago and he ventured west, first to Pike Lake, and then to the Brule River, having heard of the natural beauty and great fishing opportunities to be found there. They camped on the stream at Ashland Lake, and coincidentally, the Dr. learned that his good friend, George Markham, was encamped upriver at the head of the first Twin Rapids.

In the late 1870s and early 1880s, the trip from Milwaukee to the Brule stretched over 3 days and involved a great deal of preparation and multiple means of transportation. The sportsmen hired a hack-driver from Ledyard's 17th Street Livery to carry the passengers and their considerable luggage to the Reed Street Depot. Almost all the food, camping equipment (including lanterns and kerosene), cookware and fishing and hunting gear were packed in chests and bags as once the train departed, shopping was not an option.

The Wisconsin Central train left Milwaukee at 1 AM and arrived in Ashland in time for dinner the next evening. The men spent the night at the Chequamegon Hotel and, in the morning, took the tug-boat *Eva Wadsworth* to Bayfield, where they piled into Mr. Cooper's wagon, equipment and all, hired to take them to the Brule River, 60 miles distant.

The last leg of the journey took two days. They spent the first night at Moose Lake at the log house and tents owned by Ojibwe Johnny Morrison. The next day they finally reached the banks of the Brule River.

Soon after their return home in 1878, Holbrook and Markham discussed the possibility of starting a club and purchasing land on the river. They returned to the Brule and their dream began to take shape. The group camped at various locations until 1886 when a more permanent site was sought. Dr. Holbrook was the leader, and his keen eye could envision just the right spot even though it was heavily wooded. He selected a site just north of the current Gitche Gumee Camping property. He was just as diligent and precise in his demarcating a campsite as he was in his dental practice. A tape-measure, pencil and paper were always close at hand.

Once the parcel was cleared, the Dr.'s instincts were proven perfect. The camp sat high on the eastern bank of the Brule on a straight-away, with beautiful vistas upstream and down. It was nestled in a thick stand of white and Norway (as they were called in those days) pines. An abundant supply of blueberries was nearby and nature's refrigerator, the brook from the north end of Jack's Lake, kept lard and butter cold. Mosquito netting hanging in the shade held venison, waterfowl and bacon away from insects and other predators. Great-grandfather Noyes and

Rev. Judson Titsworth joined the group, and the Gitche Gumee Camping Club was organized. The days were spent fishing, hunting and canoeing, and at night, the campers sat around the fire joining in song and listening to the dulcet tones of Great-grandfather's reading voice.

"The Judge' who couldn't live without
Ginger Ale at 5 PM for a day,
He had good luck and went home
Because he couldn't stay longer
But he left in glory and with a bottle."
Gitche Gumee Camping Club register entry, May 30, 1889

★ ★ ★ ★ ★

While not the first mention of Judge Noyes' presence in camp, this is the initial one with an accompanying comment, a sort of north woods sonnet, with a cryptic message and perhaps an inside joke not unlike the entries in today's Noyes Camp guest book. May remained the domain of men on the river, but soon women and children started visiting in August. Grandmother Margaret's first signature in the register appeared in the mid-1890s when she made her mark with an "X."

The Milwaukee Club's first structure, a multi-purpose board cabin, was built in 1889 and the first large, log lodge soon followed. The glory days of the Gitche Gumee Camping Club were the 1890s. The fishing was still decent and the men enjoyed each other's company unfettered by the conflicts that were to come. The comradery of the Milwaukee friends was at high tide. The club members brought deerskins to the nearby Ojibwe village to have moccasins and other articles of clothing made. The process involved many steps: soaking, stretching, scraping, smoking and tanning until the hides were ready for cutting and stitching. Faint reminders of the Ojibwe paths to the river existed in the mid-1900s. Late in summer, they would walk to the north end of Ashland Lake to pick ripened blueberries before the bears arrived to feast on their favorite food.

In 1895, the Winneboujou, or St. Paul Club, purchased the land on which the Milwaukee group camped. Magnanimously, they "rented" the site to the Gitche Gumee Camping Club for the price of one trout annually. The stipulations were clear: the fish was to measure at least 9" and caught and presented by Dr. Holbrook's wife, Josephine, and delivered to Winneboujou Club leader, Mr. Christopher O'Brien, who accepted with a big hug and enthusiastic kiss. The festivities were held at the

Winneboujou clubhouse, and enlivened with many toasts of champagne gingerly transported from Milwaukee.

In 1898, the Saunders family, Winneboujou Club members, announced they would build their lodge on the Milwaukee Club site. The next year the Gitche Gumee Camping Club was incorporated and 20 acres were purchased for $600 from Col. John Knight, just one bend upriver from the old campsite. Elaborate by-laws and annual meeting schedules were meticulously crafted and followed, which was no surprise with a judge and attorney involved. From this point on, discord became the order of the day.

The first challenge was to move the two buildings upriver to its new location on what is now called "Frog's Point." Under the supervision of Joe Lucius, the structures were carefully dismantled and each plank, log and beam numbered for the ease of reassembly. The parts were carried and pulled by sled through the snow to their new destination.

There were many decisions to be made, not the least of which was the splitting the land into individual sites. George Markham floated the proposal of dividing the parcel and then having a coin toss decide the order of selection. He wrote in 1900, *"This year I have fully concluded that I must either have a place of my own by myself, or quit the river. It would be quite needless to go into details that have led me to this ultimatum."* The Markhams moved to the southernmost end of the property and built a lodge in 1903. Rev. Titsworth took note of the burgeoning crowd of youngsters and had already withdrawn from the club. This left the Noyes and Holbrook families to battle over the most desirable site on the point where the original lodge stood.

Reams of paper were used as letters crossed in the mail discussing the minutest, and in retrospect, silliest details. My Great-grandfather was the most aggressive with his parries, thrusts and misdirections. His legal training came in handy. In one letter to Dr. Holbrook, he played it coy, pretending he had no interest in building another lodge or spending money on the current one to expand and improve. He feigns disinterest in a most disingenuous manner: *"You have been desirous for some time of having a separate lodge for you and your family. I have had no such special desire for myself and family. You have suggested making a number of additions and improvements to the camp, while I have not felt disposed to increase my investment there. You have been anxious to build a separate house for your private use, while I have not cared for one myself. You want to locate such separate house on what is known as the third site, but I think that would not be consistent with the agreement we have had that such location should be used only as a site for a family lodge. Furthermore, if you should occupy that site with a lodge for your personal use and still retain a joint use of the present lodge, you would be taking the entire use of one site and sharing equally the other site while I would only be sharing in one site, and this you will readily concede would not be a fair proposition."*

JULY 31, 1905, LETTER FROM JUDGE GEORGE NOYES
TO DR. ARTHUR HOLBROOK

★ ★ ★ ★ ★

Dr. Holbrook considered building on the west side of the river where the club also owned land. He used his tape measure and planted stakes for his proposed boundaries. In the end, he demurred as he preferred the breeze which came down the river to the spot between the Markhams and the point. The view was also thought to be more picturesque. The Holbrooks finally chose the middle site and received $500 for their share of the original lodge, but not before quarreling over the independent estimate of value they received from Joe Lucius.

One might think after the "Battle of the Sites," as Dr. Arthur T. Holbrook later called it, was over the arguments would cease. Next on the docket, however, was the issue of individual shoreline length. Great-grandfather once again took to the typewriter and made his case that it was not important: *I do not agree with your statement that 'it has been generally conceded by the owners of the land that it was the river more than the land that has taken them to the Brule; therefore in a division of the land between the owners the river frontage should be made the basis…' I think you will agree with me that it was not the river frontage which has taken us to the Brule, but that it has been various other attractions such as freedom from hay fever, freedom from work; the fishing, hunting, boating, pure air and love of the woods…."*

★ ★ ★ ★ ★

The Judge then proceeded to remind the Dr. that he could have had the entire frontage if he chose to build on the western side. The men continued to argue about the division of personal property in the first lodge and the location of the separate kitchen/dining building which was commonly separated from the main lodge in case of a kitchen fire. The building, which became the Holbrook's Guide Cabin, still stands. Arthur T. Holbrook, at the age of 19, scurried up a pole supporting the shingled roof of the front porch and used a grease pencil to neatly write GITCHE GUMEE 1899 on the front peak of the cabin. The inscription remains as distinct as the day it was written.

The garbage site was another bone of contention. The Judge wrote the Dr.: *"… inasmuch as we have to bury the bottles, broken dishes and sundry articles aside from the ordinary garbage, it has been found that a considerable space is required, and that a large number of holes have been dug and filled on the garbage site."*

The Judge's end game was to ensure no Holbrook building, garbage pit, guide house or out-house would be located on his property north of the roadway.

Nothing was left to chance. The two men quarreled over the custody of the GGCC Log Book which chronicled the comings and comings of members and guests as well as interesting events that occurred on the river. Dr. Holbrook said there were ninety stately Norway pines on the Noyes site worth $3-$5 each and felt he should be compensated. Great-grandfather countered that all locations had large pine trees. It would be difficult to ascertain the value of all. When buildings were dismantled the families split the remaining logs and boards. Great-grandfather did not want the ice when the ice house was taken down, but he desired the sawdust that insulated the blocks and kept them cold.

Semantics were an issue. The Judge complained that the Dr. neglected to sign one of his missives. Great-grandfather took exception to the wording in a letter, deeming it a deal-breaker: *"…you say in your letter of the 18th [October, 1905] that 'the terms are not satisfactory to me, but that a change is forced upon me.' If you mean by this that I am forcing you to the acceptance of terms that are not satisfactory to you, I must decline to continue the negotiations for the reason that I am not willing to receive your acceptance of my offer of $400 on that condition. I would prefer to let matters remain as they have been in the past, if we are unable to reach an adjustment of the matter upon terms which are perfectly satisfactory to you, and which you are voluntarily willing to make or accept. This feature of your letter, therefore, must be eliminated before proceeding further with our negotiations."*

★ ★ ★ ★ ★

Understandably, Dr. Holbrook lost his temper. He suffered from the effects of a stroke and his son, Dr. Arthur T. Holbrook, began to take over the management of the Holbrook property. An apology was given and the Judge accepted it. Great-grandfather wrote to the younger Holbrook, *"I accept with unfeigned pleasure the* assurance of your father's regret for the unfriendly words used at the interview at his office, and I cordially join in his desire that the incident may be forgotten,'"

Great-grandfather was also feeling the effects of aging as shown to this rather dramatic letter to Dr. Arthur T. on June 25, 1912: *"I have come to the conclusion that it is not profitable for me to visit the Brule if I am to lose my memory as I did on the last trip. To repeat the experience of the morning at Ashland of leaving the dress-suit-case in the lunch-room. I left my overcoat containing your letters in the waiting room at the Brule Station, and did not remember about it until on the train en route to Ashland. I telegraphed back to the station keeper, who wired me that the overcoat was found after I had left, to stamp and mail the letters and to send me the coat by express… I would suggest in the future in view of this episode that you entrust your mail to a more responsible and careful party."*

There were some cordial moments in the correspondence between the old friends. They agreed brush should be cleared for croquet grounds for the younger generation. When the Judge wrote his friend to relate his recent fishing story, the Dr. responded with some skepticism in 1912, but couched his words nicely: *"…your account of the capture of a 'German Brown Trout' in the Brule is very interesting, and as you may not have a picture of the species I am enclosing one…. [You] may be glad to have the reverse side of the picture called to your notice. My poor side will not permit use to compete for a prize fish, but I am hoping it may be able to make a few casts before the season closes. The dogwood is beginning to show its teeth…and it is time to get away from it, so we are arranging to reach Camp next Saturday the 10th. Please leave a few trout in the River as I may get a taste."*

The Judge treated Dr. Arthur T. Holbrook in a more fatherly manner, reminding him that *"this is a business matter and however settled is not to interfere with the cordial relations which have for many years existed between you and me and our respective families."*

By all accounts my Great-grandfather was a loving and gentle man in his relationships with his children and grandchildren, and his wife was probably the main disciplinarian. According to the *Memoirs of Milwaukee County, Volume 1,* George Noyes *"established a high reputation as a sound, able and upright Judge* [who] *discharged the duties of his office as to win the entire respect and confidence of the Bar."* But when it came to protecting his interests, and those of his family, he wore his attorney's hat and was a fierce negotiator.

The two friends and combatants of the Gitche Gumee Camping Club died within 3 years of each other—the Judge in 1916, and the Dr. in 1919. Col.

Markham passed away in 1930. Today rare complaints disturb the harmony of the organization. The only current bone of contention is the necessity of tree trimming along driveways to allow space for fire-fighters to reach the lodges. Quarreling over river frontage and door yards are a thing of the past.

George Noyes Portrait

Agnes Haskell Noyes Portrait *Photo by Alice Boughton*

[6]

FITS, STARTS AND LIFT-OFF

"What? Huh? Write something? I'd like a subscription."
"It's great to be back but who keeps inviting Ross?"

Scott Shorten, May Noyes Camp guest book entries

★ ★ ★ ★ ★

NOYES CAMP WAS BUILT for our extended family to gather and it wasn't until 1966 that I was allowed to bring a friend. Rob Pearson joined us much as his mother had joined mine at Brule as teenagers in the late 1930s. Canoes, guitars and ping pong were our focus, and Rob frequented Noyes Camp every year since until his death in 2017. We had the run of the woods and the river, and our energy was boundless. Rob was so dedicated to the Brule that in 1974 Marty Schuster and he visited my family on the Brule without me when I was working in Vermont and unable to join them on the river.

Marty was on double secret probation stemming from an incident in 1970 when Mickey and he made my father wait for them an additional hour at the Ranger Station as they tumbled their way down stream, walking the last few yards to the landing. Adding insult to injury, the metal cooler that accompanied them was battered beyond recognition after cartwheeling through a series of rapids the hard way. My usually affable Dad was not pleased. Thankfully Mr. Jimmy and Tall Paul were on their best behavior in 1972 when my Grandmother Fruen was in residence.

In early May 1975, Dana Fitts, Rob, his-wife-to-be, Heidi and I piled into Marty's white van and headed north to Brule. Winter had yet to release its grip on the south shore of Lake Superior, but we went old school and pitched our tents around the bonfire ring in the Noyes Camp dooryard just as the members of the Gitche Gumee Camping Club had 85 years before. The house had not been opened and cleaned so we hauled a wicker couch from the porch to provide some seating. We improvised a spit and rotated a chicken over the open flame for dinner.

In those days we didn't let the weather interrupt our time on the river. We canoed in snowstorms, pelting rain and frigid temperatures. We paddled down to the Ranger Station in the late afternoon cold and Bobbo took an unexpected plunge into the snow-fringed river when his Old Towne tipped. Chilled to the bone, he spent most of the weekend in his tent staving off hypothermia. He emerged periodically to sit by the fire, play the guitar and eat a meal. Heidi fit right in and enjoyed her honorary status as a member of the inaugural outing of the nascent "Boys of Brule." It would be another ten years before the annual event began in earnest.

During the intervening period marriage, children and careers took center stage, and time at Brule usually revolved around our young families. We loaded the cars with porta-cribs and strollers after work on Friday afternoon and headed north spending less than 48 hours at Noyes Camp before cleaning the house on Sunday and leaving for home. In 1981 our infant son Kyle slept in a dresser drawer. The next year he was strafed by a hungry Great-horned-owl as he sat on a blanket in the front yard. The toddlers took communal baths in the large porcelain tubs and wore tiny life jackets when riding in canoes.

In 1979 the concept of "couples' weekends" was introduced as we left the young ones with grandparents and babysitters. Long canoe trips with picnics, spirited ping pong tournaments and various games including Jeopardy, Trivial Pursuit and Guesstures were played. We laughed until it hurt. One October, we took an ill-advised paddle down to the Ranger Station. The sky was spitting snow and after a tipping we rushed back to build a roaring fire to take the chill off and nurse a broken finger and an asthma attack.

Nineteen-eighty-five marked the seminal Boys of Brule weekend. It was a small group, but it represented a core of the friends who still attend 30 years later. Rob, Jim and I were there as well as Marty who made the trip from Laguna Beach, California, where he was living. It took about five more years for the participants to coalesce into the core that exists today.

Mickey returned to the fold after being off the grid for a decade. His brother Tom joined in a memorable virgin voyage, exploding like the 4th of July, displaying some of the traits that make him distinctive. Bud, Chip and Dana appeared.

College friends Scott and Wils arrived. So did Jim's brother Charlie and best friend from high school, Charlie Hullsiek. They met in home room, sitting next to each other due to the alphabetical similarity of their last names: Hur…and Hul…

Latecomers into the fold include my ex-neighbor Lorny, Marty's business colleague Rus, Bobbo's brother-in-law Glencoe and his friend Steve, AKA "The New Guy."

"All through the winter the members of the Club had been, as usual, talking of the 'beautiful river' and seeking to hasten the time when they could, for a few days, lay aside their cares and lay their heads in the lap of Mother Nature while the river soothed them with its silvery murmurs."

C.D. O'Brien, *Brule Chronicles*

Every May we emulate the swallows returning to Capistrano and the participants can be categorized like birds: Common, Occasional Visitants and Extinct. Every now and then there will be a conflict. 1998 was noteworthy as Mickey was in Scandinavia and Tall Paul bagged at the last moment for a secrecy-shrouded meeting. Their absences were mitigated by Chuck's return from cancer treatment. Occasional Visitants are often Mystery Guests whose appearances are kept secret.

A few Boys of Brule have become extinct, but just like long-lost species, one will resurface every now on then. Wives, for the most part, understand the sanctity of this tradition. In 2018, Marty's wife, Marti (yes, very confusing) declined her husband's invitation to her niece's wedding. She understands. She has similar female friends' get-togethers. They are called the Ya-Yas. She calls us the Yo-Yos.

Scott Shorten (L) and Jim Hurd (R) watching the river flow *Courtesy Marty Schuster*

Dana Fitts cooking and Marty Schuster supervising

[7]

MALE BONDING AND RITES OF PASSAGE

"TIPS FOR MALE BONDING
—Show them you care. Always maintain steady, intimate eye contact while bumping chests.
—To get any new buddies up to speed, compile a Power Point presentation of consensus choices for famous actresses you and the guys would most like to have sex with.
—Take time out each day to admire and appreciate each other's work bench set-ups.
— Slap some steaks on the grill and see who wants them rarest in an elaborate game of chicken.
—Don't be afraid to really open up and share your feelings about how the last penalty call was bullshit."

THE ONION

WHILE THE ABOVE IS satirical, much of it rings true, particularly in view of American society's take on male comradery. In the elementary grades Rob Pearson and I walked the halls of Breck School hand in hand. Studies show the same behavior in Chinese school boys until the country was exposed to Western culture and its social mores that considered such behavior effeminate. The habit disappeared.

Recently I attended a baseball game with three other Boys of Brule. Apparently Mike Melander and I engaged in some of our typical banter with roots dating back to the fourth grade when we met. After a few innings, an obviously ine-briated Millennial woman behind us leaned over and assured us that she didn't understand the fuss over gay marriage and wanted Mike and me to know that she supported us totally. After the initial surprise we had a good laugh, never realizing our ingrained way of communicating could be misconstrued for homosexuality *"not that there's anything wrong with that,"* as the characters on our favorite TV show, "Seinfeld," say. It seems that chucking your friend on the shoulder is the extent of social intimacy tolerated today.

We dismissed the incident, but it was revelatory as an indictment of our society that men can only be "buddies" and not close friends without being considered "girly." It was not always the case. In its earliest form, male bonding provided food and protection necessary for survival. Letter writing in the 19th century shows no stigma in expressing deep feelings and genuine affection between heterosexual male friends. Abraham Lincoln and his friend Joshua Speed shared a bed, and it was not considered odd in an era of small, porous dwellings where heat and space were at a premium. It was not until recently that historians, in a reflection of today's attitudes, speculate the men were lovers.

Niobe Way, in her book *Deep Secrets*, points out that research reinforces the importance of friendships: *"Close friendships provide a sense of self-worth, validation, and connectedness to the larger world and significantly enhance psychological, physical, and academic well-being."* Way also believes friends lead to a better immune system and less illness offering healthier and longer life spans.

Interaction with friends not only reduces the chance of heart disease but lowers the incidence of abdominal fat, high blood pressure and diabetes. Comradery reduces memory loss and the incidence of Alzheimer's disease and dementia. Such interaction stimulates brain function and promotes mental acuity. Perhaps most importantly, strong relationships create a support system giving one's life meaning and a sense of kinship.

A study at Germany's University of Gottingen of Barbary macaques, a primate that closely mirrors human behavior, revealed that male bonding decreased anxi-ety and stress and increased the perception of safety. Contact with friends releases oxytocin, producing a soothing effect on one's emotional state, which contributes to overall health.

Berkeley doctoral candidate Elizabeth Kirby participated in a study of rats under stress and concurred with the results of the macaque experiments. She wrote, *"A bromance can be a good thing… Having friends is not un-masculine. These rats are us in their rat friendships to recover from what would otherwise be a negative experience. If rats can do it, men can do it too. And they definitely are, they just don't get as much credit in their search for that."*

Geoffery Greif, when interviewing people for his book, *Buddy System*, met more than one person who said, *"men don't have friends."* Although this is certainly untrue, it also illuminates the perceived difference between male and female friendships.

The two genders tend to approach relationships in dissimilar manners. Greif says men interact *"shoulder to shoulder"* and women are *"face to face."* Boys often grow up learning to mask and internalize their feelings. Males tend to focus on activities while women take time for intimate discussions. Many men do not possess a template for male bonding, but most of the Boys of Brule grew up with fathers who provided examples of the benefits of comradery.

Some of our dads were members of Pearson's Pucksters, who not only attended the three-day Minnesota State High School Hockey tournament annually, replete with a hotel room to gather between sessions, but socialized throughout the year and participated in charitable activities. Other fathers had weekly golf dates and long lunches.

Our generation of Brule Bonders includes some who attended boys' schools, belonged to a college fraternity, played sports and attended summer camp. Rob Pearson had the ultimate bonding experience when he attended the Boy Scout Jamboree in New York, in conjunction with the 1963 World's Fair, which was considered so newsworthy that the Viking Council leader reported the activities daily on the Upper Midwest's most listened to radio station, WCCO. Not only did Rob meet fellow scouts from all over the globe, but he returned with an encyclopedic mastery of profanity from every conceivable language which we use to this day, even in the Noyes Camp Guest Book, when we prefer our lapses in gentility to be cloaked in mystery.

★ ★ ★ ★ ★

Voyageurs looked forward to the annual rendezvous, which took place in various locations. One of the largest was at Grand Portage on Lake Superior near the present Ontario-Minnesota border during the late 1700s and early 1800s. Canoes from Montreal, laden with trading goods, would meet others piled with furs from the interior and an exchange was made. Beaver pelts were the most desirable commodity but otter, skunk, fox, muskrat, wolf, bear and deer were also valued. Soon cloth was the coveted commodity for the Native Americans. It was highly regarded for its color, adaptability, light weight and easy washing.

Although the main purpose of a rendezvous was to conduct business, it was an excellent way to blow off steam after a long, arduous and tedious winter marred by hernias, drownings, twisted spines, rheumatism, knife wounds and broken bones. Smoke from fires caused respiratory and vision problems. The carnival-style festivities did not begin until a substantial number of participants arrived, but usually lasted until the end of July.

While voyageurs were considered heroic and legendary, their lives were fraught with danger and men looked forward to the respite from back-breaking work. The activities included carousing, feasting, relaxing, singing, dancing, gambling, brawling and various competitions: shooting, archery, foot and canoe races, wrestling and hatchet throwing. After a grueling winter of bitterly cold conditions, a rendezvous was male comradery in fast motion.

Historically, the Ojibwe were much more tolerant of the blurring of gender roles than Europeans. A third gender, known as *niizh manidoowag*, was considered to be present in certain Ojibwe. They had both masculine and feminine aspects, combining roles such as warrior and clan mother and contradictory animal spirits. Far from being ostracized, the "two spirited" Ojibwe were thought to be "the Gifted Ones," able to mediate, nurture, counsel, heal maintain traditions, foretell the future and restore balance. They often wore clothes of both genders and were allowed to perform whatever roles in the community suitable for their personality.

A famous Ojibwe "Two Spirit" was Ozaawindig, or Yellow Head, who was not only a "pillager" but one of the chief's wives. A pillager was a member of the band's advance guard during an attack, much like a special operative. Yellow Head led the Ojibwe in various incursions against the Dakota. The "Two Spirit" tradition was all but extinguished when the Jesuit missionaries and other Europeans found the practice to be a perverted abomination. Today it is being resurrected by Ojibwe LGBT members who are working hard to remove the shame imposed by outsiders on their heritage.

Hanging Cloud was the daughter of Beautifying Bird, the chief of Lake Superior Ojibwe, and thought to be the only woman to participate as a warrior.

She was said to be of average height and a thin build. Hanging Cloud attended war councils, danced in war ceremonies, wielded weapons, wore paint and sported eagle feathers in her hair representing her kills. She was a fierce participant in raiding parties and battles. While native girls usually took a husband at an early age, Hanging Cloud would not marry until a man could match her skills.

The Ojibwe called the sport of lacrosse *bagataway*, and it transcended the significance of a mere game and meant many things to the men who participated. It could be a prelude to war or a substitute for battle. It was called "the little brother of war" by some and "the Creator's Game" by others. Lacrosse was thought to cure the sick and reinforce bonds. It had spiritual aspects to honor the Great Creator and involved intricate ceremony.

The hickory sticks were decorated with feathers, carved designs and paint. The balls were initially made of wood from tree knots and later consisted of deer hide stuffed with hair. Participants adorned their bodies with colorful paint, and spectators placed bets on the outcome. The Clasping Hands Dance performed during lacrosse strengthened the bonds of the men and was a symbol of strength believed to protect them not only from the dangers of war but the injuries, and sometimes deaths that occurred during the rough sport. Games lasted from dawn until dusk and sometimes extended for a period of a few days.

The city of La Crosse, Wisconsin, situated on the eastern bank of the Mississippi, was named for the large parcel of flat land adjacent to the river. When the stream flooded, the receding waters flattened the prairie grass, providing the perfect playing surface. The boundaries for *bagataway* were limited only by the landscape, and hundreds of men often played on each side. The purpose of the game was to propel the ball into the wooden stake located at the end of the playing field. Lacrosse faded into obscurity for the Ojibwe in the mid-20th century, but is being resurrected with youth today as part of learning the old traditions.

The ancient Ojibwe rites of passage involving the metamorphosis of a boy to a man were not that different from mine, minus the killing of a large mammal and showing bravery in warfare. When a native boy reached the age of 12 or 13, he was sent on a vision quest, a *bawajigaywin,* which took place in a sacred, natural location, sequestered from the community and included fasting, praying for guidance, isolation and dreaming for four days and nights. It was hoped that these activities would bring forth a vision, sometimes called an *apowawin,* providing an awareness of the child's purpose with a merging of mind and body. The vision often revealed the boy's animal spirit guide to help him in life.

When I was nine I was outfitted for a quest of my own on my Uncle Ralph's ranch in Montana. My older cousins explained I was to go check out the distant winter ranch on horseback. My horse was an old nasty creature. It tried to get rid of me by rubbing against a fence. When the saddle was strapped on, the sway-backed old nag expanded its belly and I when I climbed on, it inhaled and I tumbled to the ground. My cousins played the cruel prank out to the very last, packing essentials in the saddle bags, slapping the horse's hindquarters, pointing to the vaguely described destination and sending me on my way. I was scared but firm in my determination not to chicken out and embarrass myself. I mounted the horse and began my journey before they finally called me back. I returned, greatly relieved and proud I had called their bluff. I proved my mettle and achieved a rite of passage. I am not sure who was happier: me or the horse who galloped back to the barn to resume its life of leisure.

My next test was to sit in the ranch hands' quarters for an hour without uttering a single word. The reward was a silver dollar. I wanted that coin badly, and watching my cousins peek through the window to monitor me, steeled my resolve. After what appeared to be an eon, I was finally rescued and received my prize. My older cousins continued my baptism by fire at Brule by pulling pranks and telling frightening stories. One of Uncle Ralph's pranks backfired. He led a group of children on a hike. He brought his bow and arrow, explaining that we needed to be on the lookout for bears that were watching us in the forest. My sister, Martha, was so spooked that he had to carry her on his back to Noyes Camp.

Traditionally at Noyes Camp, a child is generally sequestered in the back of the house at night and, in my youth, I ate in the kitchen or the children's dining room, now used for laundry. I knew my transition to an adult was progressing when I moved to the front of the house and was allowed to eat with the adults. When my canoe skills improved I moved from the bow to the stern, which was more demanding in its role as "captain" of the craft. Making the fire in the Council Room fireplace was also a big step. For the Ojibwe, fishing mastery was a final step in the transition from boy to man and I was proud to land my first brook trout on a dry fly, right off the Noyes Camp dock.

★ ★ ★ ★ ★

Loggers in the Brule Valley entered the camps when the ground was frozen hard in November or December. They used humor, storytelling and a rough and tumble brand of comradery to pass the bitterly cold months of winter and hopefully refrain from killing each other. The more outrageous the tale, the better. Jane Pearson Grimsrud, in her *Brule River Forest and Lake Superior: Cloverland Anecdotes,* relates one such fable: *"It was so cold that words froze right in the air. All winter long the weather remained that way. If one said 'Hello' he could see it hanging in the air. If a teamster swore at his team, the sound of his voice would freeze also. That spring when the thaw came you could see all of those oaths thaw out the same day. Never in all history since the beginning of man was a more terrible profane barrage thrown over than there was that spring on the Brule River."*

★ ★ ★ ★ ★

The use of tobacco has long been a ritual on the Brule River Valley for centuries. The Natives used sacred tobacco, *asemaa,* as part of many ceremonies: offerings were carefully placed on the ground in a variety of rituals or ice before spear fishing in the winter. It was inhaled and exhaled so the smoke rose to honor the Gichi-manidoo or any number of other spirits. *Kinnickinac,* or "mixture," was more of an everyday form, most often a blend of willow bark, dogwood, sumac leaves and tobacco as well as other medicinal plants. The bonding aspects varied from praying, greeting, declaring friendship, an introduction for trading, the start of an undertaking or an offering to an elder when asking for instruction. Today the Ojibwe use more palatable blends of tobacco.

Tobacco has continued to be part of the Brule ritual. John LaRock, the French-Ojibwe fishing guide who taught Calvin Coolidge to fly fish, greeted his old friends along the river, *"It has been a long time since we smoked together."* Even though my Great-grandfather George Noyes was General Counsel for an insurance company, and the younger Arthur Holbrook was a physician, tobacco use was omnipresent when the Gitche Gumee Camping Club founders were in residence on the Brule.

Cigarettes, cigars, pipes and chew were all common. Neighbor Morris Holbrook remarked, *"…GGCC was a hotbed of tobacco consumption in all its forms… the habit seemed to be contagious because nearly everyone at Gitche Gumee, except those underneath the age of about fifteen, considered smoking a full-time avocation."*

The old guides were addicted to the most unpleasant form of tobacco use. Dr. Arthur T. Holbrook, in his *Log of a Trout Fisherman*, described chewing tobacco as: *"that indispensable round, brown, cardboard package that looks like a shoe-blacking box, and has a label reading 'Copenhagen Snuff' and without which to provide a wad of strong, black, powdered tobacco to slip under his upper lip, the guide would indeed face a glum day."*

There's something about a group of guys in the north woods that promotes smoking. Some of my friends take the opportunity to sneak their yearly ration of cigarettes away from the watchful eyes of their wives. Cigars are common. And pipes appear on occasion.

C.D. O'Brien of the Winneboujou Club captured the essence of a men's outing to Brule that resonates still almost 130 years later: *"It was a merry and happy party that, in May 1889, trooped through the woods, stopping, as usual, at the Saints Rest, and halting at the top of the hill where the colors of the camp are first visible, saluting them with bared heads and lifted hands. And then when the beautiful river flashed up its smile of welcome and the rapids murmured their sweet greetings, those world-worn men, clasped hands and looking lovingly into each other's eyes, exchanged with each other their happy congratulations, for Mother Nature had led them to her choicest home and there lovingly wrapped them in her brightest robes…."*

Noyes Camp seems to nurture comradery. There is a cadence to the continuum of the Boys of Brule concept through the generations beginning with Great-grandfather George Noyes and his friends. Hack Noyes Jr. and Uncle Ralph Bagley followed suit as did my mother's cousin Billy Dalrymple. My cousins Hack III and twins Chris and Blake Noyes have similar groups and a fifth generation, Will and Andrew Parke, has continued the tradition.

Cousin Blake displayed the ultimate dedication to his Brule guy's outing. His nine-months-pregnant daughter Tricia was overdue but he went to Wisconsin to co-host the annual outing. Soon after his arrival he received an early morning text and rushed back to St. Louis with eight hours to spare. Relieved after meeting his grandson, congratulating his daughter and secure in the knowledge of everyone's good health, Blake was tempted by brother Chris to hustle back to the river for the last few days of their stay, but wisely declined.

Even the most mundane rituals sustain the bonding nature of the Brule. Caroline Marshall recalled the rhythms of the Winneboujou Club annual meetings when she: *"sat there on the periphery imagining Dad and his vision among the others… who'd been there when he was. And how the vestiges of the 100-year-old fishing club's original comradery still seemed to echo in their fusty, deferential committee reports on the pond and clubhouse, trees and treasury.*

Comradery is forged by a number of circumstances: through adversity, necessity, common interests, backgrounds, goals and experiences. Nowhere is this more evident than life on the Brule River over the centuries. It takes work, however, to keep old friendships current. Time commitments of family and career plus the mobility of today's society are impediments. Boys of Brule live in Arizona, Colorado, Florida, Texas, Minnesota, South Carolina and Ohio. Long work hours and the advent of cocooning tend to make men spend their leisure hours at home staring at large screen, high definition televisions, computers, Kindles and I-Pads. They tune out with headphones.

Participation in political, community and religious activities has waned. Mailing of letters and greeting cards has dwindled. The sport of golf is not growing. Bowling leagues and card clubs are disappearing. Boyhood friendships, so important at the time, seem to fade away as adulthood beckons. Men often experience loneliness and isolation.

The Boys of Brule keep in touch by e-mail, text and cell phone. We share core values regarding friendship. We "get" and trust each other. We generally use straight talk when communicating. Sometimes feelings are hurt but we get over it. We have well developed sardonic senses of humor. The Boys of Brule use each other as sounding boards to discuss different issues and ideas. We enjoy conversation but try to refrain from political discussions.

Our bonds are not limited to each other but include the river and the strong pull of place. The most rewarding part of our annual long weekend is the opportunity to be ourselves without pretense or pressure to act otherwise. The chance to feel young again for a fleeting moment. If some of this appears a bit sophomoric, it's because it often is. It is reassuring and heartening to revert to the old ways. And it doesn't embarrass us one bit.

Noyes Camp card game, 1950s, Uncle Ralph Bagley sitting backward in chair

Dinner is served, left to right, Bud Chambers, Tom Melander and Mike Melander *Courtesy of Marty Schuster*

[8]

THE NAME GAME

"It ain't what they call you; it's what you answer to."

W.C. Fields

★ ★ ★ ★ ★

THERE ARE VARIATIONS OF the Ojibwe creation story, but almost all include this beginning: Gitchi Manido, the Great Creator, sent Way-na-boo-zho, the Original Man, down to Earth to wander the world and name the plants, animals, and geological formations like mountains and valleys. The wolf was sent to accompany the Original Man on his journey.

The meaning of the name Ojibwe is clouded in obscurity but it was given to the branch of the Algonquins by outsiders. They called themselves Anishinaabe, or the First People. The French first encountered the Ojibwe at the falls of the St. Mary River where Lake Superior spills into Lake Huron. The Europeans called the natives *Salteurs* or "People of the Rapids." The English gave the natives the name Chippewa, simply a mispronunciation of Ojibwe.

During their migration west the Ojibwe split in two with one group traveling the north shore of Lake Superior. They were known as, *Zagaakwaandagowininiwag.* "Men of Thick Fir Woods." The group occupying the south shore of the Great Lake nearest to the Brule were called *Kechegummewininewug,* "Men of Great Waters."

The Ojibwe identified themselves through *doodems*, or clans, and the five main original kinship groups included the Crane, Catfish, Loon, Bear and Marten. Many more were spawned from the initial totems. The Cranes were prominent in the Brule River region and were known for their strong, pure voices and their skill in negotiation and mediation. The clan system helped identify family groups, define roles and assign divisions of labor.

The Ojibwe Naming Ceremony, *waawinndaasowinan,* is an important rite of passage. Someone with the reputation of skilled name-giving is approached by the child's parents and given insight into the spirit of the child. Through fasting, prayer, dreams and vision the name giver receives input from the Spirit World. It can be a long process lasting many months.

Eventually a ceremony is held and the name giver will offer tobacco to the grandfather spirits representing the four points of the compass while announcing the final decision. It is recommended that the initiate speak his spirit name to the four winds every morning for an extended period of time. The parents select a group of men and women to act as mentors to the child with the newly minted name.

Some examples of intriguing and descriptive Ojibwe names are Hole in the Day, Rice Maker, Feathers End, Little Bee, Bright Forehead, Neck of the Earth, Flat Mouth, Crows Flesh, Sharpened Stone, Speckled Lynx and Snow Glider.

The Brule River has had a litany of names depending on ethnicity and the time period. The Ojibwe used birch bark scrolls to etch symbols and designs to keep their history, spiritualism and ceremonies alive. Europeans interpreted oral language into French and English versions. The indigenous referred to the Brule as the *Wiisaakode* (Ojibwe) or *Naeisaquoit* (Dakota).

Sieur Du Lhut mentioned the stream in the first written accounts but not by name. In the 1650s maps referred to it as *"La Riviere Aux Aunage,"* the River of Alders, likely due to the frustrating tangle of the shrub-like plants that block the Brule's upper reaches. Various explorers and traders called it *"Goddard's River," "Mad River"* (probably during high water), and the *"Burntwood"* due to charred timber caused by lightning strikes or perhaps controlled burns started by the natives to clear trails to channel deer or moose to desired hunting areas. The French translation stuck: *"La Riviere de Bois Brule,"* now simply shortened to "Brule." At times during the last century one could hear the name pronounced with an accent aigu at the end, but that type of pretension has disappeared.

Michel Curot, a French trader, perhaps had the most poetic approach to naming various parts of the river although it is difficult to determine with precision where these sites lie. He spent his first night on "La Grande Prairie" after entering the stream at its mouth on Lake Superior. He called quiet stretches of the Brule "l'eau qui dort," ("sleeping water"), and one short but tricky stretch of white water "La

Rapide a Vassal," what is today called "the Falls." Another camping spot was a combination of French and Ojibwe "Le Petit Pakouijawin." Curot named the now Long Nebagamon Rapids "L'or Qui Dort" ("Sleeping Bear Rapids").

French Canadian voyageurs had a pecking order depending on the roles they fulfilled. *Mangeurs de Lard*, or Pork Eaters, were rookies at the bottom of the barrel. They handled the most menial of tasks and were paid so little they frequently ended their five-year commitments in debt. The Pork Eaters, sometimes called Montreal Men, paddled to Rendezvous locations delivering trading goods and returning to Quebec with furs. This type of "soft" duty was scorned by the *Hivernants* who ventured into the interior and spent their winters in the frontier.

Coureurs des Bois, Runners of the Woods, worked as independent traders performing double duty as trappers and traders combining arduous physical activity with financial acumen. Their operations outside the auspices of the French government were considered illegal. A *bourgeois* was a British stock holder or proprietor in the North West Company who usually was the highest ranked member of a voyageur expedition to interact with the Ojibwe and handle the negotiation process.

The voyageurs used different methods for handling rapids. A "decharge" involved walking either a full or emptied canoe up or down the fast water while a "portage" was used for more treacherous rapids as the canoe and its contents were carried around the impediment.

An interesting distinction is made by year-long residents of the area who refer to the river as "the Brule." When going to town, they say "going to Brule." Summer people tend to use "Brule" as a catch-all, hence our self-title group "The Boys of Brule." A subtle matter of semantics, but important nonetheless.

A common nickname is "The River of Presidents" to commemorate the Presidents who have stayed on the Brule. U.S. Grant, Grover Cleveland, Herbert Hoover and Dwight Eisenhower have fished its waters and Calvin Coolidge spent the summer of 1928 on the stream at the Cedar Island Lodge, his summer White House. JFK was a near miss, making a quick detour to Big Dick's Buckhorn Inn in Spooner, Wisconsin, during the 1960 Badger State puddle jump campaign to grab a quick beer and use the rest room. There is a plaque on the men's room door. He also visited Ashland and Superior, both just a stone's throw from the Brule River.

Upon the arrival of the first English settlers, various sites on the Brule were named, some poetic and some prosaic. Rapids' names include, "McVickers,"

"Station," "Little Joe," "Long Nebagamon," "Green Bridge," "Clubhouse," "Williamson," "Shale Falls," "The Twins," "Hall's," "Mays Rips," "Doodlebug" and "Hungry Run." "Lenroot Ledges" and "Mays Ledges" are a series of smooth sandstone "steps" best navigated in a kayak or portaged. The two sets of ledges deserve more ominous names. They feature precipitous drops and while the sandstone is smooth, the other downstream rapids are boulder-strewn.

The Lenroots are almost ¾ of a mile long and, if one does not keep the bow straight, the vessel will careen horizontally into a large rock, tipping the canoe, which will quickly fill with as much as 2,000 pounds of water, a life-threatening scenario for the paddlers. I have witnessed one of Noyes Camp's irreplaceable Lucius canoes smashed to pieces in the Ledges as well as an aluminum Grumman bent into a horseshoe, wrapped around a rock in the Falls, from the force of rushing water.

The "Wildcat Rapids" must be named after a sighting of an animal as they are not at all ferocious. My friends and I simply call the Station Rapids "The Wall" for the ill-placed rock edifice on the east bank located at a quick turn in the strong current. The crumbling bulwark is the last vestige of the old railroad bridge.

Lakes on the Brule are simply wide, shallow stretches of calm water. Early European explorers referred to some of them, such as Big Lake, as "Flag Lakes" due the presence of patches of reeds waving in the breeze. The closest ones to Noyes Camp are a short trip upstream, Ashland Lake, Spring Lake and Joe's (or Lucius) Lake. Hart's Lake provides a perfect habitat for trout while Sucker Lake is named for the less appealing rough fish lurking there. Rocky Lake lives up to its moniker, presenting an obstacle course for every passing canoe.

Some of the more evocative place names on the stream are "Finlander's Delight," "Pinetree Landing," "Rainbow Bend," "Blue Spring," "Swiftwater Farm," "Porcupine Crossing," "The Narrows" and "Forget-Me-Not Landing." When Henry Wadsworth Longfellow published his epic poem "Song of Hiawatha" in 1855, it advertised and romanticized the north woods and was simultaneously loved and reviled. The writer borrowed liberally from the Finnish national epic poem, "Kalevala," even using the same meter, trochaic tetrameter, which mimics the beat of a drum.

Longfellow also drew from the works of Henry Schoolcraft who traveled the Brule-St. Croix-Mississippi corridor. The Ojibwe language was mangled somewhat but many words were adopted by avid readers. Minneapolis is home to lakes Nokomis and Hiawatha. The creek, and its falls, which empty into the Mississippi from Lake Minnetonka are named Minnehaha, after the wife of Hiawatha.

The Noyes family has a colorful history of unusual and sometimes inexplicable names. In earlier times we had a Peleg, Orlando, Prince and Eutheria. Later the habit of first names derived from last names became in vogue. Haskell, Perrin, Benson, Colt, Leslie and even an unfortunate cousin named Noyes are a few. Waldo lasted only one generation. My name, Ross, is also a last name generations ago. Nicknames are equally creative. My Grandfather Harrison was nicknamed "Cleve" after Grover Cleveland. Hack, Tuck, Bolt, Dal, Forth, Mossy, Kitsy, Chick, Chici and Mimi are other examples.

In the Puritan days, our family nicknames included Teacher, Elder, Deacon and Witchcraft. Rev. Nicholas Noyes has the dubious distinction of the longest nickname in the family given to him by Judge Samuel Sewald during his despicable role in the Salem Witch Trials: *"Malleus Haerticulum"* or "Hammer of the Heretics."

My Great-grandfather Noyes and his Milwaukee friends used the Longfellow spelling for Lake Superior, "Gitche Gumee," for their camping club, and the Judge named his red canoes after animal and human characters from the poem. They included "Opeechee" ("the Robin"), "Shu shu ga" ("the Blue Heron"), "Kokokoho" ("Great Horned Owl"), "Wawanaissa" ("Whip-poor-will"), "Adjidaumo" ("Squirrel"), "Owaissa" ("Bluebird"), "Wenonah" ("Mother of Hiawatha"), "Wah wah tay see" ("Firefly") and "Te te nica" ("Blue Jay").

The Winneboujou Club was founded in 1886 by the ex-mayor of St. Paul, Chris O'Brien, and was also known as the St. Paul Club as a nod to the hometown of its membership. It was named after the key person in the Ojibwe Creation Story. Winneboujou was said to be a benevolent character whose domain included the shore of Lake Superior and tributaries like the Brule that flowed into the Big Water. While chasing a deer down the stream to the shore of Superior, he emptied his quiver of arrows and then threw rocks that became the Apostle Islands.

Benjamin Armstrong, an interpreter for the U.S. Army, married the daughter of Ojibwe Chief Buffalo and walked comfortably in both worlds. He wrote, *"Henceforth, their great spirit, Winneboujou, could work in his blacksmith shop in peace. Much of his work was done by moonlight, the legend says, with the ringing blows of his hammer being heard by Indians as far away as Superior."*

The sparks from the hammer strikes are said to remain in the sky as the Northern Lights and the copper deposits on the south shore of Lake Superior came from his blacksmithing.

Another story relates the time Winneboujou fell asleep on the banks of the Brule and the South Wind played a trick on him, blowing his canoe downriver and into Lake Superior. When he awoke and whistled, the North Wind sent it back. For that favor, the North Wind became the favorite of Winneboujou.

The founders of the Winneboujou Club were never mentioned by name in the annual *"Brule Chronicles"* of the 1890s but referred to by nicknames related to their professions: "Lawyer," "Banker," "Brakeman," "Surgeon," "Merchant," "Banker" and "Doctor." Club founder C.D. O'Brien took it a step further giving the members Ojibwe names which translated as, "Medicine Man," "Young Buck," "Raven," "Robin," "Beaver", "Bear," "Helldiver," "Turtle," "Prophet," "Wizard," "Prophet" and "Fisher Weasel." The Gitche Gumee Camping Club followed suit with my Great-grandfather being called "Judge." Others were known as the "Commodore," "Colonel" and "Doctor."

Legendary French/Ojibwe guide John LaRock, who called himself "Moose Hide," addressed Dr. Arthur T. Holbrook as "My Dear Doctor Waboose Holbrook" in letters. Waboose is the Ojibwe word for rabbit. The rabbit was central in native lore as the instrument of the Great Spirit who came to Earth as a founder of the Midewiwin, the Great Medicine Society. A perfect example of Dr. Arthur's nurturing nature is a photo of him gingerly cradling an abandoned fawn in his arms. The appellation "Waboose" was a tip of the hat to Holbrook's profession.

Our Boys of Brule group has its share of nicknames: Big T, the Klomper Brothers, Tall Paul, Chip, Lumber, Roscoe P. Coltrane, Dr. Bud the Fish Surgeon, Mints, Bobbo, Glencoe, Wils, Mickey, Two Syllables (or Lorny), Du (or The New Guy), and the late, great Chuck. Dana is just Dana. I call Scott "Old Doc Shorten." Rus, while in desperate need of an additional consonant, remains Rus although it creates confusion with Ross, or should we change it to Ros? "Farm Boy," "Doctor" and "McGillicuddy" are generic, applied to anyone when deemed necessary. Some short-timer Boys of Brule include Riff, Suckface, Skogs, Spino, Tiny Dancer and Greenie. Bud coined the phrase "Boys of Brule" which is somewhat of a misnomer now, but rings true when we are able to relax and shed our daily responsibilities in the woods.

Over the years the BOB have developed our own lingo. As a timesaver we just repeat the punchlines of jokes. Many of us will speak in French. When someone "stirs the pot" (instigates), it can precipitate a "meatcake" (dispute). The bathroom is known as the "growler." A catch-all expression of surprise or pain is "Call the Dr.!" An adult beverage is a "tasty." A quick game of golf is an "emergency nine." "Who's got you doing that?" is a thinly veiled crack when a subtle change in behavior is noted perhaps insinuating spousal influence. "Drop the Puck" is a generic term used as a greeting or an exclamation, much like aloha or ciao.

If someone cuts their May visit short or can't come at all, it is considered "bagging" and triggers my automatic response, "just one weekend!" Big "T" has the most convoluted, and lame, excuses. Once he missed the annual outing to attend the wedding of his "wife's cousin's daughter in Alabama." Another time he had to witness his "daughter-in-law's sister's first communion in Iowa." One wonders why he even admits these transgressions.

Some mishaps occurring during our annual events are followed by the phrases: "I blame Hurd," "that was unnecessary," "that's just mean" or "it makes a difference." Misdeeds incur a status of "double secret probation," although it is a hollow threat with no real consequences. "Pearson, here's what we're going to do," was always a prelude to task delegation by Tall Paul.

An unannounced attendee is a "Mystery Guest." There have been a few over the years. Once college friend Bill Wilson appeared from Texas under the guise of a new pseudonym, "Dr. Bevo." In 2016 Scott Shorten snuck back to Brule from Ohio after a 21 year absence. Jim Hurd was a surprise attendee when he cancelled a meeting in Costa Rica. Whatever their nicknames, it adds to the experience when old friends make the effort to preserve and enhance the tradition.

Gitche Gumee
Camping Club
luggage tag

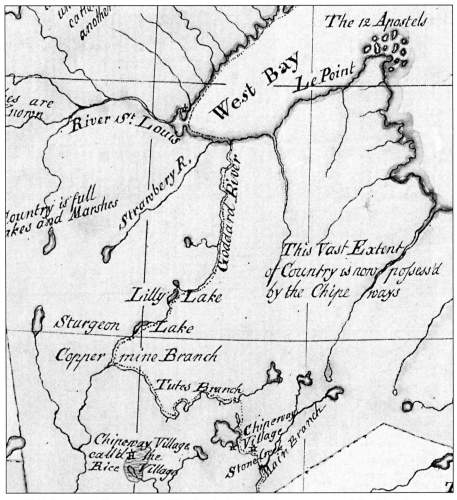

1766 Jonathan Carver map. The Brule is briefly known as the "Goddard".

[9]

THE BOYS OF BRULE WET A LINE

"Once I knew a man beset with business cares who came to the little turn around at the end of the road and camped for three months in a trailer. He was as happy a man as I ever knew. He caught up with himself there… Old Doc Brule cured him. He went to sleep with the river's lullaby and woke up to the song of the birds. He built himself back by slogging up and down the Brule's rocky backbone. He caught and ate more trout than mortal man is entitled to these days."

GORDON MCQUARRIE, *When the White Throats Sing*

★ ★ ★ ★ ★

THIS COULD HAVE BEEN written about other streams emptying into Lake Superior, but it was never truer than the fishery of the Brule River when my Great-grandfather George Noyes and his companions first ventured into Douglas County. They used split-bamboo rods and the Judge was also known for his prowess spearing pike and pickerel on nearby lakes and suckers on the Brule.

At the time of European discovery, the Ojibwe also used spears, but with obsidian tipped points. The men performed a fish dance and offered tobacco to honor and respect their prey. The Ojibwe fished local lakes, primarily at night. Some used baskets of fire secured to the bow of the canoes not only to attract fish but to reflect off the eyes of the walleyes. The French named a favorite fishing spot "Lac Flambeau" (Lake of the Torches), where the Ojibwe used pine-sap impregnated birch-bark torches, called *waaswaagon,* to light the way.

The natives fished for subsistence, not sport. In addition to spears, they used traps, hook and line, gill and dip nets, lures and bait. They preserved their catch in the winter by freezing and by smoking and drying the rest of the year. One method of cooking fish was to wrap them in clay, bury them in the coals for hours and, when ready to eat, extract them. The scales would stick to the clay.

To catch fish through the ice, the Ojibwe cut a hole and built a small tent from tree branches draped with blankets to block out the sun. Snow was swept from the area around the hole and the angler laid face down on a mat for insulation. Lures were intricately carved from cured wood and painted to resemble walleye, pike, bass, pan fish and bass. These lures, considered to be one of the earliest forms of North American folk art, were attached to a line and jigging stick. The lure was jerked to imitate a fish in distress, and when the prey approached, a spear was launched into the frigid water.

For centuries, the Brule River was used as a highway, a means to get from point A to point B. The Ojibwe paddled up the stream to reach the Folle Avoine region. Translated literally, it means "false oats," but was used to reference wild rice. Eventually, European fur traders, explorers and missionaries traveled the Lake Superior-Brule-St. Croix route to reach the Mississippi. The beaver had blocked access to trout, leaving little room to spawn or feed as fallen timber and dams littered the stream. Eventually the detritus was cleared and brook trout flourished.

By the mid-1800s, Ojanimaavu, an Ojibwe man, built a bark lodge at the mouth of the Brule and established a fishing operation, netting whitefish, cisco and lake trout. The fish were shipped east to La Pointe on Madeline Island where they were salted, packed in barrels and sent down the Great Lakes waterway. The fishing cornucopia on the upper river was still largely untapped. Ojanimaavu was often joined near the mouth by ships sailing a bit upriver seeking safe harbor from violent gales of the Great Lake.

By the mid-19th century the fisheries of New England had been seriously depleted and Robert Barnwell Roosevelt, Teddy's uncle, ventured west in 1862 to the shores of Lake Superior and extolled the virtues of the Brule: *"The finest trout-fishing in the world is to be obtained at Lake Superior….in the neighborhood of this village two hundred and fifty pounds, weight of speckled trout have been killed in one day by one good fisherman and one poor one… The Brule River, and the many streams that empty into the lake in the neighborhood, although often choked with drift, are filled with fine trout."*

Until 1876, the Bayfield Road, stretching from Superior to Bayfield, was only open to stagecoach traffic in the winter. Its year-round use opened the Brule River to men with $ signs in their eyes, and large amounts of brook trout were extracted for commercial purposes. John Bardon unashamedly relates his pillaging of the trout population in 1877: *"Our purpose on this expedition was to hunt and trap and also catch speckled trout, the latter of which was accomplished by the Chippewa-made trap net. No hunting laws or licenses had yet reached here… We had not the slightest difficulty in securing all the trout we could load on the three dog teams, probably 1,500 pounds or more. We let the fish freeze and then packed them in packs for ease of handling. I remember watching the millions of trout in the Brule, through the clear ice. There seemed to be a never ending procession passing up and down. The 1,500 pounds we took hadn't made the slightest dent."*

Great-grandfather Noyes and friends first congregated on the Brule near the zenith of its fishing majesty. A convergence of factors led to this idyllic circumstance. The headwaters, and much of the upper river, were spring fed and fertile with excellent habitat for spawning. The riparian environment offered vegetation and wood cover on the banks and into the stream, which kept the water temperature cool. The Pine Barrens adjacent to the river filtered rain water and melting snow, and there was little fishing pressure. Beaver that had dammed the water flow and affected the habitat and mobility of trout were nearly exterminated. The Judge and his friends used wet flies for many years. Dry flies appeared on the scene around 1907.

Unfortunately, a perception of endless resources permeated the region, whether it was for fur-bearing animals, deer, fish, or timber. By the 1890s avarice was taking its toll. Logging gouged the river and its banks, destroying spawning habitat. Leveling of soft timber for paper eliminated shade on upstream tributaries and raised water temperatures. Railroad construction left burning slash piles and ash and cinders fell into the Brule. Downstream clay bank erosion muddied the water. Unmonitored winter harvesting of brook trout from the spring ponds was devastating.

Easier access increased fishing pressure, and large removal of trout to sell to restaurants and retailers was particularly damaging. In the spring of 1890, Judge Noyes arrived at camp to find a note pinned to the lodge door, *"Thanks for your hospitality. We caught 161 trout on your bend of the river."* Finally, ill-advised stocking of non-native rainbow trout increased competition for food and habitat. It was the perfect storm, and fishing regulations and bag limits came early to the Brule.

At the end of the 19th century, Winneboujou Club members were up in arms over the shortening of the trout season from August 5 to September 1. The May Men's outing was limited to hunting, hiking, canoeing and shooting the breeze. C.D. O'Brien, in his highly stylized manner, described the situation, *"….in secret and in by dark and winding trails they stole into the great council of the chiefs of the country called Ouisconsin…to make a law…by day and night the Brule trout should only breed and spawn, that they should not during that time feed or leap or play, seize at the twisting worm or spring at the daring fly. Then Wendigo, our chief, called a council of the braves, and loud and long the war call pealed, and bitter were the denunciations of the skulking wolves who had done this wrong…others said, 'Upon this beautiful river it has always been peace. We will go to the lodge; we will visit the river; we will wander through the trails among the pines, but we will obey the law, bad as it is….'"*

Captain Alexander McDougall was disturbed by the decline and, in 1920, he took matters into his own hands. He owned land on both sides of Joe's Lake, just a half-hour's pole upriver from Noyes Camp, and he placed concrete anchors to the river bottom supporting iron posts connected by wire fencing. This cordoned off the lake except for a passage on the east side for canoe traffic. McDougall had created a 2,000-foot-long private fishing sanctuary.

Despite the predictable outrage, the Captain showed no remorse regarding his new personal fishing hole. Angry fishermen pushed under the fencing to cast their flies while waiting two years for the Wisconsin State Railway Commission to make a decision. McDougall ignored the ruling to dismantle the fence and threatened those who testified against him at the hearings. One September morning in 1921, with a hint of autumn in the air, the river awoke to snipped wires and toppled anchors and posts. Vigilante justice prevailed. Rumor has it that guide Willie Cheesir was the culprit.

The 3 species of trout that swim the waters of the upper Brule have their distinct styles of dueling with a fisherman. The rainbow will break the water to strike and vigorously shake to dislodge the fly. The brookie prefers to fight underwater and seeks a rock or log and heads to the bottom to break the line. The brown may not be as gymnastic as the rainbow or as crafty as the brook trout, but it will usually provide the longest and hardest battle.

Great-grandfather unwittingly added to the competition among the species by stocking the carnivorous brown in 1910. He and his Anglophile friends preferred the term "Loch Levens" as a tip to the tam-o-shanter to the Scots. Whatever the name, they are hogs and bullies, eating smaller fish and taking over spawning and feeding grounds. The most storied Brule brown, "Big Nelly," was said to weigh 9 pounds and frequented a deep pool in one of the Cedar Island spring ponds. Jack "Smokey" Ordway hooked her once but was unable to land the leviathan.

Brown trout can endure warmer temperatures. There are two philosophical camps regarding fishing for browns. Brook trout aficionados look askance at the Johnny Come Latelys, but there are avid night fishermen who love the challenge of doing battle with the cannibalistic denizens of the dark. Night fishing is difficult, exciting, contrarian and a bit spooky. A pleasant stretch of water by day becomes a different animal by night, and navigating a stream with so many obstacles and fast water in the dark is not for a rookie or the faint of heart.

James Jesus Angleton spent many summers on the Brule at his lodge just downstream from Noyes Camp. While he tried a variety of lures, his favorite was the "Angleton," a mouse style fashioned from deer hair and saddle hackles, the feathers of a rooster. Our downstream neighbor, Caroline Marshall, had the opportunity to spend an afternoon with James, fascinated by his revelations: "'Browns are vicious, atavistic creatures,' Angleton says....'They eat mice and frogs, baby chipmunks, their own kind.' He stretches his forefingers to demonstrate, matching them in a flame shaped arc. It must be five or six inches wide. 'This is the mouth of one,' he says. His eyes gleam, 'Look what it could snap on to.' He describes the life-size mouse lure he uses when the moon is down and mist a lid on the river. I saw him once as a child-coming suddenly wet, slippery, and silent as a huge brown from the dark, trailing rain, his fedora pinched and dripping, pulled low over his eyes, a fisherman wholly unlike others."*

★ ★ ★ ★ ★

The usual night fishing plan is to depart Noyes Camp at 6 PM with trailered canoes to launch at Stone's Bridge and drift downstream. Fishing from a canoe has its advantages over wading. You are always floating into new environments and the negatives of thrashing around the brush or disappearing in a drop-off are non issues.

There is always the issue of snagging a tag alder since it is imperative to cast as close to cover as possible, and if you don't get hung up a few times you aren't reaching the lairs of the big browns. They lurk under exposed tree roots, overhanging trees and sweeper pines that have fallen with branches touching the water. When night fishing, the placement of the fly is more important than matching the insect hatch.

A great spot to cast is the Noyes Landing, where the Twin Rapids spill into the widening of the river that is Big Lake, a perfect example of a transitional zone conducive to catching trout. A night fishing outing usually ends around midnight as the canoe reaches the Noyes Camp landing. Neville Connolly, a Noyes in-law, recalled one magical evening: *"….we had been fishing late, we suddenly saw tremendous lights ahead of us. We were convinced the Camp was on fire and paddled the rest of the way as fast as we could. When we got closer we realized it was no earthly fire but one of the most dramatic displays of Northern Lights imaginable. It was almost midnight but we woke everyone at Camp and they staggered out in their night clothes to appreciate the spectacle."*

Hank's Creation is the unholy co-conspirator of night fishing on the Brule. Designed by local grocer Hank Denny, it is the duckbill platypus of fishing lures, so ugly it could not inspire a mother's love. It is the bastard child of a bass fishing favorite, the Hula Popper, and resembles a voodoo doll. The body is made from a tapered, silver-painted cork with bug eyes symptomatic of a thyroid condition. It sports deer hair and the tail is accented with red and white buck tail, Mallard flank feather and red kip, a crinkly material used to resemble insect wings. Aesthetic issues notwithstanding, Hank's Creation is the subject of Noyes family fishing lore. Jim Flather, my mother's cousin, was one of our family's finest fishermen.

"One of the best night fishers I have ever had the pleasure of bringing down river lost a Hank's Creation to an enormous Rainbow in one of the big pools in the upper river. Jim Flather had fished the Brule at night for most of his adult life. He had forgotten his night fly box with his Hank's Creation tucked inside. He asked if he could borrow one of mine. After a few drifts, that rainbow took the fly hard midway through its swing. It

surged back upstream then broke water in a cartwheeling jump. The fish broke its heavy leader as it drove for the rocky bottom of the pool. Two nights later while out with a friend, that fish was caught and released, mangled fly still in its jaw."

STEVE THERRIEN, *Brule River guide*

There are many first-rate fly fishermen on the Brule River. As an aggregate, our next door neighbors, the Holbrooks, may be the finest. My Great-grandfather Noyes mastered the tricky style of casting while standing up, a habit he passed on to his son, Haskell. Sadly, I am not in their league. I am a distracted fisherman and my mind wanders. I am often unprepared when a fish strikes. I caught my first brook trout from the Noyes Camp landing under the strict tutelage of my Uncle Ralph.

Once I came in second during a children's fishing contest in the White Mountains of Arizona but was overshadowed when my cousin Virginia hooked a duck. My son Kyle and I caught brook trout and salmon in a high altitude volcanic lake near Bend, Oregon. Fish were first stocked there in the early 1900s via strings of pack horses trudging up mountain trails hauling 10-gallon galvanized milk cans filled with trout.

Perhaps the most fun I have had dry fly fishing was on a small Wisconsin lake about 60 minutes from Noyes Camp with Tall Paul Schuster. Using borrowed equipment, we fished for smallmouth bass, ounce for ounce one of the feistiest and most gymnastic fish one can find. Maybe they have a Napoleonic Complex trying to compete with their hog-jawed big brother, the largemouth. When French explorers first encountered them they nicknamed the smallmouth, *"the fish who struggle."*

When hooked the smallmouth will take to the air and turn somersaults to shake free. That day we fished with dyed deer-hair flies and although I was getting strikes with almost every cast, I kept losing them before they reached the boat. Marty scolded me for my lack of skill but I discovered the fly had a barbless hook. We released all the fish we caught in hopes of returning the next year but the lake froze to the bottom during winter, killing all the bass.

As we get older, fishing as an activity for the Boys of Brule has waned. The most talented of us was Charlie Hurd, who works hard at it and fishes streams in

Montana, Oregon and Idaho. One Sunday as we were preparing to leave, Charlie was getting in some last casts down at Frog Point. We heard him shout, *"Somebody bring a camera!"* A few seconds later he yelled, *"Bring a blankety-blank camera!"* He had landed a 26" rainbow and wanted some photographic evidence before he returned the beauty to the stream.

There are many accomplished anglers among us. The Melander brothers are avid stalkers of the muskie, the "Freshwater Barracuda." Noyes Camp is less than an hour's drive from Hayward, Wisconsin, gateway to world class muskie waters. Tom and Mike catch and release their muskie catches on Lake of the Woods where they have a place. Marty has caught his share of salmon in Alaska and Dana has spent countless hours trolling and casting in Lake Minnetonka, just west of Minneapolis, considered one of the nation's best bass fishing lakes.

Bud Chambers is our go-to all-around fishing specialist and early bird. He catches, cleans and cooks for a fine Boys of Brule breakfast. The traditional shore lunch consists of freshly caught trout after a paddle from Stone's Bridge to the Noyes Landing picnic grounds.

The fish are gutted, covered in flour and cornmeal, and cooked whole, head and all, in one of our huge frying pans preheated over the fire until the coating of bacon grease sizzles. The goal is to turn the skin a light shade of brown while keeping the meat moist and flaky. I rank the brook and brown as the tastiest while the rainbow comes in a bland third.

Fishing stories abound on the Brule. Uncle Ralph Bagley told one of my favorites. A fine fisherman, one evening he was out on the river when he snagged himself on the back cast, sinking the fly into his bald pate. He paddled back to Gitche Gumee and sheepishly walked up to the Holbrook's lodge, interrupting the cocktail hour.

Dr. Arthur T. removed the barb, cleaned the small wound, applied a Band-Aid and sent him on his way. Not long after, my uncle repeated the uncharacteristic mistake, and trudged back to the neighbors. After seeing the second fly embedded in his head, the Dr. wryly commented, "Ralph, if you wanted an invitation, all you had to do was ask."

Over the years, anglers have fished with guides, wearing expensive apparel and using equipment of questionable utility purchased from Orvis, but few were more successful than Mrs. Digle, who spent her summers near the Brule. She fished wearing a dress while sitting under a tree on the east bank of the river above a deep hole favored by trout seeking a cool spot. Her perch was just north of where the spring-fed, well-shaded Little Brule tributary empties into the river at the town of Brule. Mrs. Digle caught her limit without the fuss of plowing through the water in waders, or riding in a cumbersome canoe.

In May 2018, the Boys of Brule had an amusing situation on the Brule. Friday afternoon I returned from a downriver meeting to find Marty wading in the stream flicking his fly into promising spots. Shocked I said, *"What are you doing? The season doesn't start until midnight!* Marty replied, *"No, it started on April 28."* Tall Paul is an intelligent man and has fished and hunted all over the world, but I wondered what he was talking about.

We consulted the 2018 Wisconsin Fishing Regulations pamphlet and sure enough, it supported Marty's contention. Upon further review, however, I noticed this date applied to the OTHER Wisconsin Brule River which forms part of the state's border with Michigan. He had unintentionally jumped the gun by a few hours. To further complicate matters, there is another Brule River which flows into Superior on its north shore in Minnesota.

Dry fly fishing can use a good de-mythologizing. It is not necessary to look natty. In fact, Dr. Arthur T. Holbrook said the early anglers (it's also not necessary to call them "anglers"), looked like "tramps." Old shirts with fraying collars and cuffs are just fine to wear under wader suspenders. A drab vest with a few flies piercing it is acceptable. A faded baseball cap is all that is needed to complete one's accessorizing.

As far as strategy, William G. Tapply says in his *The Truth about Fly Fishermen:* *"We happen to know that any time trout are feeding on the surface, dry-fly fishing is the easiest, deadliest—really the only way to catch them. We can pinpoint the exact locations of specific feeding fish by their rise forms. We don't have to guess what they're eating, because we can see the bugs on the water, and we can tie on a fly that imitates them with confidence. We can watch the way our fly drifts over our target fish. If we can see him eat it, we lift our rod and catch him. If we see he doesn't eat it, we know that either the fly or the drift was wrong, and we know how to make corrections… Sportsmanship, tradition, artfulness, fancy equipment, and aesthetic values have nothing to do with it."*

★ ★ ★ ★ ★

Fishing can be a solitary salve for the psyche or a lifelong memory, strengthening the bond between family, friends and the river. Cousin Chris Noyes, accepting the first annual Wisconsin DNR Green Tie Award on behalf of the Noyes family, related a story firmly lodged in his Brule River psyche. Joanne Haas of the DNR reported his experience: *"It was a cold night. Chris starts, and he was about 11 or 12. His twin brother* [Blake], *their father and Chris—three substantial humans, you might say…climbed into a single canoe to fish for brown trout. There was also a guide with the three big guys in the same canoe on the Brule River. 'That poor guide was in a canoe with three big guys.' He said and laughed at the memory, 'My dad caught one big fish after midnight. I remember how excited I was that he caught it. I was so cold but excited.'"*

Greg Lonke and a group of friends have fished the Brule for decades. They have a cabin tucked in the woods downstream simply known as "Trout Camp." Like the Boys of Brule, they have nicknames: "Sven Lonkila," "Big Dog" and "Old Sap Ass." One night sitting around the fire they discussed the relative merits of Wisconsin streams when Greg opined, *"Boys, those guys fish the Root to fill their ego, you fish the Brule to fill your soul."*

There are still some magical moments for me when time seems suspended and every cast brings renewed hope.

President Coolidge Summer White House postcard, 1928

[10]

WIIGIWAAMS, TENTS, SHACKS AND LODGES

"The log buildings typically favored for wilderness camps and western ranches were closely associated with a log cabin myth that romanticized the hardy outdoor life of American pioneers and identified the cabin with a democratic frontier spirit and the dream of the good life."

RACHEL CARLEY, *Cabin Fever*

★ ★ ★ ★ ★

WHEN GREAT-GRANDFATHER NOYES and his sportsmen friends first camped on the Brule River they pitched canvas tents. There were tents for sleeping and one each for cooking and dining. Beds consisted of balsam boughs placed on the ground. The campers, when very cold, slept in their clothes and a coat as they burrowed under a heavy blanket. On at least one occasion, the campers' wake-up call was a volley of lead whizzing over their tents when a deer wandered into the clearing. In the 1880s the Brule Ojibwe village, near the Gitche Gumee Camping Club campsite, featured shacks, tents and wiigiwaams. One structure had a modern convenience: a birch bark porch added to one of the huts housing a camp stove for cooking.

The western Great Lakes Ojibwe built dome shaped wiigiwaams as more permanent dwellings. The frames were constructed from thin, flexible saplings about 2" in diameter at the bottom, tapering to no more than 1" at the top. The pointed ends were secured in pre-dug holes and bent and lashed near the top. Tree bark covered the exterior in the winter months with cat-tails used in the summer, with a gap for an entrance. After interaction with European traders around 1700, canvas was often used on the outside. Sleeping platforms were fashioned from hardwood branches and a hearth hole was dug in the middle with surrounding stones to contain the fire. A hole at the top allowed smoke to escape.

After a long, hard day on the water, the voyageurs snatched some sleep in the most rudimentary of places. They chose a bed along the river on a level piece of sand, moss or ground. They slathered themselves with bear grease and skunk urine to ward off the persistently swarming mosquitos, black flies, gnats and other noxious insects. During inclement weather, the voyageurs tucked their heads under their canoes to deflect the sheets of pelting rain.

The wintering voyageurs, or *hivernants,* spent the bitterly cold months in forts like the North West Company Fur Post on Wisconsin's Snake River, near an Ojibwe village. John Sayer was a *bourgeois,* the leader of the Fond du Lac trading department. The fort was constructed in 1804 and included quarters for Sayer and his Ojibwe wife, a trading room and rooms for supplies and the voyageurs. The men slept in bunkbeds near the fireplace with chinking material between the vertical logs to keep out the wind and precipitation. A wall circled the building to protect it from marauding Dakota and there was only a single gate, making the installation easier to defend.

Loggers slept in poorly made, windowless bunkhouses on narrow wooden slats. Bunkbeds, sleeping two on each level, lined the long sides of the building. There was no ventilation and the shacks were ill-kempt, and reeked of wet socks and tobacco. Their dirty straw or pine bough bedrolls were infested with lice and bedbugs. A small wash tub, with pails of water, was available at the door for the men to shave or perform a cursory wash. A grindstone was located in the rear for the loggers to sharpen their axes.

Little did the Swedes know when they built a log cabin in the mid-1600s on Darby Creek, that they were creating an iconic symbol of the American Dream in what was to become Penn's Woods. Their log cabin design became the prototype for not only housing, but defense, industry and animal husbandry when English speaking settlers arrived. Round logs, still covered with bark, were notched, eliminating the need for nails.

Imported glass was expensive and the Swedes used a method of sliding boards to create windows. Clay floors were tightly tamped to assure firmness. A combination of mud and clay, supplemented with animal hair, grass and straw were crammed in crevices to keep the elements at bay. The Darby Creek structure, inhabited for nearly 300 years, is believed to be the oldest North American log cabin still standing.

To the British, cabins were known as sleeping quarters on a ship. On terra firma in the New World, they were a new phenomenon called "cabbins," "cabanes" or cabinns." Slight, slapdash shacks were sometimes known as "English Wigwams." Little care was given to construction and the log buildings were leaky and drafty.

Cabins were not always romanticized. Ben Franklin made a class distinction between cabin dwellers and those with more dignified homes in a 1770 letter to grandson Benjamin Franklin Bothe. He claimed there are *"two Sorts of People,"* ones who *"live comfortably in Good Houses"* and those who *"are poor and dirty and live in miserable Cabins and garrets."* The author of *Poor Richard's Almanac* was suffering from a Puritan hangover. America still viewed the wilderness as a malevolent force to be conquered rather than enjoyed. The back to nature movement was still decades in the future.

Andrew Jackson was the first pioneer President. He was born in either North or South Carolina. Borders were ill defined in those days. He was neither an aristocratic Virginian nor a New Englander, but a child of the frontier. Jackson massacred and evicted Native Americans and lived in a log farmhouse from 1804 to 1821 with his wife, Rachel, on a parcel of land that would grow to be 1,000 acres. Once Jackson's mansion, the "Hermitage," was finished, the log building was then converted to slave quarters as the future President was well on his way to becoming a prosperous cotton plantation owner. Despite his growing wealth, and contrary to the image of the U.S. as an egalitarian nation, Old Hickory's election was a victory of the common man over the elite

The log cabin became a stepping stone for Americans looking to better their station in life. Author James Fennimore Cooper almost single handedly took the frontiersmen from social outcasts to respectability and even hero status in his books, *The Pioneers* and *Last of the Mohicans.* Thomas Cole and the Hudson Valley

School of artists further moved the dial with paintings like *Daniel Boone Sitting at the Door of his Cabin at the Great Osage Lake.* This was pure Americana without colonial vestiges of the Old World.

The great camps of the Adirondacks were the forerunners of the cabin renaissance in the late 1800s, and writers and artists flocked there to chronicle the shrinking wilderness of America. Industrialists commissioned these prodigious, oversized camps seemingly designed to hold all the grandeur of nature under one roof. Natural materials such as hand-peeled pine logs, river stone and decorative accents fashioned from twigs and branches were used to create these forest havens. A sense of impending loss of the frontier and the impulse to escape the complexity and power of advancing technology fueled this passion for more natural surroundings, providing a respite from the city.

Americans viewed retreating to nature as a restorative return to simplicity, honesty and wellness. The log cabin became a symbol of the American Dream before the term was coined. It was first politicized when the Whigs and William Henry Harrison appropriated the cabin to evoke the image of a common man with humble roots. The facts were ignored as he was actually born to Virginia aristocracy in a large farm house.

Harrison handed out small log cabin replicas representing the comforts of home, security, self-reliance and patriotism. My ancestor, Edward Wilder Haskell Jr., participated in the Vermont leg of the campaign in 1840. He traveled in a group of fifty men with a miniature cabin mounted on a large, low-slung cart, pulled by a train of twelve matched horses. The entourage included a complete commissary, an oft refilled keg of hard cider and a short-barreled artillery piece fired to signal the townspeople of an impending rally.

The log cabin, and what it symbolizes, endures in politics. A gloomy Adlai Stevenson, the unsuccessful Democratic nominee in the 1952 election, admitted, *"I wasn't born in a log cabin. I didn't work my way through school nor did I rise from rags to riches, and there's no use trying to pretend I did."* Bill Clinton, stumping for Barack Obama in 2012 quipped, *"Bob Strauss* [Democratic Party Chairman] *used to say every politician wants every voter to believe he was born in a log cabin."*

The Finns, who came to farm the lowlands adjacent to the Brule River, were proficient log home builders during the early sportsmen's era. The logs they used were rarely sawed, but chosen carefully for existing fit. They made their own shingles. The Finns were so skillful that they helped build many of the first wave summer homes for the city campers.

The original Noyes Camp burned to the ground on May 14, 1924. A defective chimney caused the inferno. Great Grandfather George died in 1916 and his wife Agnes took the reins and supervised the building of the beautiful lodge that remains one of the finest in Wisconsin. Joe Lucius was the contractor and lovingly managed the project from beginning to end. The Adirondack style design was an architectural gem using the best materials to construct the building with meticulous craftsmanship.

The tall, straight pine logs were shipped by rail from Oregon, off loaded at the Winneboujou whistle stop and floated a short distance upriver to the construction site where they were draw-knifed smooth. The logs were cut to the proper lengths and laid horizontally with the Swedish Cope method which created such a tight fit that no chinking or insulation was necessary. Perfectly perpendicular ends protrude from the corners in the saddle notch style. Granite of various colors from different quarries was shipped from far off locations to build the massive Council Room fireplace while river stone was employed for the two other hearths. The broad multi gabled roof is interrupted by three chimneys and has generous open eaves.

The 6,500-square-foot monument to Agnes Noyes features a two story, log vaulted Council Room, wrapped by a three-sided balcony that provides access to the seven bedrooms in the front of the house. The upstairs back hall leads to four more bedrooms primarily for children and overflow guests. The house has five bathrooms and fourteen sinks. The ceilings are comprised of countless planks of tongue and groove fir while the floors feature oak and fir. The dining room is perfectly placed with an upriver view, and a 1,500 square foot, three-sided screened porch flanks the river as it serpentines around Frog Point. Three swinging beds hang from the porch ceiling on chains: popular places to read a book or take a nap.

The windows throughout the house and doors in the Great Room have diamond pane glass, which have now been sullied by generations of children's handprints, difficult to clean but sentimental reminders of what is cherished in the continuum of Noyes Camp life. On the doors leading to the ping pong table, the heights of all Noyes family children are marked with a dash, their name and year. The sizes range from infants who spent their first visit to Noyes Camp sleeping in a dresser drawer to 6'6" teenage boys.

Change comes slowly to Noyes Camp. The bedrooms are decorated nicely but dainty, frilliness is eschewed as we try to preserve the heritage of a fishing camp. Old photos and art work are hung on the walls. Iconic items include a heavy, black metal dial style telephone and a wicker "fainting couch" that is the single most uncomfortable piece of furniture ever made. The flatbed wheelbarrow used to haul four-foot- long logs from the wood shed to the wood box sports a new tire and a refurbished platform. Another wicker couch is the only item that survived the fire. There is something comforting in the familiarity of these old relics There are modern conveniences such as a dishwasher, microwave, icemaker, two refrigerators and two ovens to handle large crowds.

The walls of the hallway in the back of the second floor are home to a gallery of old portraits, artwork and other photos. My favorite is one of in-law Donald McLennan riding an ostrich. There are paintings by Great-great-aunt Ida Haskell, an impressionist, who was one of the first women artists to break through the barriers against females in this field. There are photographic portraits of my Great-grandparents and my Grandmother by Ida's companion, Alice Boughton, also a celebrated artist. A door in the pantry leads to the old ice box that held large blocks of sawdust covered ice that were cut from local lakes in the winter in the days before refrigerators.

Upkeep is expensive on wood buildings in the wet and cold north woods but we make a commitment to keep the lodge in excellent shape as our first priority. This can lead to difficult decisions. Our Guide House was the summer home to the French/Ojibwe men who skillfully navigated the waters of the Brule avoiding rocks and back-casts. When the U.S. entered World War II the guides left for better paying factory jobs in support of the military efforts. The Guide House deteriorated and needed to be addressed before it was beyond repair. It was a painful decision but we decided to concentrate on the main house. Pragmatism over ruled nostalgia.

There is a market for deteriorating log cabins. There are companies who take them down and rebuild them on the customer's property. We sold the Guide House which has been given a new life elsewhere in Wisconsin. The dismantling process exposed a peevish porcupine's home and some relics like old glass jars. Some of the old iron cut nails made their way into the tires of our cars as final retribution from the old structure.

[11]

CANOES, GUIDES AND RAPIDS

"When I must leave this great river
O bury me close to the wave
And let my canoe and paddle
Be the only mark over my grave"

Mon Canoe d'ecorce" ["My Bark Canoe"]
Translated by Frank Oliver Call

★ ★ ★ ★ ★

THE EARLIEST EVIDENCE OF a canoe in North America is a 7,000-year-old dugout style found mired in Florida mud. In the Upper Midwest, the canoe opened up the vast waterways of rivers and lakes, providing access to the hunting, fishing and wild ricing areas previously impenetrable in the dense, deep forests. The dugout was a primitive, heavier vessel made from tree trunks of available softer wood, usually maple, basswood or cottonwood. An 11-16' section was cut from the selected tree and the insides were scooped and scraped by bone knives or sharp clamshells until iron tools were developed.

The dugout was unstable and difficult to maneuver in tight, fast spaces. Dakota bands were more likely to use this style. The Ojibwe were the most skilled mariners of their time using birch bark canoes while traversing the waterways of North America's interior. As foretold in the Seven Fires Prophecy, they chose Madeline Island as their home, just off the southern shore of Lake Superior near the Brule River under 50 miles away, partly as a defensive strategy, since no indigenous enemies could challenge them on the open water.

Although early explorers like John Cabot encountered birch bark canoes on the Canadian east coast, Jacques Cartier was the first European to write about them after his 1534 voyage. The Frenchman had sailed across the Atlantic hoping to discover a northwest passage to Asia and gold, spices and jewels. Instead he found fish and furs. Cartier met a band of Beothuks and wrote, *"They have canoes made of birch bark in which they go about, and from them catch many seals."*

Later the explorer came upon a fleet of birch bark canoes probably paddled by Mi'kmaqs and commented, *"the whole lot of them had not anything above the value of 5 sous, their canoes and fishing nets excepting."* Birch bark vessels were superior to the traditional dugouts in regard to light weight, maneuverability, speed, cargo capacity, ease of construction and water tightness. The fur trade demand for the boats eventually outstripped the natives' ability to produce them so the French built a factory in Trois Rivieres around 1750.

By the 17th century specialized canoes were used in North America by the French voyageurs. Ships from Europe unloaded trade goods which were reloaded into *canots du maître,* also known as Montreal canoes, to be transported to the interior by way of the St. Lawrence River and the Great Lakes. Their massive 36' long size was effective in slicing through the battering waves of the huge lakes.

When the boats reached what is now Thunder Bay, Ontario, the cargo was split into smaller voyageur canoes constructed of cedar planking and ribs and covered with birch bark. The canoes held six paddlers and had a total weight capacity of 3,000 pounds. They were easier to portage over the many trails in the frontier. Birch bark canoes could only be loaded in the water and portaged empty as tears and holes were common and required frequent repairs. Later a shorter style was pressed into service, the Fond du Lac canoe, with a flat, wider bottom designed to slide over shallows and navigate corners of interior rivers like the Brule.

From the early 1600s to the last quarter of the 1800s, the Brule River was used as a thoroughfare. Actually, it was more like 44 miles of bad road due to the many rapids and impediments such as fallen trees and beaver dams. The route from Lake Michigan using the Fox and Wisconsin Rivers was faster to the Mississippi, but it was more dangerous due to native unrest. U.S. Army Lt. James Allen led a force of ten soldiers to serve as an escort for Indian Agent Henry Schoolcraft's expedition to find the source of the Mississippi River in 1832. Lake Itasca was discovered and the party descended the Mississippi, ascended the St. Croix, and portaged a short way to the source of the Brule River. They anticipated a much more comfortable last leg of the trip, which would lead them to Lake Superior. They were wrong.

By the time Lt. Allen's troops reached the meager start of the Brule, they were running days behind Schoolcraft's group. The canoes were leaking, the men's feet were bleeding from the sharp rocks of the St. Croix and they were running low on food and morale. The soldiers were physically and mentally exhausted.

With vague maps from Ojibwe chief *Gaa-bimabi* and some verbal input, Allen's men emerged from a cold, spring-fed marsh into the start of the Brule River. They waded, pushing the canoes along as the water was shallow and the alder branches from each shore were so enmeshed that the birch bark vessels were more like battering rams forced through the tangled vegetation. On August 6, 1832, they reached the "Little Falls," known today simply as "The Falls." Allen and seven men took off into the woods while the two remaining canoes continued downriver. It was a brutal hike as the terrain was alternately uneven and swampy. The men then walked in the water doing their best to protect the canoes from rocks.

Using the rest of Allen's pine tree sap-gum to cursorily repair the craft, the troops once again limped downriver. The repair lasted for a short while until the canoe, once again, took on water. Allen desperately grabbed clumps of clay from the riverbank and rubbed it all over the vessel's bottom, momentarily plugging the leaks. Repeating the process every half-hour or so, the canoes finally reached the mouth at Lake Superior about 10 PM that evening. The soldiers and their commanding officer were greatly relieved to be rid of the Brule. Part of their mission was to demonstrate to the Ojibwe the agility and capability of the U.S. Army in the wilderness. Instead they were the laughingstock of the north woods. The Ojibwe were not impressed by the *chimookomaan*, Ojibwe for "Long Knives," which is what they called U.S. soldiers. The comradery of the regiment was at ebb tide. In hindsight Lt. Allen explained in his journal why his trip down the Brule was ill-fated from the start. He also managed to insult the natives in the process: "[T]*he management of bark canoes, of any size, in rapid rivers, is an art which takes years to acquire; and, in this country, it is only possessed by Canadians* [mix-blooded voyageurs] *and Indians, whose habits of life have taught them but little else.*"

★ ★ ★ ★ ★

The most outrageous boat to ply the waters of the Brule was a 42' long and 3' wide dugout purchased by William Spaulding and three other miners who set out to explore the copper deposits at the mouth of the stream in 1845. They traveled up the Mississippi and the St. Croix until they reached the boggy portage to the Brule. Once the canoe was loaded with supplies, mining equipment and the four men, it was extremely heavy, making a traditional portage unfeasible.

Spikes were hammered into the wood of the dugout and straps were attached to the harnesses of nineteen Ojibwe men and women who dragged it over rollers made from small trees. They had to dam the stream to make the boat clear the bottom and shave the edges from the river banks to navigate the crooked stretches. The expedition took thirty-four days to complete.

When Great-grandfather George Noyes first visited the Brule River with his Milwaukee friends in the early 1880s, Ojibwe were constructing canoes much as they had decade after decade before. Every year they set up camp adjacent to the long, narrow spring-fed trench later called Jack's Lake. Their operation was vertically integrated with a large supply of birch trees for the outer skin, nearby white cedar for the frame and gunwales and pine and spruce providing the sap used for the sealing gum. Roots of jack pine, tamarack, or spruce were utilized to stitch the bark to the stern and bow.

The pristine waters of the pond and level ground provided a perfect habitat for their camping and building operations. The process of making this style of canoe remained unchanged for hundreds of years. The early club members from Milwaukee, St. Paul and Duluth paddled and poled birch bark canoes. One of them is on display hanging from the porch ceiling of the Holbrook's lodge.

Frederick King Weyerhaeuser, grandson of the lumber baron, spent a great deal of time in Lake Nebagamon as his father oversaw the operations of the Lake Nebagamon Lumber Company. He described some unique methods of recreational canoeing on the Brule in the early 1900s: *"It goes into Lake Superior, but it has its origin near Lake Nebagamon. It was possible to go down what we call Nebagamon Creek…into the Brule. But what we generally did was take canoes with a team of horses and haul them over to what we called Stone's Landing. We'd ride over in carriages and put them into the Brule at that point, and we'd take guides either on the Brule or we'd take one or two men from Nebagamon. They'd guide the boats down to a place called Winnibijou [sic]… Then we'd pull them out. It was a station on the Duluth Railroad, and the train came through from Duluth about six in the evening. We'd put the canoes in the baggage car, climb aboard, and ride back to Nebagamon.*

It only took about fifteen minutes to get back. But those were great experiences. As years went by, we came sufficiently expert with canoes to run the rapids ourselves."

A major step in the evolution of fishing the Brule River was the advent of the Lucius canoe, a hybrid boat and canoe which looms large in the lore of the Brule River and its early sportsmen. Joe Lucius was a northern Wisconsin Everyman: a builder of lodges and canoes, a guide, caretaker and hotelier. His canoes were designed for use between Winneboujou and the Twin Rapids—book ends for the Promised Land of Brule fishing. While somewhat cumbersome for running rapids, they provided stability, durability and low wind resistance, as well as giving the fisherman the flexibility of casting standing up or sitting down. The ribs, laminated bow and stern pieces and the keel were of oak or ash construction as were the gunwales and spreaders.

Most Lucius canoes were 18 or 20 feet long, but Great-grandfather ordered a mammoth 24 footer to the delight of my mother's generation who crowded into the massive interior in large numbers. The Judge also flouted convention by his insistence on bright red canoes. Others thought the color to be detrimental to fishing, but the Judge disagreed and to this day, the canoes of Noyes Camp remain red. Lucius canoes were modeled loosely after the Peterborough Canadian style, which were sold as far afield as Europe. The city of Peterborough, Ontario, sent one of their 16' cedar-rib styles to Princess Margaret in England in 1948 as a wedding gift.

In the early 1900s a Lucius could be commissioned for $50 including adjustable seats, foot grates, a custom-fitted live box and paddles and poles. An adjustable captain's chair could be ordered for the bow, offering comfort and the ability to modify the level of the seat for upstream or downstream travel. The invention of a sliding stern seat allowed the guide to adjust forward or backward to compensate for the weight in front of him to suit his style.

Joe built his last canoe, the Mush-ka-mud, for my Uncle Ralph in 1957. It was a work of art. Lucius detailed the specifications: *"40" Beam, 20 ft. long, 12" deep Keel, sliding seat and* [bow] *seat white pine, Planking: native white cedar, nailed and glued together. Ribs: white oak, Floor: white pine, Decks and thwarts: African mahogany. Gunwales: Philippine mahogany. Inlay in bow deck out of first passenger and freight boat on Lake Superior, built on Lake Erie, 1834. Inlay rear deck: mahogany from a broken chair out of the commander room on airplane Carrier Essex."*

Most of the Noyes Camp Lucius canoes are gone through attrition and misuse. Previous generations didn't realize how irreplaceable they would become. A few remain and are treated gingerly, as it is wonderful to have my Grandsons ride in the same canoe their Great-great-great-grandmother used.

It is comforting to know, when recalling one's own canoe mishaps, that even the larger-than-life characters of the 19th century had similar misadventures. Dr. Arthur T. Holbrook's childhood memories include a disastrous canoe trip with his friend Powlie. The boys were sent on an errand to buy a bag of flour. The outing was uneventful until they left "Davey" Crockett's store and headed back to camp. They had barely pushed off in their canoe when they heard an ominous clap of thunder. The boys paddled furiously as the skies opened, soaking them and the paper bag of flour. They struck a submerged rock in a rapids, slashing an opening in the canoe which started to take on water.

A plan was hatched to disembark and keep them and their purchase dry until the storm passed. As they exited, Arthur and Powlie lifted the flour sack, which immediately ripped. Dr. Arthur T. reminisced: *"The rain, having successfully played its villainess role, now let up and permitted the paste to cake more or less over our caps, faces, shirts, and trousers above the water line. We were able to manipulate the canoe after a fashion, and finally reached our camp to receive the jeers and hoots for our party costumes, and the cussing and bawling out for the loss of the flour."*

Brule guides were a tight community with big egos when it came to their craft. James Angleton, haunter of the Brule River and Noyes Camp neighbor, crystallized the pride of the Brule guide in a night fishing story. He had a favorite, Ed Dennis, who had *"a lot of Indian blood in* [his] *veins. A canniness."* Angleton was a denizen of the dark, much like the brown trout he stalked. Ed and Jim tried to beat a storm back to the lodge. Angleton recounted the episode to Caroline Marshall: *"I held two flashlights just like he liked them, one to each bank and any rocks too, of course. Next thing I know it's total darkness, and I'm up to my neck in water, and all our gear—poles, lines, fish, wood, pans, you name it—is bobbing around me, and I'm trying to get my footing and at the same time gather it all against my chest. And there's nothing but the rush of water. No other sound. I'm wondering where the*

*hell he is! Then this voice from the top of the Falls, 'you OK?' Somehow we get the
canoe to shore and all the gear, completely water-logged and he builds a huge fire. We
sit there in front of it, must've been a couple of hours at least, until our clothes are
merely damp or soggy. He never says a word. That's him. And then, just as the fire's
down to embers, and the chill is tolerable and we're getting up to go, he says, 'you ever
tell anyone I flipped I say you was drunk and rocked the boat over.' That's all. Then we
got to the canoe and shoved on home."*

There is an old guide's tale from the Brule. A new client says, *"I bet you know every
rock on this river."* Just then the canoe collides with an obstacle and the guide says,
"Yup. There's one now." The Ojibwe guides may not have known every stone, but
they knew to steer to the middle right of the Falls, where the hidden shallows lurk
in the lake section and how to navigate the river on a cloudy, moonless night.

To the Noyes family, John LaRock was the dean of Brule River guides. He was
of French-Ojibwe descent, reserved in speech, fastidious in manners and dress
and abstemious in behavior. He became a celebrity in 1928, serving as Calvin
Coolidge's guide and fly-fishing mentor for $2 a day. Once the President made
him remove the canoe grate and search 20 minutes for a split lead shot that cost
one penny for 15. The press reported his activities as well as those of Silent Cal.
One day when LaRock hurt his back cranking an automobile, the headline read,
"Guide Injured, President Tries Trap Shooting,"

LaRock liked the President but walked a tightrope between the pranks of
Coolidge and the stern Secret Service men paid to protect him. He finally put his
foot down when the Chief Executive persisted in his antics: *"He was always playing
tricks on the service men. One day he asked me to hide him and I slid the canoe behind
the roots of a big windfall in East Twin Lake. The secret service men started blowing
whistles. Finally, the president said it was time to show up and I poled the canoe out on
the lake. The woods was swarming with secret service men. Col. Starling bawled hell
out of me, so next time Cal asked me to hide him I wouldn't do it."*

There are two versions of the gratuity LaRock received when the Summer White
House residents returned to Washington D.C. One story has Coolidge giving his

guide a cheap cigar while the other purports a photo was all he received. John planned to write a book about his experiences but he never did. It would have been a great read. LaRock remembered a time when the Brule was home to only brook trout. He witnessed J.J. Watson catch a 4 ¼-pound brookie. Later, he observed 20-pound rainbows pulled from the stream and even larger browns.

John was first introduced to the Brule River as a young boy by his Aunt Agnes Govan. She promised that if he were good, and diligent in his school work, she would take him to a magical fishing spot where he could catch all the trout he wanted. Eleven-year-old John lived up to his part of the bargain, and when school was over in 1886, they headed to the Brule with packs on their backs and moccasins on their feet. The first night they spent at an Ojibwe encampment with seven wiigiwaams on Lake Millicent, part of the Pike Lake chain near Iron River. The natives appeared to know and respect Aunt Agnes.

The next day they reached a little cabin on the Brule not far from where Noyes Camp now stands. Aunt Agnes removed some tree boughs from a large brush heap and revealed a birch bark canoe. LaRock said, *"...she helped me bend a nail, gave me a piece of store string and a little piece of meat and I began to catch fish. All of them Brook Trout."* At the end of summer, the boy and his aunt returned to Ashland, and John spent two more years in school before he heard the siren call of the river where he spent the rest of his life.

During the summer of 1928 when LaRock guided Coolidge on the Brule, reporters were fascinated by his Ojibwe heritage. A reporter described him as a *"tall solidly framed man"* who was not *"a great talker"* but displayed *"a natural dignity and reserve"* and *"a twinkle of his shining black eyes."*

The Noyes Camp guides were housed in the Guide House, formerly known as the Man's Cabin, located back in the woods east of the garage. Their days began at 5:45 AM when they awoke, had breakfast, washed down the canoes and loaded them for the day's activities. There were usually two varieties of trips: a serious fishing expedition or a more casual outing with women and children culminating in a picnic.

The fishing outings began at 7:00 AM with a guide and two fishermen in each canoe as well as food, beverages, fishing equipment, cook kits, waders, paddles and foul weather gear. The retinue would travel against the current all the way to Cedar Island, where a hot lunch was served. The fishing party would continue upstream, eventually turning around, with only a stern paddle to steer noiselessly to drift fish. The next stop was "Noyes Landing," our picnic ground on Big Lake which sits at the outlet of the Twin Rapids. After a dinner of trout and beans, it was time for night fishing for big brown trout that prowled the "lake section," cautious by day, hungry and reckless at night. The guides would silently glide in the dark with the bow soundlessly slicing the water. If a fish struck, they could halt and hold the canoe stationary while the fisherman played the trout.

In the early days a guide would repeat this process of 18-hour days throughout the season with a pay rate of $1 per day, plus room and board, or $1.50-$2 per day if he were a good cook. This system stayed in place until the Allies entered World War II and factory jobs lured the guides away with better paying employment. Fishing was just part of a guide's job. He ventured into the woods to collect branches from fallen trees, dry enough to make a fire for cooking. He hauled water from the springs and, when the trout weren't biting, the guide would make Sucker Head Soup, a chowder made by adding onions, potatoes, tomatoes and bacon to the boiling pot of fish heads. The Ojibwe called it *naboob*. The winter did not provide a respite for the men as it was time to repair canoes, paddles, poles, boathouses and picnic grounds. For guides looking for other sources of income during the off-season, logging was an option. Antoine Dennis exemplified the versatility of the Metis guides:

His life seemed to span eons of activity on the Brule. He was born on the sacred Madeline Island to a Hudson Bay Company French fur trader father and an Ojibwe mother. He was a fur trapper and a logger, according to a newspaper article, known for his *"squirrel-like skill in keeping his footing on the slippery tree trunks"* as they proceeded downstream. There was no fishing guide on the Brule more respected than he. Antoine was a bridge from the beginning of the sportsmen's era well into the 20th Century.

The old school Brule River guides embraced their trade, the long hours and sometimes back-breaking work their jobs entailed. The Gordon family belonged to Winneboujou from 1918-1939 and Dick Gordon related a downriver trip he made in 1928 from the club to the mouth of the Brule. His friend Alec Watson and he raced downriver and the exuberant boys bragged about their accomplishment without considering the fallout.

"On that trip the two of us paddled continuously with no stops for fishing and with canoe paint left on countless rocks. When word of our nine-hour record made the rounds, it naturally upset the guides who figured it might spoil their profitable week-long employment. Antoine Dennis was particularly concerned and inferred that we youthful canoeists were lying. I countered with the offer of a wager on another trip,

forestalled when Benny Dennis, Antoine's son and a huskie ex-Carlisle football player, intervened. He told me to pay no attention to his father, but also suggested that I stop mouthing off so much about our speedy trip down river."

The elder Dennis was in his 80s in 1928 when the Wisconsin Conservation Commission suggested he guide the President on the Brule. His advancing years had dimmed his vision and sapped his strength and a reporter wrote that he didn't *"care for the glare of publicity."* Antoine told the writers *"he didn't have time for them…*[and] *"declared he was too busy* [and] *swung a bag of potatoes over his shoulder and started off."* He was protective of his Ojibwe heritage and didn't want it turned into a caricature by the Eastern press. Into his 90s he would produce a copy of the broken treaties the U.S. government used to fleece the Ojibwe of their traditional hunting and fishing grounds.

Tony Dennis lived for years in a cabin on the fringe of Winneboujou property, what is now the southeast corner of the intersection of Highway 27 and County Road B. Upon his death, his daughter, Lizzie, and her husband, John LaRock, moved in. My cousin Bob Banks spent two summers in the cabin when he was guiding on the river and "one very cold winter."

World War II not only harkened the end of the guide system on the Brule, but its technology gave birth to the aluminum canoe made popular by the Grumman Corporation as the war was ending. Over the years Grumman made a variety of aircraft, and the same manufacturing techniques were used to manufacture nearly indestructible boats. They were lighter, portable, tougher, and inexpensive and almost maintenance free. Dents could be pounded out with a hammer. They were easily portaged and could be tied to the roof of a car. They bent but they did not break.

This revolutionized the rituals of canoeing and fishing on the Brule. Now canoes were trailered and dropped off upriver at Stone's Bridge, eliminating the need to pole upstream. A major downside was the noisiness of the metal and the tendency to spook trout. Purists called them "ashcans." While the old guard turned up their noses at what they considered to be the advent of the "aluminum hatch," they were excellent training vessels for children. The Grumman also gave novices access to the Brule as they could now career down the river from rock to rock without destroying an expensive canoe. River traffic increased dramatically.

For many years, even decades, Noyes Camp owned a large aluminum tub affectionately dubbed "Big Red." As teenagers, the members of my nascent Boys of Brule coterie paddled the long, broad-beamed canoe down to the Ranger Station, which was an hour-and-a-quarter trip, shorter in high water or if we hustled. Many days we took multiple trips, and my dad dutifully picked us up. Eventually Big Red's bottom was almost tin-foil thin from scraping over rocks and shallow gravel beds.

We slid over stones with ease when any other canoe would be stopped dead, perched and pivoting on a rock and rapids. Big Red lay in state at Noyes Camp for a few years, propped against the side of the garage in all her crimson and silver glory, facing the wood shed before being taken to the Canoe Graveyard. We weren't ready to let her go.

The next step in recreational canoeing came in the 1970s as the Old Town Company from Maine introduced fiberglass canoes, which were even lighter, quieter and steadier in fast water. Lighter canoes meant easier transport and saved hours of time poling up and paddling down dead-water for those interested in night fishing or quick trips for fun.

My dad initiated a major development in Noyes Camp transportation in the late 1970s when he rescued a canoe trailer from a junkyard. I came home from work one night to find it parked on life support in my driveway. My father breathed life back into it, adding new tires as well as making a few repairs and slapping a fresh coat of paint on the relic. This addition allowed us to haul multiple canoes upriver and pick them up downstream without relying on our caretaker or scratching our cars. Forty years later the old workhouse is still in use, held together with solder, Rustoleum and a prayer.

Poling a canoe upriver is an old-school technique somewhat out of style now with portability eliminating the necessity of traveling against the current. The poler stands in the stern, or sits with a shorter pole, in the manner of a Venetian gondolier. The metal-nubbed end is moved forward and planted in river bottom. The top hand drives the canoe forward, and it advances a few feet. The motion is repeated with some body English pushing the pole out or pulling it in if the direction needs to be adjusted.

My mother, Leslie, was an expert poler and taught us the art. One perfect autumn day, the kind that makes one wonder if it is the last of Indian summer, she unintentionally demonstrated the pitfalls of wielding the pole too aggressively. We were about half an hour into our outing, having reached the south end of Spring Lake, and after a strong push, the canoe shot forward but her pole stuck to the bottom.

She dangled precariously on top of the pole as her legs flailed in mid-air until gravity took over and unceremoniously dumped her in the cold river. All the canoes in our entourage parked at the shore while Mom assessed the damage. She eventually emerged from the woods wearing Dad's sweatshirt and shorts.

My father Roger was stripped to his boxers and T-shirt for the rest of the trip. The children were incredulous. We had never seen her knees as she always wore skirts and dresses. It was a great day for us: a teachable poling moment, and the opportunity to see our mother falling from a canoe, wearing men's clothing and sporting a ruined hair-do.

"Bobby: 'Hey what happens if we flip this thing over?'
Lewis: 'Now that you brought that up, hang on to your paddle. And if you hit any rocks, don't hit 'em with your head.'"

Deliverance, 1972

Nature's finest waterpark may be the Brule River stretch between the Copper Range Campground and the Highway 13 Landing. It is almost a non-stop series of rapids and ledges; most fairly easily managed with some thrilling heart-stop-ping moments in the middle. It is wise to scout as many of the rapids as possible and, even though the majority are Class I and II, there is trickiness involved. It is an almost continuous stretch of whitewater with few respites as the rest of the fast water includes more minor ledges. The rapids finally let up just before the High-way 13 takeout. There are some steep clay banks along the way but sightseeing is the last thing on one's mind on this stretch of the Brule.

As one approaches Lenroot Ledges, advisedly in a kayak, it is easy to get swept downstream before being able to stop and survey what lies ahead. There are two series of sandstone ledges with drops of 2-3 feet. Backsplash waves wash over the bow of the watercraft. There is a brief break in the action with some gentler rapids before one encounters Mays Ledges. The first challenge has two options: a rectangle-shaped slot or a V. The river then proceeds for a football field length until the final series of ledges appears.

The Boys of Brule have had many river adventures over the years. Once, Mickey and I were stuck on a rock right under me in the middle of the Long Nebagamon Rapids. I had a dilemma. The canoe would not budge an inch unless my considerable weight was lifted from the spot. No amount of scooting would free us. If I exited, I ran the risk of not only losing my footing in the fast water, but watching the canoe take off downriver, leaving me in its wake. I tip-toed forward, until I was standing directly behind Mike in the bow. When we dislodged and continued heading down the rapids, I slowly moonwalked backwards until safely reaching my seat in the stern. Rarely have I been so impressed with myself.

Depending on conditions, the same location can take on a different character. After a deluge of rain the level of the river rapidly rises and it is an excellent time to take a ride down to the Ranger Station. The current is swift, rocks are submerged and the length of the trip can almost be cut in half. Bill Lorntson and I once ventured downstream after a storm and pulled up on the sliver of land jutting into the stream where Nebagamon Creek empties into the Brule. When we shoved off, the current swept us wider and faster than expected and we swamped. It was a tricky situation since the water was deep and there was no place on the bank to climb and empty our canoe. We somehow managed and, thoroughly chastened, finished our trip, wetter and wiser.

Boarding and disembarking from a canoe can be tricky. Once at the Ranger Station landing, where the current is swift, I lent a helping hand to Bud and Mike as they pulled up. I was offered the blade end of a paddle to pull them closer and as they stood, the canoe capsized and they took an unexpected dip. The blame game rages to this day.

Ojibwe birch bark canoe builders at Jack's Lake *Photo by Truman Ingersoll*

[12]

CLANS, CRITTERS AND KINDRED SPIRITS

"It is a general saying…that the Bear clan resembles the animal that forms their Totem in disposition. They are ill-tempered and fond of fighting, and consequently they are noted as ever having kept the tribe in difficulty and war with other tribes, in which…they generally have been the principal and foremost actors…"

WILLIAM WARREN, *History of the Ojibway People*

★ ★ ★ ★ ★

AT ONE TIME THE Ojibwe Bear clan was the largest of all the doodems, so numerous that they were divided into sub-groups of types of bears and body parts. Eventually the different totems merged into one called the Nooke. They were guardians of the bands, known for their thick, night-black hair, and patrolled the camps for protection. To this day, Nooke clan members perform the same service even in city settings. Their knowledge of forests led them to become healers, using their familiarity with plants and trees to make medicine.

Sometimes the Boys of Brule and black bears, *mukwa,* arrive at Noyes Camp the same time in early May. The bears shake off the cobwebs from hibernation, and are hungry, well, as a bear. Until the blueberries ripen, usually in July, they will forage, eating whatever is available: insects, grass, tree shoots and roots. Bears will consume mammals and fish, dead or alive. They climb trees to pilfer black oil sunflower seeds from our bird feeders. It is a celebrated time for the Ojibwe when the berries finally ripen. A bowl of *miinan* is picked as an offering to the spirits. The presented portion is either set on fire or put outside with a gift of tobacco.

We eat well at Brule, and our garbage is kept in galvanized trash cans locked inside the old garage. One morning we awoke to find the building ransacked with garbage strewn about. A scavenging bear had swatted the hinge, padlock and a large chunk of wood from the door and helped himself. When the animal returned the next day the DNR was contacted and an agent arrived and installed two traps, placing some wafers inside.

The bear came back, took a cookie but ventured no further inside the trap. Our caretaker, Marsha Anderson, advised the agent that the bear had become accustomed to high quality garbage cuisine and would not be impressed by a bland cookie. Meat was added to the traps and this ploy succeeded. A medium-sized black bear was captured, loaded into a truck and relocated to another part of the state.

Black bears will rarely attack humans, preferring to make aggressive snorts and blowing noises, clawing the ground and making false charges. It is still necessary to remove all traces of food on the porch so a bear doesn't slash the screen and enter. Any remnants of the fish cleaning process must also be erased. A September 6, 1906, entry in the Gitche Gumee Camping Club log book reads, *"Huge black bear around kitchen creating considerable alarm, clawing about the doors and window screens, tearing off the netting. Maids blew the horn but failed to awaken anybody in the lodge."*

When Noyes Camp was rebuilt in 1925, Great-grandmother Agnes commissioned one of the guides to kill a bear to mount in the Great Room. She stipulated, *"It must have a pleasant expression so as not to scare the Grandchildren."* The head of a cub still hangs over a doorway. Bear cubs climb trees and occasionally one will get stuck in a yoke of tree branches. The resulting skeleton is venerated and used in Ojibwe spiritual ceremonies.

We used to go to the town dump once every summer around dusk. The car was parked facing the refuse heap as if we were waiting for the drive-in movie to begin. Soon the bears arrived, lumbering toward the mounds of garbage, indifferent to our presence. After a while some of us would exit the car, although I never strayed far, my hand surgically attached to the door handle.

To the Ojibwe, the *googooko* is a bird possessing a great duality of character. The great horned owl is considered an omniscient prophet, a messenger of change, and even death, and a spirit guide to the afterlife. A nocturnal creature, it is associated with darkness and mystery and thought to be a shape shifter capable of turning into a witch and then back to its original form.

For decades, female great horned owls have laid eggs in the window boxes of

Noyes Camp. The mostly inaccessible location provides protection from predators, which might eat the eggs or the young owls after hatching. Not all eggs produce a living owl, but if they do, when the Boys of Brule arrive the first week of May, chicks will be found huddling in the window boxes to shield themselves from the elements. They are fed by their parents, who hunt during the period just after dusk and again right before dawn. When we awaken in the morning we observe the carnage that occurred while we slept. Remains of fish, rabbits, mice, snakes and birds can be seen. Once a mallard duck had been killed and delivered to the owlets.

In May 2016, we arrived to find three healthy owlets in the flower box outside my Great-grandmother's bedroom. Determined to do our part in nurturing the fascinating creatures, we did not use the room and only peeked through the curtains a few times. When disturbed, fledglings will hiss and make a clacking sound with their beaks. As they mature, the chicks sometimes move to the pitched roof over the porch doorway. Moving up and down the shingles, they follow the rays of the sun in an effort to keep warm while the north woods shake off the vestiges of winter. One could use the chicks as a sundial, so predictable are their movements.

At seven weeks the owlets are usually on the ground, learning to fly. They are most vulnerable to predators at this stage. Their welfare is monitored by the parents for months. The Boys of Brule also felt an avuncular duty to the three youngsters and were pleased when they hit the ground and perched on a stump and two trees near the house.

From the dawn of my Noyes Camp memories a stuffed great horned owl, perched on a cross section of birch, has stood sentry on the mantle of our dining room fireplace. As a young child I respected the duality of the *googooko*: fascinated and scared at the same time. When alone, I gave the owl a wide berth, using the other entrance to the pantry and kitchen.

Ojibwe legend relates how *gawg* got its quills. The porcupine was tired of being attacked by the bear. One day it brushed against the sharp tipped branches of a hawthorn bush and a plan was hatched. *Nanabush*, the Trickster, was watching and spread *gawg's* back with clay and attached some hawthorn branches. The next time the bear approached, the porcupine rolled itself into a ball and the attack was thwarted by the pointed barbs. From that day forward *gawg* was protected by quills.

The summer my Grandmother Margaret turned ten she started an art project at Brule. She needed some porcupine quills and knew one of the primitive looking rodents had burrowed under the Guide House. Armed with a canoe paddle, she began to poke the area under the bottom log. The animal took exception to this intrusion and sent Grammie screaming through the woods. *Gawg* had used her as a Northland pin cushion.

When my mother was a child, there were some domesticated animals at Noyes Camp. Due to the presence of Ojibwe in the area, the children were fascinated by their way of life and ran whooping through the woods in native regalia including feather headdresses. There were some Banty hens kept in the yard. This type is smaller than common chickens and requires less space. One of the McLennan boys, sarcastically nicknamed "Darling Donnie" by his adversarial cousin Nancy, tormented the Bantys and kittens in the yard with his toy bow and arrow, hopefully the suction cup variety. Top of mind decades later, Nancy still seethed saying, *"I do not believe he was ever punished either."*

In 1905, the Winneboujou Club had a problem with domesticated animals. Mr. Saunders sent a letter to members describing the issue: *"A good number of the members of our club have been very much annoyed during their visits at the clubhouse, incident to the fact that there are now a good many cattle roaming the woods in our vicinity, that haunt the place nights, and, when accompanied with cowbell attachments, cause the members to fear nervous prostration."*

Grace and Calvin Coolidge were animal lovers and turned the White House into a menagerie during their stay. Canaries, cats and even a raccoon named Rebecca were in residence. Rebecca, caged at night but free to roam in daytime, was eventually banished to the National Zoo after damaging furniture and apparel, but not before she made an appearance at the annual White House Easter Egg Roll. The first family received unsolicited gifts from their admirers including a pygmy hippopotamus, a wombat, a horse, a mule, an antelope, a bobcat and assorted waterfowl.

Dogs were the Coolidge family favorites, however, and they had quite a few. Rob Roy, a white collie, was considered a close family member and travelled to the Brule to spend the summer of 1928 at the Cedar Island Summer White House with his masters. He often went fishing with the President and looked like a huge cotton ball in the canoe, resting between Coolidge and guide John LaRock.

Grace Coolidge's affection for animals even extended to trout. A wooden foot-bridge crossed the narrow river linking the small island and its living quarters to the other shore. The First Lady wrote in her Autobiography of a "fish story."

"It was underneath that bridge where President Coolidge met his toughest challenge yet, among 'several large trout who were rather tame and looked to us for their daily food consisting of crumbs from the table.' A particular trout, a very greedy one' [In Grace's words] *was named by the President. He called him 'Danny Deever' 'for,' said he, 'I'll hang him in the morning.' Referencing Kipling's popular 1890 poem, Coolidge relished not only the play on words but also the personification of his piscatorial nemesis....In the trout's case, despite repeated efforts to lure him up with 'pretty flies'... Grace kept Danny fed so well that the 'hangin in the morning' never took place."*

The Importance of the Obvious,
On Coolidge, Cleveland, Kipling and Fish Stories

Paddling to the Ranger Station we often encounter a great blue heron, *zhashagi*, fishing in the shallows for trout fingerlings. They have an awkward, primeval appearance, resembling an avian version of Ichabod Crane. When disturbed they will fly a ways down river and repeat the process as we follow. Sometimes they ingest a fish too large to navigate their narrow throats and choke to death. The Heron clan is a sub-group of the Cranes, who are considered orators and interpreters. A recent theory regarding the origin of the name Ojibwe suggests it mimics the call of the crane.

White-tailed deer may be the most iconic mammal of the Brule forest, visible when they are on the move during feeding time in the early morning or late afternoon. The Ojibwe call them *wawashkosh* and the secondary Hoof totem includes gentle, kind people: poets and mediators. Its members are pacifists who take care of others and eschew strife and harsh language.

Hunters and dogs are the deer's most common predators as well as coyotes, wolves and, most recently, cougars. Bears can run down and kill fawns. Sensing danger, the deer will raise its tail, displaying the white underside as an alarm and a beacon for fawns to follow the adults who can run at a rate of 30 miles per hour. In the late 19th century, deer shining, or fire hunting, was an acceptable method of shooting deer on the Brule.

Usually on a moonless night, a canoe was launched, hugging either bank, depending on the wind, to reduce human scent. Paddles were filed to remove slivers and frayed edges to prevent excess dripping and kept in the water as much as possible to limit noise. A black box-like contraption called a "jack" was positioned in the bow with a Ferguson lamp attached. The shooter was stationed in the bow with his shotgun resting on the jack. The stern man not only maneuvered around rocks and fallen trees but also kept lookout for deer.

When a white-tailed deer was spotted, the stern man grabbed the gunwales and gently rocked the canoe as a signal to flash the Ferguson lamp. The deer froze in place and the shooter blasted away, aiming for the neck. The fallen animal was dragged to the river bank, field dressed and packed in the canoe for return to camp. We have a few deer heads hanging in Noyes Camp, including one named "Rosie the Dew Eyed Doe." Uncle Ralph dispatched most of them with a bow and arrow without the benefit of blinding lights.

The Wolf clan is called *ma'iingan* and the animal was present at the beginning of the Ojibwe. The Gitchi Manido sent Original Man to the newly created Earth giving him the task of naming every object in nature, animate and inanimate. The wolf was his companion, even speaking the same language. Wolves are considered guides, scouts, and a source of knowledge and strength. The animal was driven to near extinction in Wisconsin and is considered a scourge by farmers and hunters who have lost livestock and dogs.

Red-haired Vic Desimval was a young man in 1875 when he and his team of horses were hired to work in a lumber camp in Amnicon, just west of Brule. He rode from Superior and spent the night alone in the forest when wolves begin to howl, scaring Vic and the horses, which whinnied in fear. When the first animal came within sight, Vic hurriedly set a fire. By the time it was shooting flames high in the air, Desimval counted 25 timber wolves sitting 50 feet away watching his every move until daybreak.

After 60 days in the camp Vic returned to town and went to the barber. A Superior newspaper told the story: *"The barber said to Vic, 'Look at this, Vic.' And the barber showed Vic a bunch of hair he'd cutoff. 'My God,' Vic said. 'It's all white.' That was the first Vic knew that his hair had turned white from the scare for no one told him at the lumber camp. Vic said, 'It never did get back its red color after that.'"*

The Ojibwe are vehemently opposed to wolf hunting as they consider the animal to be a family member. They feel the *ma'iingan* is misunderstood. They say the wolf is a kindred spirit and lives a parallel life to theirs. When the wolf prospers, so do the Ojibwe, and the opposite is also believed. Like the Ojibwe, the wolf has been persecuted, removed, hunted, killed and now on the road to recovery.

After the naming journey ended, the Great Creator separated man and wolf. As a parting gift the *ma'iingan* gave the Ojibwe the dog, *animosh*, to keep them company. The wolf controversy continues in the Upper Midwest. Robert DesJarlait, Ojibwe activist, says, *"If you take the fur of ma'iingan, you take the flesh off my back."* The high and lonesome howl of the wolf can be heard at night in the Brule River valley and the head and pelt of a *ma'iingen* hangs prominently on the wall of the Great Room.

The most mystical experience I have ever had at Brule involves the rare appearance of a Cecropia Moth. One night at Brule, I accidentally came upon the most beautiful, strange sight as I went to the porch, hoping to lure a partner for ping pong. As I flipped the light switch I saw a huge Cecropia perched on the screen, which covers the upper two-thirds of the loggia-style porch. Not wanting to disturb the stunning creature, I went back inside the house and exited through the kitchen door and circled back to observe the moth's front side.

The Cecropia is the largest of the giant silk moth family with a wingspan from 5-7". Its larvae are found on maple and birch trees, and the moths only produce one generation per year. They are nocturnal, live for only a few weeks and do not eat as they solely exist to mate. The Cecropia has a red body with a white color and horizontal white stripes on the abdomen.

As I faced the moth from the edge of the woods it was backlit by the porch light, and I could see the muted colors of the wings ranging from charcoal black in the center to dark red, fading increasingly to lighter bands of brown until the edges were tinged with tan. The subtle beauty was enhanced by two crescent-shaped spots on each wing and a round spot resembling an eye on each upper tip. The exquisite texture and blending of the colors on the wings resemble frosting.

The river valley and forest are a birder's paradise, home to rare species such as the saw-whet owl and various warblers: Connecticut, Canada and Cape May. The woods and river are home to 28 species on the Wisconsin List of Greatest Conservation Need. Grouse, osprey and geese are prevalent.

A rainy day at Brule is a good time to retire to the porch with a book, and with water dripping from the roof and trees, engage in some bird watching. The feeders are filled with black oil sunflower seeds which attract finches, chickadees and woodpeckers that thrive in the old growth forest surrounding Noyes Camp. Blue Jays are colorful, but annoying, as they shriek and bully other birds. White-breasted nuthatches walk head first down trees looking for insects and seeds. My favorite is the Rose-breasted grosbeak whose white, black and red coloring is even more striking when they visit the feeder in groups, which they frequently do. The French named them for their large powerful beaks tailor-made for cracking big seeds.

Chipmunks and the odious red squirrels often join the fray, chattering and fighting. Dr, Arthur T. Holbrook was a kindly gentleman who fashioned chipmunk traps from tree twigs for the children of Noyes Camp. They did not harm the little critters and he made us promise to release them by nightfall. We loved him and called him, "Dr. Chipmunk."

Bald Eagles, once of the verge of distinction, are often sighted using the river as a flyway or sitting in their huge stick nests, which over a period of years can reach nine feet across and weigh well over three tons. The eagle is named *migizi* by the Ojibwe.

Perhaps the most famous American bald eagle, Old Abe, was from northern Wisconsin. Ahgamahwgezhig, Chief Sky of the Flambeau Ojibwe, sold the eaglet in 1861 for a bushel of corn. The bird was acquired by Company C, 8th Wisconsin Volunteer Infantry Regiment, which became known as the "Eagle Regiment," and the bird was named "Old Abe" in honor of President Lincoln. The regiment spent the Civil War in the Western Theater and the eagle "marched" into every battle on a pedestal carried by a sergeant.

The mascot got under the Rebels' skin as a Confederate General vowed, *"that bird must be captured or killed at all hazards. I would rather get that bird than capture a whole brigade or a dozen battle flags."* Old Abe ventured into combat with the regiment in all of its thirty engagements, including Corinth, Nashville and Vicksburg. He was grazed twice by enemy fire. After the war, Old Abe was a celebrity, touring the country to raise funds for wounded veterans and participating in America's Centennial Exposition.

In retirement, Old Abe resided in Wisconsin's State Capital Building until 1881 when he died of paint and solvent fume inhalation from a fire that began in an adjacent storage room. He was then mounted and given a place of honor in the Grand Army of the Republic Memorial Hall. A 1904 fire left only a few feathers, which are now on exhibit in the Wisconsin Veteran's Museum. In an example of Ojibwe symmetry, Old Abe's feathers, revered in native spiritualism, are a gift to the people of Wisconsin. The profile of the Civil War mascot has been used by the Army's 101st Airborne Division since 1921.

In December, eagles flock by the dozens to the shallow "lakes" just south of Noyes Camp, feeding on spawning rainbow trout and salmon. Elegant, graceful trumpeter swans use the stream as their winter habitat preferring remote, undisturbed environments.

Mergansers, or *anzig,* are perhaps the smallest, but most entertaining, waterfowl species on the river. They often feed on our stretch of the stream, drifting down river first and fishing their way back. Their bill has a hooked end and serrated edges to snare their prey. The birds have distinctive crests on the back of their head giving them a "duck tail" hair style. In order to lift off the water they flap their wings on the river for some distance. Ducklings trail behind the adult, running on the stream's surface.

Dogs are generally banned from the Boys of Brule May outing. They smell, stain, bark, growl, bite, chew and generally get in the way. Bud's yellow lab has been grandfathered, however. When Bella was a pup, Dr. Bud's wife Linda said, *"Either the dog goes with you or stay home!"* When most of us took off for golf, Bobbo and his brother-in-law Glencoe stayed back at camp and made a play pen outside for her. The experiment was short lived when a bald eagle strafed the puppy, looking for a meal. Bella was whisked inside. She is a good companion and behaves better than we.

Early in the 20th Century our upstream neighbor, Mr. C.B. Couch experienced the heartbreaking, senseless loss of one of his beautiful bird dogs trained to flush partridge and woodcock for Mr. Couch to hunt. The dog was cruelly poisoned and the grief stricken master buried her at the foot of a large red pine with an accompanying note: *"Not a sparrow falls without God's notice. Also vengeance is mine, saith the Lord. Let the murderer of my dog and my faithful friend, BONNIE MAY, read. May he be accursed by God and despised by man."*

C.B. Couch

In addition to the spiritual aspect, the Ojibwe Clan system has also served as an organizational vehicle, assigning roles to the various totems to fulfill all the needs of a band, from emotional to physical. The doodems provide an individual with an extended family and help keep the various bands together in the Ojibwe Nation.

The Noyes Camp family now consists of four clans. We do not have animal totems but the clans feature different characteristics. One is very large and the others are relatively small. There are varying degrees of organizational skills and compliance. One branch separated over the years but seems to be returning to the fold. The Boys of Brule are a clan the first week in May before we disperse as the Ojibwe proverb suggests: *"A great wind carries* [us] *across the sky"* until we meet again when the Sugarbushing Moon, *iskigamizige-giizis,* returns.

[13]

RITUALS, ACTIVITIES AND PRANKS

"The need for ritual is a basic human instinct, as real, as urgent and as raw as our need for food, shelter and love. Ceremonial observance adds lucid layers—depth, dimension, drama and distinction to our lives, making the ordinary seem special, and the special, extraordinary. Through the practice of ritual we are privileged to experience ourselves as prepared, present, passionate, principled and potent."

Donna Henes, *Huffington Post*

★ ★ ★ ★ ★

THE CENTURIES OLD MIDEWIIWIN Society, or Grand Medicine Society of the Ojibwe, remains a mysterious entity. It is believed that the sacred rites were delivered from the Great Spirit in a time of great need. The path to full-fledged initiation involves four degrees. It is difficult with no guarantee of success. Each stage grants the aspiring practitioner more knowledge and power.

"'My Grandson,' said he, 'the megis I spoke of, means the Me-da-we religion. Our forefathers, many string of lives ago, lived on the shores of the great Salt Water in the east. Here it was, that while congregated in a great town, and while they were suffering the ravages of sickness and death, the Great Spirit, at the intercession of Man-ab-o-sho, the great common uncle of the An-ishin-abug-ag, granted them this rite wherewith life is restored and prolonged....'

'This, my grandson, is the meaning of the words you did not understand; they have been repeated to us by our fathers for many generations.'"

William Warren, *History of the Ojibwe People*

The *midew*, both respected and feared, possess knowledge of medicinal herbs and plants to be kept in the ceremonial bag or *biindegeysaasin*, often made from the pelt of an otter. The *migis*, sacred cowrie shells, are also included. Tobacco, the Water Drum and rattles are also used in the healing rituals designed to maintain physical and spiritual balance. The ceremonies take place in the *midewigaan*, a dome-shaped lodge.

The Midewiiwin Society interprets the sacred birch bark scrolls, *wiigwaasaba-koon*, which contain the history of the Ojibwe people in the form of hieroglyphics. Carbon dating has proved some to be many centuries old. These scrolls contain the early maps of lakes and rivers in the Lake Superior region as well as history, music, mathematics and folklore.

Our Noyes Camp next-door neighbor, Arthur T. Holbrook, had the rare chance to observe an Ojibwe Healing Ceremony on the Odanah Reservation near Brule at the age of eleven in the 1880s. He was mesmerized and a bit frightened by the proceedings. An old woman, obviously sick and weak, was sitting in the middle of a large circle. The *midew* presided over the ceremony, described by Arthur: *"Before this sick woman was a large, impressive Indian with highly painted cheeks and fore-head gorgeously attired in a long feathered bonnet with buckskin blouse, belt, leggings, and moccasins, all elaborately beaded and decorated with feathers, claws, bones, and fur. At one side were two or three drummers...."*

Dancers chanted to drive away the spirits causing the woman's illness. Kettles of stew were passed around the circle for the observers to sample. The impressionable boy from Milwaukee tried a piece of meat which he found unappetizing. He was later told it was either puppy or porcupine.

In 1899 the Gitche Gumee Camping Club was incorporated and, in 1936, upon the death of my Great-grandmother Agnes Noyes, my family formed the Noy-es-Brule Corporation. It was a wise move by my Grandmother Margaret's genera-tion, forging a bond and creating harmony that continues today. We have officers and committees that govern with a steady hand and shareholders who support them. Leading up to our annual meeting every Memorial Day weekend, there may be a bit of sabre rattling by family members, but any discontent is almost always alleviated by the time the gathering is over.

Beyond the business component, the Family Meeting reinforces our legacy and provides fellowship and comradery. It is a chance to touch base and introduce younger family member to their relatives and expose them to the process of operating Noyes Camp. People take turns hosting the meeting, planning meals and collecting the money for the weekend's expenses. The annual ritual of planting geraniums and other plants in the window boxes on the lodge and boathouse is accomplished with crossed fingers in hope that the last hard freeze has come and gone. Properly tended, the red flowers that match our canoes can last into mid-October.

Most Ojibwe games are separated by gender and usually have an educational element rising above mere entertainment. Men play *makazanitaagenwin,* the Moccasin Game, a complicated activity that encourages trust, rewards concentration and reinforces comradery, communication and teamwork. Sleight of hand and misdirection are key components.

While the rules may vary from band to band, the teams often have three players per side: one who hides the tokens under the moccasins, another who guesses the location of the marked token and a drummer who tries to confuse the other team with his insistent beat, which resembles the sound of horse hooves in motion. There are counting sticks to keep score and scoring sticks, which are used to flip the moccasins in search of the marked token. Gambling adds to the excitement. Ojibwe girls play the Butterfly Game, a version of hide and seek. The seeker sings the Butterfly song while the others run and hide. Tracking skills are used to follow footprints.

Snow Snake is an Ojibwe winter game of skill. It is a combination of javelin throwing, luge and curling. A crevice is dug in the snow by dragging a log and is often coated with water to increase the speed of the wooden darts as they careen between the walls of the trough, which is sometimes constructed with bends, obstacles and a rise at the end. The snakes can be highly stylized, colorfully decorated and as long as eight feet. They are sanded, polished and coated with wax. Snow snakes can be played individually or as a team sport. Skilled players toss the snakes underhand at great speed and for long distances. After each round, children run to retrieve the darts.

The voyageurs looked forward to the annual Rendezvous held in locations like Grand Portage, Fort William or Trois Rivieres in the earlier days. The Great Gathering was held in June or July depending when the agents from Montreal and the voyageurs from the interior (hivernants) reached the destination. Business was conducted and the packs of furs were exchanged for trading goods to take back to the natives via rivers like the Brule. It was also a time of great celebration: feasting, singing, dancing and drinking. Competitions included tomahawk throwing, wrestling, archery and canoe racing. Rendezvous was an effective release from the arduous and dangerous work performed by the voyageurs.

The men played a game of Cat and Mouse requiring great dexterity, balance, strength and strategy. The two players stood on the gunwales of a canoe facing each other with a long rope between them. At the count of three they pulled in the slack and tried to knock the other off his perch and into the water. At times one would loosen the tension to the surprise of the other contestant.

Like the voyageurs, north woods lumbermen lived in a macho culture. The various crews competed in contests to see who could down the most timber, creating rivalries and comradery. Their long days consisted of dangerous hard work, prodigious amounts of food and chewing tobacco and nights spent in cramped, smoky shacks. Sundays were their only day off. Some went to church services, mended clothes or bought the wares of the itinerant peddlers visiting the camps. They played cards and horseshoes and whittled. There were tree climbing, log rolling and arm wrestling contests. Some rough housed or ran through the woods to blow off steam. It was no life for the faint of heart. Alcohol was banned from most lumber camps due to safety concerns.

One of the most successful ways to set a trap for a prank is to play to the victim's vanity. Truman Ingersoll was a renowned photographer and hunter, called "The Artist" at Winneboujou. Chris O'Brien tells the tale of the perfect trick played on Ingersoll in his *Brule Chronicles*.

"...*The artist is a mighty hunter...his rifle has waked the echoes from crag to crag, upon the summit of the Rockies, the elk, the Grisley* [sic]*, the mountain sheep, the black* *tailed deer and the bounding antelope have fallen in hectatombs before him…. He said with modest complacency, that his senses were trained more sharply than those of the common man, that he could not only hear a deer but could SMELL one, even at a distance of a quarter of a mile…."*

To prove his point before heading upriver for the day, Ingersoll mentioned to his fellow campers that a deer had been feeding on the vegetation below his window during the night and vowed that he would "kill a deer IN THE YARD" before they broke camp. The three men remaining at Winneboujou plotted the perfect prank. The Club was in possession of a stuffed albino white-tailed deer, with distinctive markings on its head and legs.

The long dead hooved creature was tantalizingly positioned in some brush and tree branches. When the Artist returned to camp after sundown he merrily recounted the details of his day until Joe Lucius, the caretaker, approached him and conspiratorially whispered, *"Wa-wa-wash-kash"* (Ojibwe for deer). Ingersoll grabbed his gun, lamps were lit and Joe and he crept through the yard to within fifteen yards of their quarry… The Artist warned Lucius, *"Be still! Now I see him—a buck! Hold the light a little higher—down a little—cast out to the left—I want to shoot him through the heart."* The animal remained motionless.

Ingersoll pulled the trigger of his 40-90 Winchester and scared every beast in the valley except the albino deer. He fired again with the same result.

"The Artist drew his hunting knife, sprang upon the back of the animal,—and, alas that we should live to tell it,—both rolled over in the brush. When the artist arose, the hay with which the deer was stuffed obscured his countenance so much that the expression was no longer recognizable. But he bore no malice, and when consciousness returned, joined in the pleasant laughter that occurred around the hearth-stone."

The Boys of Brule have our own set of activities and rituals. We are fortunate to have some excellent cooks in our midst who prepare great meals. The downside is the carnage left in the kitchen by those who don't believe in pre-coating pans or soaking bowls, feeling such precautions have a deleterious effect on taste. Post meal clean-up duties are determined by a game featuring five dice called Ship, Captain and Crew, requiring rolling a 6, 5 and 4 in that order and then adding the total of the final two. The cook and one kitchen helper are exempt from the competition. It is common for others to make pitiful attempts for exemptions such as setting the table or lighting the candles. These scams are immediately quashed. When Marty cooks, the atmosphere is darkened by anxiety and dread. The kitchen is littered with singed pots and pans.

The dice game is a raucous event resembling the wild Chinese casino games on the island of Macau, with cheering, booing and disputes. It has spawned its own language with terms like "no qually" when one fails to roll a 6, 5 and 4 in his three turns. The "Pearson Gap" is a slight opening where two tables are pushed together for large crowds. Once, Bobbo threaded the narrowest of needles with a die and automatically sentenced to dish duty when the die fell to the floor. The term "dice yips" was coined when Lorny had a particularly bad streak of luck, stranded in the kitchen all weekend. The most exciting aspect is when one inadvertently drops a die on the floor, resulting in automatic banishment to the kitchen.

This rule was instituted when suspected fraud occurred as someone would pick up the offending die claiming it was a six, or whichever number he was missing. Lorntson executed the most egregious violation once when he fumbled the leather dice holder, dumping it and all its contents on the floor. This event coined the often-uttered warning, *"keep them on the table."*

In 2017, Glencoe fabricated a set of dice that did not include the number 4, which, of course, is critical to winning. The dice made the rounds and as no one qualified, it was chalked up as an odd coincidence. Eventually Dana studied the dice and detected foul play.

★ ★ ★ ★ ★

"The Trickster is a transformative figure. Nenabozho, in his interactions with creation, transformed the landscape, and his actions had varied impacts on those he encountered… when Nenabozho took the form of a rabbit to steal fire, he was marked by this action. Nenabozho's actions affected all hares from that day forward, as their white fur would become brown in the summer as a result of their ancestor's act of carrying fire on his back… Nenabozho's stories explain how the land and earth's beings came to be, reinforcing an understanding of how our own actions and engagements create lasting impact."

HEIDI KIIWETINEPINESIIK STRARK, OJIBWE AUTHOR,
Transforming the Trickster

The Trickster character is common in Native American lore: complicated and ethereal. There are various versions even within the Ojibwe Nation. There are many Nenabozho stories, and spellings of his name, and his characteristics vary widely, but he is generally kindly, playful, humorous and giving. Nenabozho often runs into trouble with his foolish antics, which serve as lessons for humans.

Folklore tells how the birch tree acquired its black markings. One winter, the Trickster's grandmother sent him on a mission to bring back fire to prepare food and provide heat in the frigid Northland. He ran like a rabbit until he reached the dwelling of the Thunderbird and asked him for a momentary respite from the elements. As the bird looked away, the Trickster rolled in the fire, igniting his back. As Nenabozho took off for home, the Thunderbird chased him, flinging lightning bolts. *Omaai mitig,* the birch tree, called to him to seek shelter at the foot of its trunk. The lightning bolts hit only the tree, giving it its distinctive black accents.

★ ★ ★ ★ ★

The Boys of Brule have their own Trickster, Jim Hurd. Mick searched Noyes Camp high and low for days looking for a pair of sunglasses, finally locating them in the toaster oven. I stash my breakfast bacon for a lunchtime peanut butter and bacon sandwich so Hurd can't steal it. In retaliation I once took my foot stone from the shower and placed it on his pillow. Payback is sweet. One spring Jim and some others took a quick trip downstream and we agreed to meet them in Lake Nebagamon for a beer later. Mr. Jimmy left his wallet on the fireplace mantle in case of a canoeing mishap.

We arrived at the bar first and I handed the bartender Lumber's pilfered credit card to start a tab. When it was time to leave, the unsuspecting victim was given the slip to sign. He took it well and we all enjoyed the retribution. They say revenge is best served cold, and in this instance it came in the form of free beers.

Jim is also known as "The Fiddler." He rarely lets a CD play in its entirety without fast forwarding or repeating a song. One year he set up a "media center" in the old children's dining room with a DVD player, a projector and screen. We played music DVDs at high decibels. Mickey and Hurd had a dispute over a selection and ended up wrestling over the remote control. Jim finally seized control and struck a bargain to change to a more up tempo artist once James Taylor was over.

Mike agreed, Lumber immediately pressed "stop" and said, "It's over." Dana slept through the whole spat sitting in his wicker chair.

Tall Paul is a frequent pranking target. One year he arrived late from California and was brought up to speed on the activities including our fictitious tale of how refreshing our swim in the river had been earlier in the afternoon. Always ready for action, eager to catch up and weary from his long plane and car trip, Marty took a running leap into the stream. The first week in May features water temperatures hovering in the low 50s, and he emerged from the water gasping and sporting a bluish hue.

A few years later, tables were turned on Suckface and Chip, who were night fishing. The rest of us piled in Marty's white van. We crept down the driveway with the lights off. At the very last moment, Tall Paul roared into the open and flashed the high beams at the unsuspecting anglers. Not only were the fishermen close to cardiac arrest but the passengers were too, expecting to plunge into the water just a few feet distant when our chauffeur finally slammed on the brakes.

Glencoe pulled off another elaborate ruse involving an antique rotary wall telephone, which he hung on a nail in the boathouse wall. A few minutes later the perfect victim, Big T, ambled down the steps to the river. Joel activated an old school ringtone from his cell phone and one of the guys said, "T, get the phone, please." After repeated "Hellos?" and gales of laughter, it dawned on T that he had been pranked.

★ ★ ★ ★ ★

There is a cigar store Indian on the Mik-E-Nok lodge dock a few minutes downriver that has stood sentry for decades. On occasion the eyes of the statue are painted looking in toward the bank, the river or straight ahead, giving frequent paddlers the uneasy feeling of being followed. A more serious prank was perpetrated when a group of boys cut the head off. To their credit, when the boys' fathers learned of the vandalism, they made the miscreants reattach the missing head and repaint the whole statue.

In the early days of the GGCC separate lodges, two of Dr. Arthur T. Holbrook's men's group sang well into the night and, around 1:30 AM, after unsuccessful attempts to fall asleep, the revelers were evicted into the cold night and locked out until they agreed to cease and desist.

Noyes Camp newcomers have been tricked. When William Flather Sr. first visited, he was sent to the boat house to retrieve a paddle. He took one step too many and fell into the river where it was exposed in the bath house. He sank to the bottom in his suit and shoes, his hat floating on the surface.

Brule River guide Antoine "Tony" Dennis pulled a prank on the foppishly dressed owner of the Cedar Island Estate, Henry Clay Pierce. The St. Louis oil and railroad tycoon had apparently offended another guide who offered Tony $5, a tidy sum in the early 1900s, to tip his canoe and launch Pierce into the cold, spring-fed river. Dennis must have had plenty of other paying customers because he accepted the challenge, and rocked the canoe until the dapper fisherman took an unanticipated dip in the stream—tweed, silk, flannel, foulard, bejeweled cuff links, white buckskin shoes and all.

During the tenting period of the Gitche Gumee Camping Club, George Markham tricked himself one day. My Great-grandfather was surprised to see him looking so bedraggled after a long absence from the campsite. Dr. Arthur T. Holbrook tells the story: *"Where on earth have you been, Colonel" asked Judge Noyes. "Out at Five Mile Lake," said The Colonel. "Oh," said the Judge, "is Patterson's cabin still usable? I want to go fire-hunting some night." "I didn't see it," said the Colonel. "Why, it's right beside the trail," said the Judge, "you couldn't miss it." "Well I didn't see it," insisted the Colonel. "In fact I didn't see any lake. I simply walked to Five Mile Lake and there wasn't any lake there."*

★ ★ ★ ★ ★

Perhaps the longest lasting prank from the Brule River is literary, and has lasted over 125 years. Benjamin Armstrong was the son-in-law and adopted son of La Pointe Ojibwe Chief Buffalo. Before he befriended the Ojibwe band he had already led a remarkable life. He was a horse jockey, logger, farmer, trader and shopkeeper. He learned the Ojibwe language and was an interpreter and trusted friend and advisor for the natives who called him, *Zhah-bahsh-kung, "the man who goes through."* In 1891, he published his memoirs, *Early Life Among the Indians.* Chapter 5 included *"The Battle of the Brule:" "The whole country from this point to Lake Superior was an unbroken forest, inhabited exclusively by the Chippewa, but their right to this county was strongly contested by the Dakota (Sioux), leading to many bloody battles... I witnessed a battle on the Brule River about October 1st of the following year [1842], a true version of which I will give you, the Sioux were headed by Old Crow and Chippewas by Buffalo, each having a number of sub-chiefs to assist them. The battleground was about midway from the source of the Brule River to its mouth and about 15 miles from Lake Superior...."*

Armstrong claimed to have watched undetected from a perch high above the east river bank where Chief Buffalo had gathered 200 warriors to face Old Crow's greater forces on the west side of the Brule. Armstrong provided detailed information which, of course, is the best way to spin a tall tale. After sunset, the Ojibwe set numerous campfires to exaggerate their numbers and planned to unleash a 3-prong strategy; sending some men up the river to cross the stream and some men down while the center force waited for the enemy to cross. The fighting supposedly began at daylight when the Ojibwe men in the center feigned a retreat drawing the Dakota across the river where they encountered a 3-foot bank. Armstrong wrote that the Dakota, *"being in the water they were impelled to scale the bank before their clubs and knives were of any use, and the Chippewa brained them as fast as they came in reach... The river ran red with blood...."*

Benjamin said the Ojibwe collected 101 scalps and lost only 13 men. There is only one problem with his account: no one else confirmed it. Some say there was a Battle of the Brule but it occurred the previous century. Historians are skeptical at best. People will do anything to sell a book.

The veracity of a story is not important if it is interesting and outrageous. Brule historian Leigh Jerrard even won the *Westerners Brand Book* tall tale award for his dubious stump story. He claimed he was taking a walk in the woods and came across the stump of an old tree, which he climbed on to get a better view. It was hollow and he fell into the crevice, unable to extricate himself. This may have been plausible, but the tale doesn't end as a bear ambled over to the stump, sat and tumbled down on top of Leigh, startling both. Neither party was happy with the situation, and as the bear scrambled upward, the woodsman hung on to the fur of his derrière and escaped. Leigh answered anyone's challenge of the whopper with, *"If you don't believe me I'll show you the stump!"*

★ ★ ★ ★ ★

The Brule's current flows toward our landing, which makes canoers tend to veer to the other side when we sit in our chairs watching the traffic. They are often stuck on the sandbar on the western shore. One sunny afternoon, two of the Boys of Brule decided to set a trap by moving rocks from a wing dam to create an unseen barrier. The experiment was foiled when some offended neighbors put the boulders back in their original home, which we would have done once the clinical trial was complete. A wing dam is a man-made contrivance. It wasn't as if we were clear-cutting original growth timber. Some senses of humor are more developed than others.

There was precedent, after all. The Winneboujou Marshalls had perpetrated the same trick. Caroline described, *"The pile of rocks brother Alan had built in front of our dock—'Frog Island' to snag the unsuspecting and quantitated and those transfixed by the calm sheen near us just at the moment of full-blown trust and relaxation, and how they turn to dockside sunbathers and say 'Oh, what a gorgeous day, isn't it?' as a vicious scrape saws the air."*

★ ★ ★ ★ ★

Any Boys of Brule outing to play golf, canoe or head into town requires, at the very least, a 15-minute buffer to round up the participants who will dart back into the house to get sunglasses or a windbreaker or other items invariably forgotten. This is just a prelude to a discussion regarding who will drive, how many vehicles are needed, who will ride shotgun and who is stuck rattling in the way back. When a canoe trip is on the docket the entire process is repeated once we reach Stone's Bridge, the upriver launching spot. It is like herding cats. Prior to leaving for golf I usually hide Big "T"'s favorite club, a 5 wood.

A game of horseshoes takes place before dinner. Jim and Dana always play Bud and Mike. The pit is a few feet from the copse of trees between Noyes Camp and the Holbrook lodge and often doubles as a gnat and mosquito breeding ground. The matches are spirited and, in 2012, a contentious rules debate turned into quite a brouhaha which simmers still.

Part of the attraction of the annual Boys of Brule tradition is the opportunity to relax. During inclement weather we gather in the Council Room, resembling toddlers who play next to each other but separately. Usually a game of Hearts or

Cribbage occupies the card table while someone noodles on the guitar or piano. Crossword puzzles and reading are popular, and a couple of the guys may be engaged in conversation. Inevitably someone is snoozing while sitting erect in his chair or on the couch. Daydreaming in front of a roaring fire is also common.

A more frenetic indoor activity is a game of Horse played with a Nerf basketball set complete with backboard, hoop and stand. Old Doc Shorten is probably the most accomplished dead-eye executing inventive shots from the balcony that swish through the hoop situated by one of the porch doors downstairs. I hate being the shooter after Lumber as he tricks me into his hurry-up strategy, which makes me jittery and my accuracy even worse, if possible. This activity has been on hiatus for many years since we stored the equipment in the garage and some critter chewed the ball into pieces.

Perhaps the most spontaneous event of our history occurred in 1993 when Marty was soon to take a matrimonial plunge. A bachelor party was deemed appropriate, and we piled into Tall Paul's van with folding chairs in the back and a designated driver at the wheel. We headed to Northern Wisconsin's most heralded den of inequity, Phipps Tavern near Hayward, about 40 miles south of Brule. Since it was the opening weekend of the fishing season, the place was packed with revelers who all seemed to be on leave from a logging camp. These were large, imposing men, and the city boys were on our best behavior. The atmosphere was like that of an Old West saloon, although I don't think anyone was shot.

Great-grandmother Noyes would not have approved of our outing, but she had some quirks of her own. She was competitive to a fault. When the boathouse we share with the Holbrooks was under construction, she pulled the contractor, Joe Lucius, to the side and whispered instructions in his ear. After the project was completed, our portion was a few inches longer. She never accepted second best. On Sundays the family poled upriver to the picnic grounds and if the wind was at her back, Agnes unfurled her parasol to act as a spinnaker guaranteeing her canoe a first place finish. She smiled from ear to ear.

[14]

DROP OUTS, EVICTIONS AND MAKING THE GRADE

"An entrance into the lodge itself, while the ceremonies are being enacted, has sometimes been granted through courtesy, but this does not initiate a person into the mysteries of the creed, nor does it make him a member of the society."

WILLIAM WARREN, *History of the Ojibway People*

★ ★ ★ ★ ★

HISTORICALLY, NOT EVERYONE IS cut out for life on the Brule. The indigenous battled each other when the fur trade pushed eastern tribes into Wisconsin, upsetting the status quo. Voyageurs were crippled and some died during long portages and shooting rapids. Logging camps experienced death either through pneumonia, accidents or murder. Explorers and soldiers arrived at their destinations bruised and battered.

Reverend Judson Titsworth, one of the founding members of the Gitche Gumee Camping Club, was nicknamed "The Commodore" for his service in the Union Navy during the Civil War. In 1903 with the burgeoning families in the club, he saw the need for separate lodges. Rather than undertake such a financial burden, he reluctantly withdrew.

The Winneboujou Club members were wary of new visitors and the possibility of upsetting the equilibrium.

"And of course the most enthusiastic of the Club were the Baron, the Engineer, the Doctor and the Lawyer. Others wanted to go, but these four would go, and of course they did. Nor would the party have been complete had the hereditary guests, the stoic and the happy one—otherwise Rhodes and Hannaford—failed to accompany them,

but they had never failed a friend and did not this time. It is true that they were a little shy of the Bishop, whom the Baron had invited to be of the party, but upon holding a secret conversation among themselves, they concluded that if he was a friend of the Baron he could not be very austere, and so, as he was known to be a good fisherman, they would chance it this time. And now they insist on having the Bishop every time."

C.D. O'Brien, *Brule Chronicles*

In the earliest days of conservation efforts, Mr. C.B. Couch engaged in a different manner of self-exile from the Brule River. One August, an earnest game warden checked his creel and found two undersized trout and arrested him for his transgression. The sportsman was so angry and embarrassed by the accusation that he packed and left the area for good.

Increased use of the river by sportsmen and the enforcement of property rights by landowners has been an ongoing issue for well over a hundred years. An early example occurred one May along the Cedar Island stretch of the stream when Dr. Arthur T. Holbrook and Colonel Markham stopped for lunch with their guides near Durant's Channel.

In those years the early club people shared a sense of great comradery, and thought of the Brule as their own and treated it with respect. Seemingly out of nowhere, the Cedar Island superintendent materialized from the forest with two formidable dogs and politely but firmly ordered the anglers to douse the fire, clean up the grounds and never repeat the intrusion unless they were prepared to be prosecuted for trespassing.

The flabbergasted Markham was an attorney and began to deliver his opening statement, and as Dr. Arthur reported, *"...stood his ground and argued quietly at first, then vehemently, and finally, abandoning restraint, heatedly berated the superintendent, his two accompanying huskies, the owners of the land, everybody connected with Cedar Island, and dared them to arrest him. The superintendent looked at his watch and very calmly and quietly said: 'If you are not off this land and the place properly cleaned up in ten minutes you will be thrown off it. Now take your choice.'"*

The evicted fishermen retreated, embarrassed and outraged, and a bit of the magic of the Brule dimmed that day. Not all evictions on the river are solely due to trespassing. One May some canoers pulled up on Gitche Gumee land and started a campfire. A few of the Boys of Brule, courteously at first, encouraged them to move on. The forest was tinder dry and fire bans were enforced to the point that power lawn mowers were verboten for fear that sparks could ignite an inferno. The interlopers balked, unmoved by the safety issues and we had to be more forceful.

Some banishments are of a financial nature. When my father was treasurer of Noyes-Brule Inc., one of my mother's cousins ignored annual invoices to pay for his share of the camp's operation. Eventually Dad sent him a letter explaining his shares would be revoked unless his account was current. A threatening letter was penned by the debtor, warning that any attempt to take his shares would be met with castration, although his words were much cruder. The shares were acquired by one of his siblings and the surgical procedure avoided.

Some sons-in-law of Agnes Haskell Noyes found life on the Brule to be less than idyllic. Donald McLennan was initially scorned by Agnes because she was unenthusiastic about his prospects and felt he was uneducated. Her instincts were wrong as he co-founded the megalithic insurance and financial company, Marsh and McLennan. He bristled at his mother-in-law's autocratic style and preferred to set his own schedule in what was supposed to be a relaxing setting in the north woods. Since he financed the new lodge after its predecessor burned down, he may have felt entitled to a little leeway. Under the guise of a better location for his allergies, he joined the Huron Mountain Club in Michigan's Upper Peninsula.

My Grandfather, Edward "Cleve" Harrison, felt the same way. He chafed at being stranded with his in-laws when the weather turned foul. He found fishing and canoeing boring. He was accustomed to the male comradery of golf, tennis and polo and found the formidable cadre of sisters-in-law and mother-in-law to be suffocating.

As a member of an eminent military family on his father's side and an old Washington D.C. lineage on his mother's, he attended social events at the White House and enjoyed the company of the nation's leaders. One of the youngest majors in World War I, a graduate of the prestigious Army War College and a longtime bachelor, Grandpa was used to giving the orders and fumed at being subjected to his mother-in law's dictatorial manner.

Participation in the Boys of Brule is no different. It is difficult for newbies to hit the ground running. Many of us have known each other from childhood, speak our own language and anticipate each other's thoughts to such a degree that we just blurt out the punchlines rather than wait for the end of a joke. It's not that the veterans are unfriendly or the neophytes are hazed or put through a rigorous initiation, but the pace is fast and the verbal repartee acerbically witty.

Throughout history there have been evictions of individuals and groups in the Brule area. The fur trade and the bellicose Iroquois League started a domino effect as native bands were rousted from their ancestral territory. The Iroquois, Ottawa and Huron served as trading intermediaries with other bands but as the profitability of the fur business grew, the Iroquois drove the other two to the southern shore of Lake Superior. The Dakota pushed the Ottawa and Huron from the environs and by the last quarter of the 17th century, the usually loosely affiliated Ojibwe bands joined forces militarily and, aided by weaponry obtained from the French, moved the Dakota west.

Further encroachment by the French, English and Yankee businessmen signaled the death knell of the Ojibwe way of life. The effects of the Revolutionary War and the War of 1812 were slow to reach northwestern Wisconsin, but eventually the Ojibwe's culture and gender roles were permanently altered. As the native men spent more time trapping beaver and other animals, the women began to take over the hunting role. Trading with the Europeans changed their weaponry as they abandoned the bow and arrow for firearms. Cloth replaced deerskin for apparel except for moccasins.

After the fur trading era ended and white settlers pushed westward, the government attempted to turn the Ojibwe into farmers who planted crops and raised animals. Native women were encouraged to embrace the roles of housewives. Northern Wisconsin was not really suited for farming and the Ojibwe increasingly turned to the outside world for their basic needs. Their autonomy was reaching an end. The natives were relegated to reservations by the mid-19th century. Hunting and gathering became a thing of the past as the Ojibwe were evicted from their traditional lands. The compression of native territory was a windfall for the expanding United States.

Once northwestern Wisconsin was stripped of fur bearing animals and fashions changed in Europe, attention was shifted to the seemingly endless stands of white pine. A series of unethical treaties and dirty tricks boxed the natives into smaller and smaller tracts of land. The Brule Lumber Company, one of many logging entities, cut 50 million board feet on 3,000 acres during its period of operation. Once Wisconsin was largely denuded, the industry left the Brule region and continued west to Minnesota. Lumber Baron Frederic Weyerhaeuser was more magnanimous. He donated 4,320 acres along the river in 1907 to jumpstart the Brule River State Forest. His only caveat was to insist the state never build dams on the stream. The lumberman, perhaps as atonement, helped ensure the river would continue to be a source of enjoyment.

The Boys of Brule have had "one and done" individuals who for various reasons haven't fit in or didn't feel comfortable. Mickey's friend Skogs, a burly ex-all conference college football player, tore his rotator cuff playing ping pong the first night and left in pain for Chicago the next morning. Jim's brother-in-law, Suck Face, did not return after his rookie season. We pranked him a bit and he was involved in the Great Cooler Dispute of 1993. He grabbed someone else's cooler to bring home and various attempts to rectify the situation were muffed.

High school classmate Clancy Dokmo visited one year but perhaps we forgot to invite him back. College buddy Steve "Spino" Dinapoli surfaces every now and then from Texas, when his love life is in disrepair and he needs some TLC from his friends. My Target Stores colleague, Dave Ruce, was a regular attendee but faded away.

Jim's younger brother, Charlie Hurd, was in the fold for many years but decided that we were really his brother's friends and made a graceful exit. It was an amicable split, and we miss him. He had a mitigating effect on some of our foibles. One year Mickey was having a difficult time separating his juicy rack of ribs, slathered with barbeque sauce. The ribs flipped off his plate, making a slow descent to his shorts, finally landing on the rug at his feet. Charlie had seen enough and, shaking his head, jumped in and cut Mickey's ribs for him after they had been quickly removed for the carpet, barely beating the 5 second rule.

There have been a couple of introverts who didn't join in the general merriment and kept to themselves. The Boys of Brule favor extroverts who add to the weekend's atmosphere. One year we had a "none and done." Tall Paul insisted that Rip Mason, a college friend, would join us. We rolled out the red carpet, saving him the master bedroom, complete with private bath. Marty has a veneer of credibility but, on occasion, his theories should be thoroughly vetted. We patiently kept an eye peeled for Rip but he never showed. The nicest bedroom went unused. "Waiting for Rip" turned out to be just as absurdist as Samuel Beckett's play. Godot never appeared either.

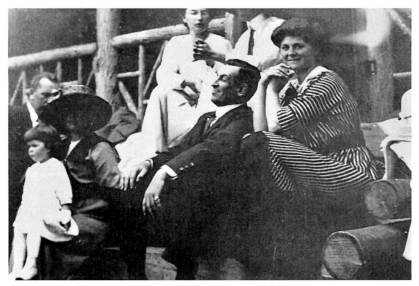

Donald and Katherine Noyes McLennan (foreground) on Noyes Camp porch steps *Courtesy of Katherine McLennan Bradbury*

Grandparents, Margaret Noyes Harrison and Edward "Cleve" Harrison

[15]

FIRE NEXT TIME

"And I dread the ominous stains of tar
That there always is on the papered walls,
And the smell of fire drowned in rain
That there always is when the chimney fails."

ROBERT FROST, *"The Kitchen Chimney"*

★ ★ ★ ★ ★

EVER SINCE FIRE WAS first used by Homo Erectus about one million years ago to warm the body, cook the food, ward off predators and extend the day it has been respected, venerated and feared. It is powerful, frightening, fascinating, mysterious and revered.

The Brule River has always been associated with fire. Whatever the language of the speaker, Dakota, Ojibwe, French or English, it has been most often named for the charred forests caused by lightning strikes or other causes. The image of the Noble Savage as a steward of the natural environment dated back to John Dryden, Restoration England poet, in 1672, and explorer Jacques Cartier, who claimed Canada for France in 1534.

Native Americans, however, often altered the landscape. The Ojibwe have used fire for a variety of reasons, both practical and ceremonial. They set intentional fires to clear the banks of the Brule River to remove underbrush that prevented their prey, moose, deer and beaver, from access to the stream's drinking water, directing them to a desired hunting location.

The natives burned parcels of land to eliminate mosquitos, flies, ticks, snakes, rodents and other pests. Fire was utilized to signal allies, remove cover for their enemies and provide a deceptive smoke screen for their own warriors. Retreating war parties left scorched earth behind to mask signs of their escape and multiple campfires were set to exaggerate strength. Land was singed to provide habitat to grow berries and roast grasshoppers and crickets to eat. Bees were smoked from their hives to collect honey and surround fires encircled rabbits. Flames cleared overgrowth from trails to facilitate travel.

The Ojibwe glorified fire and incorporated it in nearly every ritual and ceremony. The story of their migration west from the Atlantic region was predicted by the Prophecy of the Seven Fires. Each of the seven represented a phase in Ojibwe history and migration and was called a "fire." The prophesies presaged a place *"where food grows on the water"* and is thought to be the marshes of the mainland at Chequamegon Bay where wild rice grew and maple trees were tapped just a stone's throw from the Brule Valley.

According to the *Midewiwiin* interpretation of the sacred birch bark scrolls, the Confederacy of Three Fires formed at Micshimikinaak where Lakes Superior, Michigan and Huron converge. The migrating Anishinaabe split into three bands, the Ojibwe, Ottawa and Potawatomi but agreed to form an alliance to support each other in political and military matters and maintain the traditions. They met periodically for the Council of the Three Fires.

The Confederacy began each forum sitting at their individual fires to formulate their proposals and then met at the large communal fire to forge final decisions. Edith Leoso, tribal historian for the Bad River Band of Ojibwe, quotes Three Fires Midewiwan Society member Eddie Benton concerning the exit from the Madeline Island "Shangi-La," perhaps due to overcrowding and scarcity of food or even something more sinister, as lore passed through the generations suggests the presence of evil spirits. The island was quickly abandoned and avoided for many years.

"The old people who had to leave built this huge bonfire and then we left. They say when we got to Bad River…we could still see the fire…We wanted to remember where our homeland was at, so that when we did ceremonies, we could always know this. That fire, it was always a part of letting go. Yet…knowing our connection. Perhaps it was part of the detachment—to try and forget and cope with the trauma of leaving."

The Ojibwe revere fire and consider it a relative of the Sun and a source of great energy. The Firekeeper was an important figure in the band and often carried live coals from campsite to campsite to start the next fire. They believe that six of the fires have been fulfilled and that now is the phase of the seventh fire when society, if it takes the right path, will be led from the darkness and the Sacred Fire will be relit.

The Upper Brule River Valley is the home of first growth, ramrod-straight white and red pines. These species can benefit from periodic fires, which eliminate competition and expose nutrients in the soil. A recent tree ring study in the area found evidence of nine fires in the area before 1910. The scientists discovered evidence of a particularly destructive 1838 fire that burned so hot that its crown scorched a stand of adjacent trees. Pines are somewhat fire resistant due to strong root systems, thick bark and long stretches of trunk before branches grow.

There is a pine tree in the Brule River State Forest that predates the Boston Tea Party. Much older fire-damaged stumps exist in the valley. The Brule was home to a white pine that measured 151 feet high with a circumference of 17 feet 11 inches. Sadly, a large limb fell from the behemoth in the 1980s and despite efforts to save the tree, the senior citizen of the river finally died. A white pine, if particularly stately, is called *zhingwaak* or Grandfather, by the Ojibwe. In February, 2018, we toppled a 232-year-old pine tree from Frog's Point at Noyes Camp. It was dead and in danger of falling on an unsuspecting canoer. The tree germinated the same year that frontier folk hero Davy Crockett was born, and Revolutionary War Major General Nathaniel Greene, George Washington's favorite officer, died. The pine now rests in the river providing new trout habitat.

Dendrochronologists have recently studied the annual growth rings of trees and stumps in the Brule River Valley to learn of the many forest fires in the area. A stump was discovered dating back to 1540, the year Francisco Vazquez de Coronado began his expedition to find the Seven Cities of Gold in what is now the southwest United States. Trees were located that survived as many as 15 forest fires.

To clear land, procure firewood and building materials, the natives killed trees with fire. They were toppled by boring holes through the trunk and inserting hot coals in one side so smoke could escape through the other. Fire was lit around the tree's base which burned the bark and the trunk, eventually killing it.

"The earth, born in fire, baptized by lightning, since before life's beginning has been and is, a fire planet."

Edward V. Komarek, fire ecologist

After the Europeans nearly exterminated the population of fur-bearing mammals in the Upper Midwest, the lumber scions of New England stripped the forests of New England of stands of white pine to feed the insatiable need for lumber and ships' masts in England. They then focused their greed on the woods of Michigan, Wisconsin and Minnesota where they believed the supply was inexhaustible. Unscrupulous lumbermen used fire to defraud the Ojibwe to drive the price of timber land downward. They set the understory of a forest tract ablaze, leaving the lightly singed virgin pine stands still marketable. The logging concerns convinced the Ojibwe the wood was unusable and then paid them a pittance for the rights.

In 1871, Peshtigo, Wisconsin, was a typical mill town. Lumberjacks felled the pine and the stripped branches lay in heaps on the ground. The mills cut the trees and left slabs where they fell. Sawdust was so pervasive it was shoveled and swept under buildings and the raised wooden sidewalks. Farmers, railroads and the weather were also complicit in the impending disaster: the worst forest fire in U.S. history. The ancient style of slash and burn agriculture was used to clear fields, the railroads cut vegetation to clear the way and sparks from the train tracks ignited small blazes. The odor of smoke was so pervasive in Peshtigo in the autumn of 1871 that it perhaps led to complacency.

The smaller fires converged into one over the town of Peshtigo, and the 100 MPH winds and the estimated 500-700 degree temperature of the conflagration fed on the carelessly scattered fuel. The fire was so intense it leapfrogged the 10-20 mile wide Green Bay to the Door County Peninsula. Few laborers bothered to extinguish the countless small fires and, on October 8th, a massive cold front moved into the Peshtigo area and caused a 40-degree drop in temperature, whipping up strong winds, which accelerated the fires burning all over the Upper Midwest: north from Chicago and west from Michigan to Minnesota.

The townspeople's hair and clothes caught fire, and they were unable to outrun the galloping inferno. The death toll reached as many as 2,500, and a minimum of 1.2 million acres of land were scorched. Amazingly, the Peshtigo Fire is largely forgotten, overshadowed by the Chicago Fire on the same day and the myth of Mrs. O'Leary's cow. Two-hundred-fifty people perished in that disaster.

History repeated itself in 1894 as, unfortunately, the lumber industry hadn't learned from the horror of Peshtigo. By midafternoon on September 1, residents in the town of Brule were carrying lanterns to see through the smoke-blackened air as two fires bearing down on Hinckley, Minnesota, 100 miles away, were about to merge into one. Three years of drought had created a critical situation. The Brennan Lumber Company sprawled over 36 acres amidst mounds of sawdust and logs. Hundreds of thousands of board feet were piled, ready to be cut. The temperature was high, the winds strong, humidity low and soil moisture non-existent.

As the two fires joined, they created their own weather system with flames licking the air 200 feet above the ground and debris shooting thousands of feet into the sky, powered by a convection column. The heat soared to 1,200 degrees, melting metal and welding the wheels of train cars to the tracks. People sought refuge in shallow, muddy Skunk Lake and the Grindstone River. Many died from deadly gases before they were incinerated.

Our immediate downstream Winneboujou neighbors, Mrs. E.N. Saunders, her niece, nephews and children, as well as Mr. C.D. O'Brien, boarded the afternoon train from St. Paul to Duluth, on their way to Brule. Flames burst through the windows of the railroad car and the smoke was so thick one could not see the other side. Mrs. Saunders huddled in a corner protecting the children by hiding them under her skirt while Mr. O'Brien did his best to keep the fire at bay. The New York Forest Commission wrote: *"When the heroic engineer, Root, stopped the train at a place where everybody thought was Skunk Lake, Mrs. Saunders marshalled her little ones and started despairingly through the flaming forest. They came upon a place that looked like water, but it was only a barren waste of hot sand. In this sand, Mrs. Saunders buried all the children and herself. But the heat grew more and more horrible, and they had to hunt a new place of shelter. They finally floundered into the morass of Skunk Lake. There the brave woman buried all the youngsters in the mud and muck and slime of the lake, and protected herself in like fashion There they all lay half-smothered from 5 o'clock Saturday afternoon until 4 o'clock Sunday morning, and they all came out alive and but little hurt."*

★ ★ ★ ★ ★

The official death toll was 418 but did not include an unknown number of Ojibwe living in the woods. Six communities and 400 square miles were consumed by the catastrophe.

In 1909, a conflagration started in a hotel almost leveled the town of Brule. Firemen from Superior soon arrived by train, and after they believed the fire to be extinguised with a loss of twelve buildings, they left. The simmering embers flared and another five structures were gone.

Forest fires are a frequent concern in the Brule River Valley. Many times in the history of our family's tenure in northwestern Wisconsin canoes have been packed with valuables and essentials in case fire threatened Noyes Camp. Later, cars were loaded in the same manner.

In early May 1910 forest fires blazed with regularity in northern Wisconsin and the woods lining the Brule River were no exception. On the morning of the 9th, Joe Lucius sent word to the downriver camps that they were in imminent danger and that his family was heading to Big Lake for protection in canoes stuffed with their possessions.

A fire ignited by sparks from a Duluth South Shore and Atlantic Railway locomotive had been racing through the dry slashings, and it was obvious that unless action was taken the flames would soon reach the long bend of the river below Noyes Camp. Backfires were set and the blaze was contained to the old logging railway and its environs. The camps on our stretch of the stream had been surrounded by fire, leaving the homes of the Gitche Gumee Camping Club standing on a small island of greenery amidst the charred forest.

An entry in the Noyes Camp Log Book chronicles a momentous occasion in family history: *On May 14, 1924, there were in camp David* [Guide] *and Ida* [Cook] *Sample, Elena Forstland* [Cook], *Katherine* [Kay] *Dalrymple and party who went up the river with Dave. About 3:45 PM Ida went to the Lodge room to put some wood on the fire which was low, when she heard a slight crackling sound above, but investigating upstairs could find nothing wrong. But looking around outside she thought more smoke was coming out of the chimney than could be caused by the few embers in the fireplace, and so at once gave the alarm to Brule and then started the pump.*

Meantime Elena telephoned to the neighborhood. Mr. and Mrs. Irving Fish and Mr. and Mrs. William Uihlein, guests of Stuart Markham, and many others, came but, unfortunately, Stuart was at Brule. Nobody knew that the water should have been shut off from the house so as to give the full force to the hose and so it was quite ineffective in quenching the fire which got such a good start that nothing could be done to save the house, and by 6 o'clock nothing was left standing but the two chimneys which sight, accompanied by much smoke, greeted Katherine and her party when they returned from their day's pleasure. Stuart at once telegraphed the bad news to Haskell in Milwaukee and he and his mother [Agnes] *took the train the following night (a sad*

birthday excursion for Mrs. Noyes) and Saturday the insurance adjuster arrived from
Superior to view the remains and provide for a decent burial.

Fortunately the day of the fire was a quiet one, for had there been any wind probably
the entire district would have burned.

The house was a total loss. No one was injured, and like the sacred Phoenix, a magnificently designed and constructed lodge rose from the ashes. It stands today as a testament to the foresight of Great-grandmother Agnes Haskell Noyes and the craftsmanship of the contractor, Joe Lucius. The new edifice is considered one of the finest on the river and includes modern conveniences like electricity and indoor plumbing missing from the initial generation of smaller, more Spartan homes on the stream. The financial support of Donald and Katherine McLennan made the new structure possible.

Another close call on our river bend occurred in the summer of 1936, a year of lengthy and extreme drought. Morning had begun like any other day in the town of Brule.

"It looked like rain when I came out of the post office, a dark cloud hung over the
timber line to the southward, and I hurriedly drove toward camp to escape it. But I
had not gone far before I discovered my error. It wasn't a storm! It was forest fire off
there, and how it was travelling."

Dr. Frank Bowman, "The Battle that Saved the Brule,"
Wisconsin Outdoors Magazine, February 1937

A small fire had started three miles south of Stone's Bridge and, within six hours, hundreds of men arrived by truck from Ashland, Superior, Duluth and many smaller towns to fight the blaze. They carried implements including shovels, axes, spades, scythes and large brush knives, similar to machetes. Portable water tanks were used to douse the flames. The barrens were a tinder box of dry fuel stretching for miles. Sparks carried on the wind ignited dead leaves.

Plows and bulldozers clawed the earth in an effort to create fire breaks, and back fires were strategically set. On the second day, over eight hundred were working to contain the blaze before it reached an area of desiccated pines that stood for miles to the north. Others darted from spot fire to spot fire to prevent the conflagration from spreading.

Homeowners along the Brule River, ready to evacuate at a moment's notice, brought water, coffee and food to the men fighting desperately to control the holocaust. Guides such as Ben and Ed Dennis, John LaRock and many others were performing the long, exhausting, dirty and dangerous work. The fire was finally contained after 36 agonizing hours. Almost half of Douglas County had been seared and many homes destroyed, leaving smoke-stained chimneys as the only recognizable vestiges. The Brule River Valley had been saved and its residents heaved a collective sigh of relief.

Every boy has a bit of pyromania in his DNA and the Boys of Brule are no exception. The massive Noyes Camp fireplace was carefully pieced together with granite stones of a variety colors and sizes hand-picked from different quarries. The fireplace easily accommodates four-foot logs of birch and pine and is the focal point of the large two-story Council Room. There is something primal and mesmerizing watching the flames on a cold north woods May day when massive Lake Superior, a scant fifteen miles away, holds the remnants of winter. The wood shed is stocked with three cords of wood over the off season, and the wood box around the corner from the fireplace is periodically filled with the logs piled on our ancient flatbed wheelbarrow.

Fire can be magical and even theatrical. In 1886 young Arthur T. Holbrook organized a downriver outing for his buddies with three canoes. Revered Brule River guide Antoine Dennis piloted one of them. Tony was employed by the Holbrook family every summer, and his family occupied the Olibwe camp adjacent to the first location of the Gitche Gumee Camping Club.

Dennis was the last of the Ojibwe mail-runners traveling the 92-mile trail between Superior and Ashland, then back again in astounding time. Every time he passed the Brule River he would stop for a moment to catch his dinner. He earned $1.72 per day to start and did not miss one day in his almost 6 years of service. When the stagecoach era on the Bayfield Road began, Tony returned to guiding. One day Antoine guided Arthur T. Holbrook and some friends on the Brule. The skies were threatening that day, and not long after they started, the heavens opened when the group passed through the Station Rapids. They persevered to the Ranger Campground where they stopped, soaked to the bone. The cloud burst had subsided to a light drizzle and Antoine began to prepare the fire. Arthur excitedly boasted to his friends that they were about to witness some Ojibwe woodland wizardry passed through the generations.

Tony cleared some space, built a circular rock barrier and arranged some small logs in the center. He then retrieved a container of semi-dry kindling from his canoe and dumped it on the wood. The young men watched with anticipation as the guide grabbed a bottle of kerosene and poured it over the fire. Holbrook was subjected to a great deal of ribbing for the effective, but hardly mystical, method of fire starting.

Jim "Lumber" Hurd is perhaps the most accomplished fire aficionado of our group. He is well known for the bonfires he set at his Minnesota cabin and the haphazard yet oddly appealing fireworks displays he orchestrates. Like Tony Dennis, he uses a strong accelerant when he becomes impatient. At Noyes Camp he lights rolled up newspaper and strips of birch bark to jumpstart our entrancing infernos. While Jim is our resident firebug, Dana is our academic, having earned a Master's degree in Forestry.

We recently dodged a potential catastrophe which could have burned the house to the ground for a second time. There were some loose stones on our exterior chimneys, made from river rocks, and we had an expert inspect the fireplaces and the chimneys. Signs of a chimney fire were discovered in the main fireplace. Creosote builds in the flue and when it is not regularly removed it can ignite and burns with such intensity that mortar disintegrates and bricks crack. If wood is exposed, the entire structure is endangered. We had stainless steel liners installed and the fireplaces are now annually inspected and cleaned.

The multiplicity of fire is amazing. It can forge to make metals stronger and can weaken them with extreme heat. It annihilates and regenerates. Fire is beautiful and hideous.

"There are three things that are never satisfied, yea,
Four things say not. It is enough the grave,
And the barren womb, the earth that is not filled with water,
And the fire that saith not, it is enough."

PROVERBS 30: 15-16

Noyes Camp Council Room fireplace *Courtesy of Kelly Griffin*

[16]

WITCHES AND CREATURES AND SPIRITS AND GHOSTS, OH MY!

"Then, as he wended his way, by swamp and stream and awful woodland, to the farmhouse where he happened to be quartered, every sound of nature, at that witching hour, fluttered his excited imagination: the moan of the whip-poor-whill from the hillside; the boding cry of the tree-toad, that harbinger of storm, the dreary hooting of the screech owl, or the sudden rustling in the thicket of birds frightened from their roost. The fire flies, too, which sparkled most vividly in the darkest places, now and then startled him, as one of uncommon brightness would stream across his path, and if, by chance, a huge blockhead of a beetle came winging his blundering flight against him, the poor varlet was ready to give up the ghost, with the idea that that he was struck with a witch's token."

Washington Irving, *The Legend of Sleepy Hollow*

★ ★ ★ ★ ★

PERHAPS THE STRANGE OCCURRENCES and apparitions at Noyes Camp can be attributed to the legacy of despicable ancestor, Reverend Nicholas Noyes, who was a presiding minister over the Salem Witch trials. He was hell bent on extricating confessions by hectoring the defendants. Nicholas was such a hardliner that he refused to pray with the accused. On September 22, 1693, he oversaw the final executions. He observed the strangled bodies twisting in the wind and commented, *"What a sad sight it is to see the eight firebrands of hell hanging there."* The Reverend, a gluttonous man, then enjoyed a leisurely lunch with friends before delivering his "Lecture Day" sermon.

149

On July, 19, 1692, on the gallows platform, Noyes tried to badger Sarah Good into admitting guilt. Robert Calef, a critic of the trials, quoted Nicholas who maintained, *"She was a Witch and she knew she was a Witch."* The prescient Good responded, *"You are a liar! I am no more a witch than you are a wizard, and if you take away my life God will give you blood to drink."* Twenty-five years later, the Reverend died from an aneurysm as blood filled his lungs and throat.

Nathaniel Hawthorne borrowed liberally from not only the witch hunt, the dialogue of Sarah and Nicholas, but also Noyes' death, in writing his gothic tale, *The House of the Seven Gables: "'God', said the dying man, pointing his finger with a ghastly look, at the undismayed countenance of his enemy,—'God will give him blood to drink,' Soon thereafter the judge is found with 'an unnatural distortion in the fixedness of* [his] *stare, that there was blood on his tuff, and that his hoary beard saturated with it. It was too late to give assistance. The iron-hearted Puritan, the relentless persecution, the grasping and strong-willed man was Dead."*

Margaret "Tuggie" Noyes of Falls Parish (Newbury), Massachusetts, was the perfect target for witchcraft accusations. She was a weaver and spinner; single without financial or political clout. She was a bit odd and fit other parts of the profile: "[She was a] *hardworking, inoffensive woman, possessing a marked individuality, strong intellectual faculties, quick perception and keen wit, united to a firm will and independence of action, characteristics which, in some way, had brought upon* [her] *the ban of the community."*

Sarah Emery, *Reminiscences of a Nonagenarian*

Tuggie walked around town in her grey lambkin cloak with its hood drawn tightly about her face. She usually clutched a skein of woolen yarn in one hand and her pipe in the other. She bought her tobacco from Emery's Tavern and enjoyed a cup of cider. Not all the townspeople were accepting of Tuggie and she was shunned by many. Thankfully the period of cruel punishment for witchery was over in Massachusetts. One chilly morning David Emery and his friend Nate Perley encountered Tuggie on their way to school. Sarah Emery relates, *"'There's that witch,' Nate exclaimed, lamenting the lack of a sixpence to place in the path to stop her*

further progress. His companion expressed his credulity regarding such an effect, but nevertheless drew a sixpence from his pocket, which he adroitly dropped immediately before the old woman; she passed on directly over it with a courtesy and a good day, and David again pocketed his coin, firm in the faith of Tuggie's innocence of the diabolical influence, with a full determination never to believe in any witch."

"The Weendigo was gaunt to the point of emaciation, its desiccated skin pulled tautly over its bones. With its bones pushing out and against its skin, its complexion the ash gray of death, and its eyes pushed back deep into their sockets, the Weendigo looked like a gaunt skeleton recently disinterred from the grave. What legs it had were tattered and bloody… Unclean and suffering from the supperations of the flesh, the Weendigo gave off a strange and eerie odor of decay and composition, of death and corruption."

BASIL JOHNSTON, *Ojibwe scholar*

Wendigo, is an Algonquin word, meaning *"evil spirit that devours mankind."* The concept of Wendigo is a pastiche of myth, moralistic folklore, an academically studied psychosis and a cultural and even legal phenomenon taken very seriously at times throughout the centuries. The story of the Wendigo is known to the Anishinaabe people located primarily in northern Minnesota and Wisconsin, and in southern Ontario around the northern shores of the Great Lakes. While descriptions of the beast vary widely, it was universally agreed that the creature was so fleet of foot that it was difficult to get a good look at him.

Wendigo was over sixteen-feet tall with a sepulchral appearance, thin, skeletal and emaciated, with glowing red eyes seemingly floating in bloody eye sockets. Its long tongue hung between dissipated thin lips exposing yellow fangs. It would tear its victims apart with long, sharp claws and talons. The Wendigo has always been equated with the north woods, winter, famine and starvation. It was considered to be the most feared of all spirits. The beast was created, according to legend, when an early member of the First People broke the taboo against cannibalism.

The Wendigo was a skilled, stealthy, hunter, eternally scouring the landscape for its next kill and controlling the weather with its strong magic. It was said to be able to cause severe weather which was a harbinger of its presence. The creature's hunger was never sated and it is said that its shape changed based on the size of its most recently consumed human.

The Ojibwe tried to ward the spirit away with fire and spells. The legend claims the only way to kill Wendigo was to use silver bullets or a silver-bladed knife and then to drive a silver stake into its heart of ice. The heart splinters would then be interred in sacred ground such as a graveyard. To complete the process, the body was chopped into pieces with a silver axe, burned and scattered to the four winds.

A human could "go Wendigo" if he resorted to cannibalism, was attacked by the monster or infected by the spirit in a dream. The creature seemed to appear in times of great hardship and stress. Ceremonies were performed to support the ideals of kinship and cooperation to combat the Wendigo's mores of gluttony and excess, as well as thwarting the temptations of cannibalism. A dance, called *wiindigookaanzhimowin,* is part of the final day of the Sun Dance with participants wearing masks and dancing backwards around a pounding drum.

The Wendigo has long been a part of traditional Anishinaabe folklore and has, on occasion crept not only into everyday life, but also the legal system. In the spring of 1879, the Cree trader and guide, Swift Runner, returned from his winter camp without the other members of his family. He claimed that Wendigo had infiltrated his dreams and eventually took over his spirit. The Royal Canadian Mounted Police began to investigate and Swift Runner took them to his camp and showed where one of his sons, who had died from starvation, was buried. This did not explain the other skulls, bones and bits of hair that littered the campsite.

Swift Runner stuck to his story and swore the Wendigo had forced him to butcher, cook and consume his wife, the remaining children and his mother and brother, even though they were camped only 25 miles from a Hudson Bay Trading Post. He had shot some, clubbed others and strangled his daughter with a rope. Some of the bigger bones were snapped in half to extract the marrow.

The police brought Swift Runner and the grisly evidence back to the fort and a trial was conducted. The judge and jury did not buy the alibi of Wendigo Psychosis and sentenced Swift Runner to death by hanging. According to Anishinaabe tradition, Swift Runner should have taken the high road and resisted the urges of cannibalism by committing suicide or asking someone to kill him.

Another court case involved Jack Fiddler, an Ojibwe-Cree chief and *midew,* a spiritual medicine practitioner who was said to have powers to defeat Wendigo, and his brother Joseph. They were accused of several mercy killings performed to kill the beast. Jack killed himself before the trial in 1907 while Joseph was tried and executed.

Over the years, the "Wendigo Condition" has been fiercely debated between the believers of the old traditions and the medical community who consider it a *"culture based syndrome brought on by a volatile combination of isolation, despair, alcohol and hopelessness."* Wendigo Psychosis has faded from the Ojibwe culture, but our down-river neighbors, the Saunders/Lindekes, named their lodge Wendigo, which stands on the site of the old Gitche Gumee Camping Club, as a nod to the old lore.

La Chasse-galerie, or the "Bewitched Canoe," is a French-Canadian folktale that has its roots not only in France but in Anishinaabe legend. There are variations of the story, but it generally consists of voyageurs working in the interior, lonely for female companionship. The only way they can visit their women and be back in time to resume their duties is to strike a deal with the devil, who gives them powers to fly their canoe over the frontier and villages until it lands in Montreal.

The agreement will be broken if the voyageurs take the Lord's name in vain or touch the spire of a cathedral during their flight. The devil will then take their souls. The men engage in a night of celebration until it is time to return to the lakes and rivers of fur country. Invariably, one of the men breaks the pact by inadvertently flying too close to a cross on top of a church or swearing. In the vast majority of the versions, the voyageurs somehow escape the fires of hell and return to their arduous labors.

The timber camps of northern Wisconsin were fertile grounds for tall tales, many of them involving Paul Bunyan and Babe the Blue Ox. A few included the creature named Hodag, a companion of the giant and his pet. The beast, also called *Bovine Spiritualus,* roamed the forests but was said to be hard to locate due to the dwindling supply of white bulldogs, its favorite prey. A lumberman named Eugene Shepard had an entrepreneurial spirit and began spreading rumors of sightings. In 1893, he claimed to have thrown dynamite into a Hodag's lair and retrieved the charred remains.

The animal was said to weigh 265 pounds with the face of a frog, the head of an elephant with bullhorns, green eyes and the back of a dinosaur covered with short dark hair. Its stumpy legs ended in long, sharp claws and the Hodag's tail sported a sharp hook. The creature had the stench of rotting meat accented with essence of skunk.

Shepard insisted he captured a live one in 1898 using chloroform and bear wrestlers to subdue it. He began to display the curiosity at county fairs in Oneida, Wausau and Atigo, charging 10 cents admission. A darkened shack behind his house was also used to showcase the Hodag. Sheperd attached electrical wires to the wooden model disguised as the creature, giving it frequent jolts to cause movement. His sons, hiding in an adjacent room, growled and moaned, sending the patrons shrieking toward the door. The Smithsonian Institute called his bluff and offered to send experts to Wisconsin to examine the beast, forcing Shepard to admit the ruse. The tradition lives on in the Badger State where the Hodag is honored with festivals, concerts and local events.

Noyes Camp has its own spirit world, many say. I have never actually experienced anything myself, but there are enough stories that the claims cannot be summarily dismissed. A common thread seems to be a blue or green light that appears in Great-grandmother Agnes' pitch black bedroom in the middle of the night. Other anecdotes have some credible back-up that I can confirm. Noyes Camp has earned a reputation in the Brule environs over the years.

We often have repair work done at the house after it has been put to bed for winter at the end of October. On one such occasion, an electrician was doing some wiring work in Agnes' room. When he arrived at the empty house, which had been unlocked by the caretaker, the windows in the room were wide open. He closed them, locked the latches, and went back to his truck to retrieve a tool and, when he returned to the bedroom, the windows were wide open. He called out to see if there was anyone else upstairs and received no answer. With the hairs on the back of his neck standing at attention, he grabbed his tool box, left a note in the kitchen and fled to his pick-up, never to return.

One evening my cousin Bob Banks' daughter Perrin was not feeling well and went to bed early in Great-grandmother's room. After a while her mother Marna went upstairs to check on her, and found Perrin talking in the general direction of a chair. When asked to whom she was speaking, the young girl responded, *"Agnes."*

We often have large groups of friends and family at the Brule as the house can accommodate 20+ people comfortably. One summer on the first evening of our stay, our nephew Ryan came downstairs and asked, *"When did Amy get here?"* My wife Kristin answered, *"She's in California, working."* Ryan responded, *"I just saw her upstairs."* Late one night, Kristin was last to go to bed and was turning out the lights upstairs. From the silence came a disembodied female voice she did not recognize saying, *"Good night, Kristin."*

"The pine forests there were trackless and spooky. The valleys were still strewn with monstrous fossils that had laid undisturbed for thousands of years: mammoths and saber-toothed tigers, dire wolves and a species of beaver that was the size of a grizzly bear—relics from the dawn of the world of the American wilderness, before the first humans arrived."

Lee Sandlin, *The Wicked River*

Noyes Camp may derive some of its disquieting atmosphere due to the presence of the first growth boreal forest called *taiga* by the Russians and found in the northern climes of the globe. The southern shore of Lake Superior, including the Brule area, represents the southern reach of the American boreal biome. The thick woods, with its tall trees and closed canopies, allow little light to permeate the interior even on the sunniest of days, giving the forest a pervasive gloom.

The trees are mostly coniferous, dropping needles and pine cones while the leaves of the hardwoods and the ferns, mosses and lichens combine to create a bog-like, spongy, rotting floor most of the spring and summer. At dusk, one's imagination takes over as tree stumps resemble wild animals and tree trunks take the shape of an Ojibwe warrior. The plaintive call of the great horned owl and the mournful whip-poor-will add to one's uneasiness.

The large logs used to construct Noyes Camp add to the primordial effect as the organic style of the house blends with the statuesque pines. My daughters, as well as others, do not like to sleep alone in the bedrooms, thinking there is strength in numbers. Very few family members have occupied Noyes Camp by themselves. I have done so a handful of times. As mentioned, I do not believe many of the stories associated with the house, but I still have a healthy respect for the woods and lodge.

The variety of animal heads, skins and mounted trout and birds lend a creepy feel to the interior. As a child I avoided the great horned owl perched on the dining room mantle at all costs, even in the daylight hours as its large, yellow eyes followed me around the room. At night when you try to fall asleep, the forest comes alive with noise from birds to things that go crash in the night, small splashes by fish and larger ones from deer and bear.

One windless night, alone in Noyes Camp, I was sitting at the card table facing the porch and playing a game of Solitaire. Suddenly the nearest porch door to the outside swung open and slammed shut. I flipped the nearest porch light on and went to investigate. Turning to my left, I looked down the long side of the porch. The light dissipated down the corridor until all I could see were murky shapes of furniture at the end. While I really couldn't detect anything out of order, a shiver coursed through my body and goose bumps rose on my forearms. I briskly walked back into the house and locked the doors.

Our gang of Boys of Brule has not experienced any paranormal activities at Noyes Camp, and while previous men's groups would probably condone our May activities, I am surprised the spirit of Great-grandmother Agnes has not manifested itself in a disapproving manner.

What a sad thing to see EIGHT FIREBRANDS of Hell hanging there.........

Rev. Nicholas Noyes, presiding minister over Salem Witch Trials

[17]

PRE-PRANDIAL DRINKING AND THE AFTERMATH

"Our fathers came into this wilderness to enjoy the gospel and its ordinances in its purity, and the conversion of the heathen, but instead of converting them, amongst other things we have taught them to be drunkards which we may have cause to fear God has permitted them to be such a scourge at the present. Plain dealing is the best I pray pardon my bluntness.
Your servant,

JOSEPH NOYES" selectman, Sudbury, Massachusetts.
Letter to the Justice of the Peace, Middlesex County, February 29, 1692

MY NOYES ANCESTOR JOSEPH went on record identifying a serious ramification of the Puritans' introduction of alcohol to the New England Native Americans. His concern was echoed at the same time by Catholic missionaries in the Great Lakes region who identified the issue in the late 1600s. Their alarm fell on deaf ears in Montreal as alcohol was an important factor in expediting trading in the interior and was not to be disturbed. The Vatican had advocated efforts to "invade, capture, vanquish" natives around the world in order to break them down and convert them to Catholicism in order to expand the Christian Empire.

When the fur traders' chicanery, bullying and brutality failed to weaken the Indians' resolve, alcohol often achieved the desired results. The indigenous could only use so many kettles and blankets, and liquor was a consumable commodity they could not yet distill themselves.

"*…for Native people, alcohol meant more than intoxication. Like tobacco, it had* *a mesmerizing influence that assumed a spiritual significance. It became centrally important to kinship and mourning rituals. Intoxication seemed to help people make contact with their departed friends and family members. By the late-eighteenth century, the addictive qualities of alcohol, along with its ceremonial importance, had made it the most valuable commodity in the trade. In fact traders, considered it impossible to carry on business without it."*

Mary Lethert Wingerd, *North Country*

★ ★ ★ ★ ★

Fort St. Louis, an outpost of the North West Company, was located at modern-day Superior, Wisconsin, and the traders would depart with canoes stuffed with provisions, trading goods and kegs of High Wine, a potable consisting of watered-down rum. They hugged the south shore of the Freshwater Sea before paddling up the Brule River en route to the posts along the Yellow and Snake Rivers. The Ojibwe would spit a stream of High Wine into a fire and the resulting flare up indicated the potency of the alcohol. The term "fire water" was derived from this practice.

The oral tradition of the Ojibwe tells of their first encounter with alcohol on Madeline Island when Ma-ae-wa-pega brought some back to La Pointe after trading with the "white spirits" to the east. Ojibwe historian William Warren called it *"the most dreadful scourge and curse of their race."* When it was first introduced to the natives at Chequamegon Bay, the braves were reticent to taste the liquid they thought might be poison and tested it on an old woman whom they deemed expendable. Warren wrote, *"The old woman drank it, appeared perfectly happy and in ecstasies, got over the effects of it, and begged for more. On which the men took courage, and drank up the remainder themselves. From that time, fire-water became the mammon of the Ojibways, and a journey of hundreds of miles to procure a taste of it, was considered but as boys play."*

Many Europeans saw the evils of what really was chemical warfare, driven by the fur trade's attempts to curry favor with the natives, create dependency and control the area's riches and waterways. Alcohol poured into Grand Portage at the rate of 20,000 gallons a year in the early 1800s. It should be noted that while the indigenous were vulnerable to the effects of alcohol, the white traders were often in a state of intoxication. The traders would go to any extent, no matter how immoral or illegal, to gain an economic advantage. Demon Rum had become an essential part of the trading process and efforts to curtail it were fruitless. It was just another form of European imperialism.

Alcohol was also key in enticing men to join the ranks of voyageurs and traders. They believed it to be part of their compensation and would not sign on for expeditions without the guarantee of an ample supply. It was considered to be a reward for their strenuous and hazardous life in the wilderness.

★ ★ ★ ★ ★

Men navigating logging rafts on the Mississippi were hard-core drinkers when they had shore leave and, when the saloons closed, they staggered into the streets to continue their besotted brawls. George Myron Meerick, in his *Old Times on the Upper Mississippi,* recalls a typical evening in his hometown of Prescott, Wisconsin, where the St. Croix and Mississippi rivers meet. He remembered the local constable watching the proceedings from a safe vantage point, gun in his hand, *"with the enlightened eye of an expert and the enjoyment of a connoisseur."*

Logging was hard work with barely enough time in the day to eat and sleep. When they received their poke (pay) at the end of the spring log-drive, many went home to their families, but others were hell-bent on blowing off steam and made a beeline to the bars. In his book, *Out of the Northwoods,* Michael Edmonds describes the scene: *"In Superior, hundreds would link arms at one end of the main street and charge through the town, mowing down everyone in their path until they had cleared the streets. Fistfights were to loggers what gunfights were to cowboys, competitive combat was a rite of passage, and drunken brawls were commonplace."*

Legendary logger Red Bob Cochran entered a Superior watering hole, plowing his way through the patrons. Another thug took exception and asked, *"What do you think you are doing?"* The reply came quickly, *"I want to get drunk and don't want you in my way."* Inevitably a fight broke out and Red Bob pummeled his opponent, a professional pugilist.

When sportsmen began visiting the Brule River valley, they let their hair down. In May they spent their days hunting and fishing and the night celebrating. The members of Winneboujou were no exception. They reveled in their brief respite from the stress of city life, and any sloppy behavior caused by bibulousness was humored and excused. St. Paul Club founder C.D. O'Brien detailed one such incident in *Brule Chronicles*: *"There were little explorations made to Lake Florence and the Little Brule. But the Counselor being charged with the Commissary Department, wandered from the others one day and gave them much trouble and tribulations ere they found him, seated on an old beaver dam clasping his spiritual advisor and gravely pronouncing a cow track to evidence the pathway of the lordly moose; argued the question in good set terms, but when, alas, he insisted he saw the horns, the men of the woods who knew that the horns did not grow in May, were forced to the conclusion that those he saw were what he had surreptitiously extracted from the missing flask, and they did not wonder that they seemed large to him, for when the party reached him, the flask was empty of horns as well as everything else!"*

Drinking was part of the daily schedule at Winneboujou, as it was in other camps, and foibles were recounted amusingly as C.B. O'Brien continues, *"You know, boys (the men of this camp are always 'boys' to each other), how opposed I am to drinking.' 'You mean to letting anyone else have a drink,' said the general manager... Well we sat there and talked, and, while we were there talking, he incidentally-like drew his flask out and offered me a drink. It was a large flask and the liquor was good, and he said it was the last he had, for he had filled it twice that day... Well being a stranger, you know, I couldn't come right out with what I wanted to say and warn him... The thought came to me all at once, and I acted upon it immediately—I would drink up all his whiskey, then he would be safe, and my duty done. So I kept sitting there, and, in about an hour, I finished the flask, and then I said goodbye and left him... Oh I love to do good by stealth."*

In the early days of the Gitche Gumee Camping Club the drink of choice was the Brule Harp, made with rum, hot water, a squeeze of lemon and a light shaving of nutmeg. It was served after a long day of fishing or hunting as a reward for the tired and chilled campers. Rev. Titsworth initiated the ritual. Dr. Arthur T. Holbrook recalls: *"I can see him now carefully mixing two harps, with Father bantering him about his rule, then placing the two glasses on a shelf, taking Father by the hand, and the two of them with long, tiptoe strides making their way to the river's edge, then dipping first one foot in the water, then the other, and scampering back to the lodge to get their harps!"*

In the mid 1880s the founding members of the GGCC joined the nascent Milwaukee Club, housed in a beautiful American Queen Anne style building constructed of red sandstone, red terra cotta and red brick. Noyes, Holbrook, Markham and Titsworth now had a place in the city to practice their Brule River comradery. The club, still in existence, has zealously maintained the original atmosphere without letting it become shabby. Dr. Arthur T. Holbrook penned a couplet in 1941 describing the philosophy: *"We'll patch her up so she will do, But we'll not change the old one for a new."*

The atmosphere remains more formal than the Brule Harp ceremony. No bare feet and toe dipping. The club has resisted suggestions to have a bar with stools and members never see the drinks being prepared as the bar and bartenders are tucked out of sight with waiters delivering the libations. An August 3, 1941 Milwaukee Journal article explained: *"They have always opposed any suggestion to have a bar in the place. A gentleman sits down to drink."*

Early members of the gentleman's club included Brew City beer making pioneers such as the Pabst family and the Uihlein's, descendants of Joseph Schlitz. The German brewing magnates broke into the previously Yankee dominated social hierarchy of Milwaukee.

"Down Vizes way zom years ago,
When smuggal'n war nothen new,
An people wurden nar bit shy
Of who they did their sperrits buy...."

Edward Slow, *Wiltshire Rhymes and Tales in Wiltshire Dialect*

The Noyes family immigrated to America in 1634 from Wiltshire County in the "West Country" of England which is still considered country bumpkin territory by many. Their home town of Cholderton lies on the Salisbury Plain in the shadow of ancient Stonehenge. Wiltshire residents were known, somewhat derogatorily, as "Moonrakers," a colloquialism taken from a tale which supposedly took place in the 1770s.

Wiltshire smugglers hid casks of French brandy in a pond to avoid detection from the tax collectors. One moonlit night they began to retrieve their contraband by using large rakes to bring the barrels to the shore. They were interrupted by suspicious excise men who inquired about their activities. The locals in their best dim-witted yokel imitations, pointed to the moon's reflection on the water and explained in an exaggerated broad Wiltshire accent that they were *"reaken var a sheese."* The revenue men were taken in by this ruse and went on their way shaking their heads at the Wiltshire "simpletons."

Author Louise Erdich spoke of alcohol in relation to the damage done to the Ojibwe, but it echoes throughout almost every ethnicity and resonates within the history of the Noyes family.

"For the disease is without pity... Alcohol is cunning, and it is phenomenally deceptive... There are no Anishinaabeg, including mixed bloods like me, whose lives have not been affected by the perplexing pains of addiction. The degraded longing and despair of alcoholism changes even the most intelligent among us."

Drinking in the Noyes family escalated in my mother's generation and became so pervasive and ingrained in everyday activities that my elders included it in their most central memories of life at Brule. Uncle Ralph remembered his Uncle Hack frequently inviting him to accompany him on his daily drive to Iron River in his station wagon: *"So I got in and I can hardly believe it to this day, but he never got out of second gear... He never got over 15-20 miles per hour and therefore never got out of second gear driving all the way over to Iron River and he had to stop at a pub or two on the way or coming back."*

Hack was the victim of a prank perpetuated by his older sister, Katherine, who eschewed strong drink but would serve it at her home to guests. Haskell was visiting in Chicago with his family, and was on the lookout for a beverage. He was easy-picking. My mother's cousin Nancy was there and relates the story: *"While we all watched, alternating our stares between Grams and Uncle Hack, he slipped out of the living room and edged through the big double doors to the dining room. As he stood in front of the sideboard eagerly eyeing the two cut glass decanters there, his normally sedate sister unexpectedly broke into barely controlled laughter.*

'Just watch,' she advised as we sat, dizzy from holding our breaths. Her hands remained quietly in her lap, but her brown eyes twinkled...and she smiled broadly... Uncle Hack cast a quick glance over his shoulder to see if he was observed. Then he took the glass stopper from one of the sherry bottles and grasping it by the neck, took a large hasty slug of the contents. Gram could barely contain herself at this point and neither could Haskell. He spat his mouthful out in a spray of amber and clutched frantically at his throat.

'Vinegar,' Gram cheerfully explained. This was followed by rueful laughter. I was the only one who hadn't yet learned that alcohol was the nemesis of many in the family. Gram's antidote was typical of her, I think. No lecture, no remonstrations. Just effective counteraction."

Neville Connolly, a very British surgeon who married into the Flather branch of the family, explained his policy regarding morning drinking at Brule: '[Brother-in-law] *Jim and I had a rule, if you wanted a drink before lunch you had to do something useful around camp during the morning. We always wanted the drink so we did lots of odd jobs including mending furniture, etc. Ben* [another brother-in-law]*, always retired to his room to write articles that he had to send off and never came down before lunch to join us for a drink. At first we gave him great credit for the abstinence but then we noticed that he took his bottle of martinis with him."*

Some of the Ojibwe guides also drank when the opportunity arose. My mother's cousin Dal Frost recalled, *"My Grandmother, Emily Noyes Dalrymple, had several of her friends at Brule and they decided to go on a picnic upriver. The young guide appeared and unnoticed by them had had several early drinks. The ladies were in the canoe dressed in summer dress. He stepped in and over went the canoe dumping them*

in the river. The young guide was a son of the cook in the kitchen at the time. Mrs. Pearson, a friend of grandmother's, went up to the kitchen where the cook was in tears. She put her arm around her and said, 'I have 5 sons and they come home having had too much to drink and I feel the same way!'"

Brule River guide Chuck Stewart was a formidable sight: big, tall, strong, dark, gruff and fierce looking. He felt sobriety was over rated. One day he was scheduled to guide for Seth Marshall, a superb fisherman and member of the Winneboujou Club. One day at Stone's Bridge Stewart asked Seth, *"Did you bring the bottle?"* Marshall replied, *"Chuck, we don't need the bottle."* The guide asked once again and when he didn't receive the answer he wanted, Chuck angrily pushed the canoe from the landing and disappeared into the woods.

Dal and my Grandfather Harrison, both wonderful when sober, frequently drank at a downtown Minneapolis bar. They were what my Uncle Joe Clifford referred to as *"habitués of roisterer's lairs like Harry's Bar."* Dal eventually took the cure and was very active in Alcoholics Anonymous, sponsoring many. Grandpa slowed down in his 60s under my Mother's eagle eye. She allowed him one drink at Sunday dinner. Once we went out of town and our friends, the Pearsons, invited him to dinner. Mom neglected to inform them of the one drink rule and they had a hard time getting the 6' 4' noodle with a walking cane into the car for his return home.

Uncle Joe, married to my mother's sister Patty, was a great guy and one of my favorites. He was brilliant, Yale educated with a great sense of humor. He was a true Renaissance man, a wonderful pianist and singer, an accomplished attorney and business executive and extremely well read in many subjects, including literature and history. He paid special attention to me, talked sports, and to my adolescent delight, swore a blue streak like a sailor, which he was in World War II, serving as his ship's legal officer. He had a talent for eloquent profanity and total command of the English language as evidenced by his letters home from the South Pacific. He referred to his cocktail hour tippling as his *"pre-prandial restorative."*

In a missive to his wife, he was impressed by her ability to acquire liquor in Minneapolis during war-time shortages: *"…where did you get that bottle of brandy? Your letters, as a matter of fact, fairly reek of stale martinis and such. Very stimulating for my morale. I am so purified and de-alcoholized that I have ceased anaesthetizing unwary mosquitoes. I think I told you about the aborted beer party the other day. It was an experience that still has me quivering with anticipation. Well, I hear Saki is a good drink once you get used to it. Anyhow I have elaborate plans for my first open house at the Imperial Hotel, Tokyo."*

★ ★ ★ ★ ★

My Grandparents, Edward Harrison and Margaret Noyes Harrison were alcoholics to the point that they were unable to care for my mother adequately and shuttled her off to various boarding schools. It was tragic as they were both well-educated and accomplished before they succumbed to the debilitating effect of booze. Sometimes their parties would begin in Minneapolis, proceed to the train station and head to Milwaukee. Friends and relatives hopped aboard and the festivities finally ended in Chicago.

Grandmother Margaret was a bon vivant before liquor robbed her of her looks and health. She loved fashion and travel. She reveled in the early days of the Roaring 20s and Prohibition had little effect on her lifestyle. Travel and the social world were top priorities for the beautiful woman. She loved scandalizing her more proper sisters by hanging her undergarments from the open windows at Noyes Camp.

Protracted winter vacations were spent at the beachfront Hotel del Coronado, which today is one of the few remaining vestiges of Victorian-style wooden resorts. It is on Coronado Island in San Diego, just a stone's throw from Tijuana, Mexico, known then as "Satan's Playground." The border city was the template for the future Las Vegas. When the United States, according to the *San Diego Reader's* Joe Deegan, clamped down on *"prostitution, erotic dancing, boxing, horse racing, gambling at cards, roulette and dice,"* it drove throngs of tourists south of the border. Liquor was next on the list of vices to be banned, increasing the appeal of Tijuana.

Celebrities flocked to Tijuana including Gloria Swanson, Bing Crosby, Clark Gable, Charlie Chaplin, the Marx Brothers, Louis B. Mayer and Jean Harlow who were seen at casinos such as the Agua Caliente and hotels like the Caesar. Boxers Jack Johnson and Jack Dempsey were there as well as gangsters like Bugsy Siegel. Margaret's friend and fellow partier in Tijuana was Wallis Simpson, later to become the Duchess of Windsor and the woman behind England's constitutional crisis and the abdication of her husband, Edward VIII.

Simpson and Grandmother partied south of the border at night. Margaret was a widower and Wallis was married, at the time, to the commander of the U.S. Naval Station in San Diego. After recovering from the previous night's Tijuana outing they would walk the beach dressed to the nines in white before heading south again, most likely to first catch the horse races before getting into party mode.

"It was by far the largest house of prostitution in the world, and probably the most successful… The Molino Rojo had no madam. The girls ran the place themselves, and they did so with the cunning of robber barons… Surely it was more than a happy coincidence that the price of admission—'fifty cents straight up,' remembers one former bug boy—was precisely equal to the pay for a galloping horse…there were so many girls to choose from, every conceivable nationality, that a kid would have to gallop three hundred horses to afford them all. 'You went through there,' remembers one client, 'like you were going through a grocery store.'"

LAURA HILLENBRAND, *Seabiscuit: An American Legend*

Grammie's dry wit was never sharper than in a postcard photo she sent from Tijuana. She innocuously posed with her rather stern and humorless Bagley mother-in-law in front of a cinder block, shag carpeted building, the Molino Rojo, also known as the Red Mill, a brothel and club occupying half a city block in the Zona Norte. It was Mexico's version of the Moulin Rouge, borrowing not only the name, but also the style of the Paris cabaret and its courtesans. A tongue in cheek one sentence message on the back of Margaret's postcard read, *"Mother B. and I off for our favorite pastime."*

Margaret was not done quipping, giving her maternal grandmother Hannah Cole Haskell a snarky, posthumous nickname, "Hadacol Haskell." Hadacol was a patent medicine of dubious efficacy, promoted as a vitamin supplement. The real attraction, however, was its 12% alcohol content. The "medicine" was particularly popular in the south and spawned many R & B and Cajun songs like "Little Willie" Littlefield's *"Drinking Hadacol."* The unfortunate similarity between the sound of Hannah's name and the cure-all elixir became an inside joke for my grandmother and her siblings.

It seems the Noyes family had a Bacchus curse nipping at its heels. The members of my mother's generation, whether they were blood relatives or spouses, seemed predisposed to excessive liquor consumption. Lives became consumed by drink or drugs or both. One common way of coping with alcohol abuse is to romanticize stories about the escapades of drunks, polishing the ragged, tragic edges until they are sanded smooth. When I was younger I bought into this mythology, making humor from the foibles of my inebriated relatives. Sometimes, though, the anecdotes ARE funny.

One night at Brule the adults were sufficiently pickled by twilight and joined us in a game of tag. The object was to circumnavigate the house before being caught. An aunt gleefully entered the fray and immediately tripped over a large tree root. Almost in slow motion, ice cubes arched into a clump of trees followed by a stream of liquid and her lowball glass. She landed face down on the ground, bounced back off her ample bosom, took a quick inventory and rejoined the action.

Deep in the Wisconsin woods during a break in our canoe trips, Dad would be prepared for a picnic. We shot the Twin Rapids and stopped at Noyes Landing where the fast water spills into Big Lake. We built a fire in the little cook shack and grilled hamburgers and hot dogs and heated a pot of beans. We had potato salad, chips, cole slaw and array of condiments. We ate at the picnic table under the shelter, often in the rain.

The adults dipped their white, blue-rimmed porcelain enamel coffee mugs in the river for a splash of clean spring water and topped the cup off with bourbon. When Aunt Patty visited from Arizona she stashed a martini shaker in her canoe. Dad had a small cooler with little racks filled with airline-size bottles of liqueurs. He had an impressive assortment of after-dinner drinks including Kahlua, Grand Marnier, Schnapps, Drambuie, Curacao, Brandy, Crème de Menthe (white and green), Cointreau and many more.

As children we took these habits in stride as it was all we knew. Growing more aware, we learned to deal with the inebriated antics of our relatives who were more stoic, with a vestige of the Victorian age, when sober. Thankfully we weren't often exposed to mean drunks, but frequently we were forced to nod patiently when an aunt or uncle waxed philosophically. As we matured we tried to escape when the revelers became messy and the conviviality became something sad. It wasn't funny anymore, just annoying.

The Boys of Brule are not choir boys by any stretch of the imagination. We have had our moments but rarely to the point of sloppiness. One night Lumber and Mickey got into some tequila and had to be separated from the CD player after repeatedly jamming a Joe Cocker disc into the cassette player opening of the device.

One late Saturday afternoon a friend who couldn't make it to the Brule that year called the Kro-Bar and had a round of shots delivered to our table as we watched the Kentucky Derby. These days we mostly drink beer and wine with dinner. Hangovers are avoided in order to greet the next morning without the handicap of acute membrane outrage.

In May 2017, Bill Lorntson introduced a new mid-morning feature: a Bloody Mary Bar, set up on a table on the porch. He went all-out, starting with a mid-priced vodka, Tito's handcrafted, and augmented with the spicy Absolut Peppar, a horseradish-infused brand that is very hot. An additional option, a pepper liqueur, was the least popular. An array of mixes was offered: the 5 Pepper (very hot!), Spooky Dill Pickle and the most enjoyed, Zing Zang. Twelve-inch wood spears were provided for the garnishes. I do not drink hard liquor, but I availed myself of the beef sticks, cheese cubes, shrimp and green olives. I left the celery for others to enjoy. Based on the data Lorny collected from his first try, he promises upgrades and tweaks in the future.

Peer pressure was never a big issue for me. In college I developed a taste for beer but luckily I have an internal governor that tells me when I have had enough. It is a mystery to me why cigarettes have been vilified and driven from acceptance in the U.S. when alcohol gets a free pass. While I understand Prohibition was a failure, turning ordinary citizens into law breakers and gangsters into millionaires, I can make a persuasive argument that aqua vitae have caused more economic, physical and emotional damage in this country than has tobacco. Not even close.

Late night at Winneboujou *Photo by Truman Ingersoll*

[18]

MUSIC IN THE WOODS

"He vass a Scandinavian hot shot,
A hot shot from Da-Loot,
He vass a triller-diller and a lady killer
And he yust didn't give a hoot."

STAN BORESON, *"Scandinavian Hot Shot"*

★ ★ ★ ★ ★

THERE ARE MANY SCANDINAVIANS in the Upper Midwest, and the Brule River region was largely settled by Finns after the Yankees snatched the land from the Ojibwe, but it took an Irish-German from St. Paul, Chip Michel, to introduce what has become the unofficial theme song of the Boys of Brule. It has been sung loudly at northern Wisconsin bars, Target Headquarters in downtown Minneapolis and even during a chance encounter in the Fort Myers, Florida, airport.

Generations before the French ventured into the Great Lakes area, Ojibwe held ceremonies emanating from their lodges, singing vision and dream-inspired songs accompanied by a drum representing a heartbeat. The songs have great spiritual meaning as the men vocalized with women, joining with a call-and-response style or adding harmony. It was believed that every time a song was performed it increased in strength. Titles include "Jingle Dress Song," "Friendship Song," "Picking Up the Eagle Feather Song," and the "Grass Dance Song."

The drum is the centerpiece of spiritual ceremonies for the Ojibwe with different sizes, colors and designs depending on the situation. Large drums were used to pound a bellicose beat to prepare for war and medium ones kept the beat for gambling games. Small hand-drums are still in use for healing purposes. Other percussion instruments include birch clapping sticks, rasps and rattles made from the dewclaws of moose and deer, which are placed on the end of a stick or wrapped around a dancer's ankles.

Drums are present in almost all Ojibwe ceremonies from birth to love to marriage to death in addition to healing, blessing and praying. Native chanting was misunderstood by the early Europeans who thought it to be meaningless utterances, but in reality they are syllables called "vocables" to set the rhythm and add layers of sound The chanting is complex rather than random, and its repetition is mesmerizing.

Ojibwe elder Art Solomon spoke to the primal sense of the drum: *I was never without the sound of the drum, without the sound of music, since before my birth. I began to hear the sound of the drum, even as I was in my mother's womb.*

Ojibwe *midew* are members of a shamanistic society devoted in easing hunger and healing disease. Their sacred drum is made with cedar or birch bark with animal hide stretched over the top. Water is added to the drum to increase resonance. The *midegwakikoon,* sometimes known as "grandfather," is a type of membranophone that vibrates when hit with a stick or hand. The color of the drum represents a clan or a shade that comes to the drummer in a dream.

By the 18th century French voyageurs were singing on the Brule River to coordinate their paddling, ease their senses of isolation and boredom. They sang to express their feelings whether joy or sorrow, and to celebrate pleasant memories while enduring hardships in the wilderness. Favorites included "Alouette," "A la Claire Fontaine" and "En Roulant Ma Boule." Rarely were lyrics written down. Today, Canadian schoolchildren are taught the tunes.

The mysterious correspondent, "Morgan," from the delegation searching the south shore of Lake Superior for silver, copper and other minerals reported from the Brule River expressing his European assessment of songs as the group paddled along the Brule-St. Croix corridor: *Jean Baptiste, our pilot, had an excellent voice, full, loud, and strong. He generally led off in singing; the others falling in at the choruses. All their songs were in French, sometimes sentimental or pathetic, sometimes comic, and occasionally extempore, made, as sung, from the preceding day, or suggested by the passing scenes.*

The Chippewa Indians are poor singers; yet they have songs (such as they are) among them; one of which is a monotonous air repeated at their moccasin game.

Daily Union, Washington D.C., July 28, 1845

★ ★ ★ ★ ★

"My name is Yon Yonson,
I come from Wisconsin,
I work in a lumber mill there.
The people I meet
As I walk down the street,
They stop and they say
What's your name?
My name is Yon Jonson,
I come from Wisconsin..." repeated ad infinitum Northwoods song, origin unknown.

★ ★ ★ ★ ★

Douglas County lumbermen had limited spare time to celebrate and entertain themselves while in camp. They enjoyed consuming prodigious amounts of food prepared by "cookees." When possible, they enjoyed card playing, telling stories and competitions like log rolling, climbing stripped trees and chopping. They also sang songs and danced with each other. Tunes included "Leather Britches," Once More A Lumberin' Go," "A Shanty Man's Life" and "Lumberman's Alphabet." Loggers played many instruments ranging from guitars, mandolins, concertinas, fiddles, dulcimers to animal bones.

Finnish lumbermen penned a lament describing the hard life of a logger, related by *The Forest History Society*:

"A wretched home, this cheerless camp;
And 'finer people' sneer, make cracks:
'You ruffians, bums, bearded lumberjacks!'
Our wages are the rags we wear,
Our scraps of food no one digests.
Our beds are bunks
And fleas our only guests."

★ ★ ★ ★ ★

In the early days of the Gitche Gumee Camping Club there were no cocktail and dinner parties or night-time bridge games like the ones that became popular when the current lodges were built. Kerosene lamps or electricity were not available to lengthen the day and provide light for reading, board games, chess and checkers or jigsaw puzzles. Flickering candles and lanterns were the usual means of illumination. Neighbor Dr. Arthur T. Holbrook remembered the post dinner campfire as the focus for the evening's activities as everyone gathered.

The tradition continued over the years around: *"the old campfire night after night... It is a pleasant echo of old days as now and then we gather at our lodge or at the Noyes', and again sit around the campfire and watch the great flames, while our gaze follows the sparks as they fly upwards. We bring the out the old guitar and sing many a song by heart, beginning always with 'We Meet Again Tonight Boys' and winding up with 'Good Night Ladies.'"*

★ ★ ★ ★ ★

Great-grandfather George played the cat-gut string guitar and his favorite tune was "You'll Take the High Road." He was said to have had a resonant speaking voice and a dramatic style of delivery. He often read to the campers on the porch or outside and in later years beside the lamp in the Council Room.

Old timers remembered a legendary party held during the summer of 1891. Canoes sporting jacklights, portable oil-filled lights, came from upstream and down to congregate at the south end of Big Lake. The Noyes family had built a picnic grounds as a stopping place during fishing and social outings. The trees were draped with Chinese lanterns and campfires blazed, lighting the cleared ground where blankets were spread for sitting. Cedar Island provided the punch to drink. Music was an integral part of the festivities and Dr. Arthur T. recalled, *"guitars, mandolins and banjos were in many canoes, and songs constantly floated from the boats on the soft evening air."*

Diminutive Brule River guide Frank George possessed excellent canoeing skills and a strong baritone voice. The "Singing Guide" dreamed of performing light opera on stage and took requests from his passengers. He knew the acoustics of the stream well and showcased his pipes at night on Big Lake, using the hills of the ancient glacial river bed to form his personal amphitheater while he sang "Golden Threads Among the Silver."

Most of the songs sung on the Brule in those days would be classified as folk songs today. The tradition continues with the Boys of Brule as guitars, the Noyes Camp piano and a harmonica mingle with voices in early May. My lifelong friend Rob Pearson and I played guitars and sang fireside at Brule for 55 years. We caught the bug during the Great Folk Scare of the 1960s when I learned to play on a cheap starter guitar which I, in turn, sold to Bobbo for $25. The deal included unlimited free lessons, and soon student surpassed master. Our first public performance was at a talent show in 7th grade. We sang "Rock Island Line" acapella as we weren't confident enough to pull out the guitars yet.

We spent hours honing our craft on the Noyes Camp porch, playing the same song over and over until the grownups chased us to the back of the house. Critics! We learned the tunes of our idols: the Kingston Trio, the Brothers Four, the Smothers Brothers and Bob Dylan, at first via Peter, Paul and Mary and the Byrds. Music lifted us from our homes and insular neighborhoods to the West Coast of "California Girls" and across the nation to Philadelphia's "American Bandstand." When the Beatles and their allies invaded we were transported across the Atlantic to magical places like "Penny Lane" and "Strawberry Fields."

Soon Beatles songs rang through the north woods. We have played for money which I guess gives us the right to call ourselves "professionals." We were still competent musicians into our 60s, although our tenuous grip of four verses of lyrics led to truncated versions of songs. Even in the idyllic setting of Noyes Camp in the woods, there are detractors. One day I was alone in the Council Room, minding my own business, singing and playing what I considered to be a pretty good version of Joe Ely's "Jericho (Your Walls Must Come Tumbling Down)." My older brother Dave walked through the room and said, over his shoulder, "That's the worst f'ing song I've ever heard."

For Rob and me, music was more than just beauty, expression and therapy. We didn't gravitate to guitars to become rich and famous. We played as vehicles to be noticed, cool and attract girls. The first concert of popular music we attended was the Brothers Four. We hung on every chord and committed every corny joke to memory, even arcane references to Americana like the John Birch Society, which we may not have understood but somehow gleaned they were very witty.

In a brush-with-fame moment in the 1990s, Rob, Marty and I had the opportunity to meet the iconic Bob Dylan at an engagement party. Our friend Bill Wilson, an occasional Boys of Brule collaborator, was marrying the Bard's cousin, Nancy, and Dylan flew in from Paris to attend. He seemed fried to a crisp and mumbled greetings and offered a flaccid handshake. At one point I spent an awkward moment with the legend alone in the kitchen. Unable to come up with anything remotely wise or witty, I blurted out a quick *"I've always enjoyed your work."* He responded with *"thanks,"* and I fled.

When my grandparents' generation wanted some peace and quiet they would send their children on various errands to empty the camp of youngsters and the accompanying racket. One ploy was an upriver errand to fill ceramic jugs with spring water where it emptied into the river. It was simply called "The Spring" and the cool, gin-clear, slightly mineralized liquid was considered ambrosia by the summer people on the Brule. My mother's older cousins, Mimi Noyes and Georgianna Flather took an entire afternoon and loaded a crank style Gramophone and some 78 RPM records into the middle of a sturdy Lucius canoe. The girls enjoyed the sounds of the Big Band era in an idyllic setting.

Decades later, Mike Melander and I tried to replicate the event on a hot summer day with an electric turntable and 33-1/3 albums owned by Mickey's brother, Big "T." We plugged the cord into an outlet in the boathouse but made a fatal error by leaving the turntable outside. The strategy was going swimmingly until the melodious strains of the Moody Blues were suddenly garbled, as if they were emanating from the river bottom. The sun had made quick work of the vinyl and the disc was so warped it couldn't even be used as a Frisbee.

When the Boys of Brule outings solidified and became annual, Rob and I played for the group who sang along to our old favorites like "Good Night Irene," "Drill Ye Tarriers," "Rock Island Line" and "Greenback Dollar" as well as more recent tunes. One year we retreated to the dining room with printed lyric and chord sheets as the ceiling was lower and held the sound better than the Council Room. Marty joined us on the mouth organ and we had a raucous, full-fledged Hootenanny.

Our reputation grew, and one night we were invited to join the next door Holbrooks, Will and Hester, and some of her friends, during the cocktail hour. We brought our guitars, played music and the wine and beer flowed. We stayed for dinner, then whipped the neighbors in a game of Trivial Pursuit. The final blow came when Bud knew the meaning of the term "Cooper": a barrel maker. He worked at Colonial Williamsburg in his youth and knew his way around a barrel stave. I walked to Noyes Camp to make a phone call and when I returned, all hell had broken loose. Rob, the only single BOB at the time, was half-naked and getting a massage from one of Hester's friends. The next day she waved to us sheepishly as she went for a run.

We also have two excellent pianists among the Boys of Brule with widely disparate styles on the camp Steinway. Wild Bill Lorntson can play almost any song by ear and sometimes serenades us with the Canadian Anthem, "Oh Canada," to announce breakfast. Marty Schuster plays an appealing improvisational blend of blues and jazz. Mike Melander adds a dose of bygone era easy listening like Tony Bennett's "I Wanna Be Around" if sufficiently prodded. Glencoe has a comprehensive grasp of Classic Rock from the giants to the one-trick ponies.

Tom Melander has a booming bass voice and enjoys singing in the church choir while lamenting there are few solos for the lowest register. If only Tennessee Ernie Ford's "16 Tons" were in the hymnal. Our old school Noyes Camp compact disc boom box is now augmented by wireless blue tooth devices playing a mix of old favorites such as Eric Clapton, Tom Petty, the Eagles, the Allman Brothers, John Fogerty and Delbert McClinton in addition to 1960s oldies and newer music.

Those on dish duty start the process by listening to the seminal British blues band Savoy Brown's "Tell Mama" and "Wang Dang Doodle (All Night Long)." When it is my turn to wash I am accused of procrastination as I move the boom box to the kitchen. I counter with the argument that I am providing a valuable service. The Boys of Brule have our own series of CDs, started by the late great Charlie Hullsiek and me. The quality of the track mix and the artwork have improved dramatically over the years and now approach the look of a professional music CD.

The CDs number well over 30 now and all revolve around a theme. Titles include: "It's Not So Much the Money, It's the Cash," "Anatomy," "Los Bruley Boys," "Douglas County Dreaming," "Color Us…The Boys of Brule" and "Time Has Come Today." There are two releases a year, one in May and the other at the annual Christmas outing, most notably "The Boys of Yule."

We may not play hockey anymore, but we can always play and discuss music. A recent Boys of Brule member is Rus Emerick, a Georgia boy with an exhaustive knowledge of Southern rock, which is right in our aural wheelhouse. He was the road manager for Lynyrd Skynryd as well as The Who during their initial "Quadrophenia" tour when Roger Daltrey cut Rus' new Saville Row suit into ribbons with a pair of scissors. Life was dangerous on the road. Touring England early in their career, Lynyrd Skynyrd had a drummer on probation, Bob Burns, who frequently saw Satan when he was drunk and high on a codeine chaser, which was most of the time. The last straw was when he perceived a demonic glint in the road manager's eyes. Kevin Elson, the band's sound engineer at the time, recalls: *"We were trying to get him to the show, but Bob wasn't having any part of it, and then he suddenly went on the offensive. Spotting a likely weapon at a nearby work site, Bob grabbed a pickaxe and chased Rus down the street. No one got hurt, but it was the end of the line for Bob."*

★ ★ ★ ★ ★

We haven't always been in sync with our musical tastes. During sophomore year in college, Marty was enamored with a cacophonous, leftist, anarchic rock band from Detroit, the MC5. Music critic Stephen Thomas Erlewine gave them credit for *"crystallizing the counter culture movement at its most volatile and threatening."*

Jim and I didn't need to analyze; their album "Kick Out the Jams" was loud and atonal. Awful. To stymie Marty's efforts to spin the disc, we placed it inside its dust jacket and hid it under a couch cushion. At the end of the school year it was rediscovered in perfect shape after enduring countless bouncings of rear ends and other indignities.

It was indestructible. Ironically, today "Kick Out the Jams" is one of the most sought after and valuable LPs. Could it be Marty's affection for the recording transcended poor taste? Maybe he was onto something.

Ross Fruen strumming his six string at Noyes Camp *Courtesy of Bill Wilson*

[19]

JAMES ANGELTON: THE BRULE'S FURTIVE FISHERMAN

"James Jesus Angleton, the famously paranoid chief of the CIA counter-intelligence branch, was a passionate fly fisherman. Even as he became increasingly convinced that the Russians had penetrated every level of America's military-industrial complex, he still managed to take the time to steal away for a day or so to a favorite fishing hole where, at his leisure among the shadows (where he felt most comfortable anyway), he would set his line, roll his casts and contemplate the inevitable fall of the free world."

CHARLES DUBOW, "A-FISH-IONADOS & ANGLER-PHILES,"
Forbes, AUGUST 1997

★ ★ ★ ★ ★

JAMES JESUS ANGLETON WAS rarely visible during daylight. The insomniac seldom ventured outside the confines of his Brule River lodge until nightfall. His brother-in-law and sister-in-law, the D'Autrements, lived three houses upriver from Noyes Camp in the summer. Jim's lodge was not far downstream from us. Angleton, the future head of CIA Counterintelligence, married Cecily D'Autrement in 1943 in a church near the Fort Custer, Michigan, military base. Cicely then went to Arizona and Jim headed to Maryland for military training.

By the time Angleton appeared in New Haven for his freshman classes at Yale in 1937, he had experiences that gave him confidence beyond his years. His mother was an exotic Mexican beauty named Carmen Moreno. James had lived a middle-class life in Boise, Idaho, and Dayton, Ohio, and after his upwardly mobile and ambitious father Hugh bought the Italian division of the National Cash Register

Company, the family moved to Milan, Italy. James went to boarding school in England and emerged speaking three languages and feeling self-assured in any social situation. His varied interests included poetry and fly-fishing. He fished for trout in northwestern Connecticut during college but, oddly, his roommate never remembered him bringing back any fish.

Cecily D'Autrement was a Vassar student when she met the Harvard law student in 1941. She was immediately attracted. *"I fell madly in love at first sight. I'd never met anyone like him… Jim was a Chicano and I loved him for it. I never saw anyone as Mexican as he was. He was Latino, an Apache, he was a gut fighter."* The young woman's parents' marriage was a merger of Upper Midwest mining, lumber and financial holdings. Her maternal grandfather was Chester Congdon, a Duluth mining magnate and capitalist. Her father, Hubert D'Autrement, was a banker and politician. Her mother, Helen, was a community activist and philanthropist.

Cecily spent her childhood summers on the Brule and the rest of the year in Tucson where the family had moved for the relief of father Hubert's respiratory issues. Angleton was friends with poets Ezra Pound and e.e. cummings and a mentor from Yale, Norman Pearson, arranged for the newly minted serviceman to attend training for the Office of Strategic Services, the forerunner of the CIA. In addition to the boiler-plate exercises like running obstacle courses and darting through the woods, James learned how to pick locks, as well as other secrets of the night.

The sixty OSS trainees, with names like Richard Helms and William Colby, sailed to Southampton where James rejoined Norman Pearson, who taught the men the rudiments of "X-2," or counter-intelligence. Pearson invited a Brit who would loom large in Angleton's future, Kim Philby, to impart the details of running an X-I station including cracking German codes.

In May 1945, Angleton transferred to Rome. Germany had just surrendered but there were loose ends to be addressed. This was where he made his bones. It was the perfect post. He knew the country and language well and was able to use father Hugh's influence to his advantage. James began collecting allies and assets. He nurtured a relationship with the powerful Vatican through the church's undersecretary of state, Monsignor Giovanni Battista Montini. Jim made connections with the Italian Mafia.

The U.S. was understandably suspicious of Soviet designs on Europe and feared a civil war in Italy between fascist and leftist elements. The fast-rising star of the OSS honed his simple but effective strategy of counter-espionage: gather as much information as possible while thwarting the enemy's ability to do the same. He directed the banishment of German informants. In his battle against fascism and communism, he enlisted the help of the church, French, Brits, Mafioso and his father. Ten million dollars, mostly consisting of confiscated Axis assets, were used to defeat the Politco Communista Italiano.

Communism in Italy was squelched, and James returned to Washington to join the newly minted CIA in 1947 to the delight of Cicely, who was in need of adult conversation as she cared for their children. The trappings of the posting were not glamorous as Jim and his staff were housed in virtual shacks near the Lincoln Memorial.

The Angletons essayed a conventional family life in Arlington, Virginia. In addition to his fly- fishing passion, James built a greenhouse to tend orchids and polished gems in the basement where he made jewelry for his friends and colleagues: tie tacks and cuff links All solitary hobbies. They entertained friends and co-workers with liberal amounts of alcohol. Even though she was well-educated, Cicely often felt intimidated by the Washington intelligentsia that frequented the parties.

She was only truly happy when the family was ensconced in their Brule lodge, where she reunited with childhood friends, her Duluth relatives and watched Jim teach their children to fly fish. There was comfort in the familiarity and memories, the tea and homemade bread spread with apricot preserves she served guests. Cicely enjoyed providing pastries to her visitors but insisted that no dairy products were used in the preparation of the baked goods. When she hired local cooks, however, eggs and butter were slipped into the batter when Cicely wasn't looking. Once when Caroline Marshall was visiting, Cicely sighed, to no one in particular*, "I must stay on. We must come for at least three weeks."* The spirit of the river permeated her DNA. She spent much of her time at Brule with the children and her mother, Helen D'Autrement, who had her own suite in the Angleton lodge. On occasion, Cicely brought her cook, Carrie Jackson, from Virginia, who hated to be left alone on the river. She rattled ice cubes throughout the night to ward off evil spirits. Cecily was reed-thin and was often seen pedaling her bicycle on the roadways and paths of the Brule Valley in a haphazard manner while other vehicles did their best to dodge her.

Husband Jim also loved the Brule. While he spent his nights fishing, he spent his days in the lodge playing poker and in the garage in the woods polishing his stones. People on the river found him to be quiet, but pleasant. James' career was never far from his thoughts, however. Even his pastimes correlated with his work. He stalked brown trout lurking under the branches and trunks of fallen sweepers intruding from the river banks on moonless nights. He preferred not to fish if the moon was brighter than its quarter phase. Jim was fascinated by orchids that used disguise and deception to lure pollen-bearing insects to aid propagation. Even in the forest he was extremely cautious. James never entered a room directly, first visually checking the nooks, crannies and corners before proceeding. He never received nor sent communications to Washington when he was at the Brule. He preferred to be apart from Cecily for her safety and considered hiring a bodyguard. The Brule River was his sanctuary.

A typical night of fishing began with a launch from the eastern side of Big Lake. A 30-45 minute wait ensued as Jim and the guide listened intently. If any lights appeared they took cover in a patch of tall cat tails near the western bank, where there was no access, until the master spy was convinced there were no threats. Angleton kept a handgun in his rucksack, explaining he brought it *"in case of bears."* He was so acclimated to the night that he could tie a fly in the dark, an incredible feat. Jim packed four pieces of bread, some mustard and picked watercress for midnight snack sandwiches.

James was always focused on his environment and tried not to stay in one location for long. His idiosyncrasies were fascinating to 14 year-old Roger Anderson. Roger's father, Gunnard, was the superintendent of the Winneboujou Club and was as close to the CIA man as anyone on the river. Roger, physically mature for his age, frequently guided for Angleton and helped John LaRock build a vessel commissioned by the spy to his exact specifications. It was more of a boat than a canoe; big, wide and stable, and not designed to run rapids. Roger worked on its ribs and gunwales. His compensation was always four cucumbers from Lizzie LaRock's garden. She monitored the construction process, sometimes offering insight as she chewed on orange peels and a wad of tobacco. The pay was better when Roger guided for Jim at night. A crisp $5 bill.

Jim's peculiarities at Brule extended to his automobiles. He had a beautiful Woodie wagon but painted it blue with a paint brush to make it appear shabby and less conspicuous. Anyone who peered inside could see the elegant birch and mahogany panels and leather accents. When he returned to the Angleton Lodge he immediately pulled into the garage. James also drove a beat-up black '53 or '54 Cadillac. He would slowly creep down the Winneboujou driveway to pick up Gunnard. They proceeded to the Little Kro-Bar in town or parked in the Pine

Barrens to drink Old Crow bourbon. When he needed groceries Jim planted a small flag at the start of his driveway as an invitation to come and get his list.

Angleton assumed the position of chief of operations of Staff A, charged with the collection of foreign information, an important distinction when it came to the denouement of his career. The work of vetting agents and reporting his findings was often prosaic, but Jim handled the tasks with his usual perseverance and his methods set the standard for many years thereafter.

Some insight into the brilliant and counterintuitive mind of James Angleton was revealed when he hired Carmel Offie in 1948 to work in the section. Offie was an openly gay man, a Washington oddity in those days, and although Jim loathed him personally, he knew a good agent when he saw one and Carmel had excellent contacts. Jim told an undersecretary of state, Sumner Welles, that Offie should be watched closely as *"he was capable of floating ruinous, scandalous rumors, wrecking careers."* Despite the danger, James thought the risk was worth it as Offie was a *"master intriguer….*[who] *knew everybody. Superb bureaucratic infighter and guide."*

By May 1948, Zionists had driven the Arabs from Palestine with the help of the Soviet sphere communists and reclaimed what they thought was their rightful homeland now called Israel. Many Jews espoused the communist philosophy, but any Western worries were assuaged after the anti-Semitic Josef Stalin waged a cleansing of all Jewish culture in Russia and began arresting the leaders of the Jewish Anti-Fascist Committee, the die was cast. Angleton was close to the Israelis and helped them establish the Mossad, their version of the CIA. Many in Washington felt he was too chummy and let them develop their own nuclear arsenal with enriched uranium conveniently filched from a Pennsylvania facility.

In 1949, Angleton was pleased to be joined in D.C. by his friend Kim Philby of the English SIS, the Secret Intelligence Service. The Brit was to act as the liaison between England's secret service, MI-6, and the CIA. They resumed their friendship, but there was a fly in the ointment: Philby was discovered to be a Soviet spy. James refused to believe it, and it cost him professionally. The upward progression of his career was temporarily stalled.

The 1950s were strange times in Washington. Wisconsin's U.S. Senator and bully Joe McCarthy was finding Communists under every rock and the only thing worse that being thought a Communist was being considered homosexual.

The Angletons wanted nothing to do with the Red Scare or the Lavender Scare and hunkered down in their tight social circle. Cicely said they were boycotting Wisconsin beers in protest of the maniacal senator.

When ex-OSS man Allen Dulles was brought back into the Agency, Angleton felt as if he had been let out of the doghouse. Jim believed the CIA had lost its focus and was concentrating on propaganda efforts rather than the garnering of information and assets. He was hell-bent on proving his point. Dulles gave him free rein and James built a fiefdom of 171 employees. He had an academic approach with counter-intelligence at the fore. He believed the priorities were information gathering, acquiring effective agents and building volumes of research so his people could better understand history and tactics.

James continued to acquire assets like a numismatologist collects coins. He hired Jay Lovestone, a rehabilitated Communist, who was the head of the American Federation of Labor's Free Trade Union Committee. Unions represented power to Angleton, and he funded Lovestone's activities with labor unions around the world. Surprisingly, James even cultivated a relationship with J. Edgar Hoover, no small accomplishment.

Jim needed information on the movements of Soviet spies within the U.S. and the FBI, for a while, was his only option. Hoover was not interested initially, but sent an intermediary, Sam Papich. He was a no-nonsense Montanan and bristled at the pretensions of the Ivy Leaguer. As soon as Angleton discovered the two men shared a common passion, fly-fishing, he invited Sam on a brown trout excursion, and the FBI agent was hooked. The CIA-FBI liaison and information exchange was forged on a West Virginia stream.

James Angleton's career could be roughly divided into two segments. From the mid-40s until the mid-60s he was brilliant, energetic and effective. Eventually cracks began to appear in his psyche. Suspicion is a professional prerequisite in the spy business, but Angleton began to take it to a level of extreme paranoia. His tolerance for ambiguity, a necessity in his trade, faltered. His focus turned to "mole hunting" rather than counter-intelligence.

He could often be found at the bar of La Nicoise in Georgetown drinking excessive amounts of I.W Harper bourbon and chain smoking Virginia Slims. In his gray suit with gray hair, sallow complexion, large glasses and gaunt, bent posture, he resembled a cross between a spider and an owl. He ordered mussels but insisted on ones with the orange-tinged meat, not the white. When James ventured outside he wore his trademark trench coat and black homburg.

JFK was livid with the CIA and blamed them for the failure of the Bay of Pigs invasion in April, 1961. They had assured the President the operation was a slam-dunk. The President denied air support for the mission because he felt betrayed by the Agency. Stephen Kinzer, in his book *The Brothers*, quoted Kennedy as he fumed, *"I've got to do something about those CIA bastards."* He vowed to *"splinter* [the CIA] *into a thousand pieces."*

Angleton went off the rails, running rogue operations outside the purview of the Agency which he kept secret from his superiors and underlings. He was making enemies in the workplace. James obsessed about the Soviet Union at the expense of China, Cuba, Czechoslovakia, and East Germany. When he did impart information during staff meetings his people often left shaking their heads, not understanding the abstruse rhetoric of their boss. *Aussie Observer* reporter Greg Marbury captured his essence: *"He was amongst the most out-there of people, a T.S. Eliot quoting/loving, chain-smoking, hard drinking, orchid-growing, fly-fishing, gem-collecting, insomniac raconteur who burned the spy-candle at both ends... In his day many considered this dude the sharpest tool in the spy shed, bar none."*

There were as many opinions of Jim's personage as he had nicknames: Ghost, Skinny Jim, Kingfisher, Oracle of Delphi, Virginia Slim, Mother, The Poet Spy and Black Knight. He was charming to his friends and staff and combative with others. He was inspirational and contentious at the same time. The word "Angletonian" crept into the vernacular meaning odd, furtive or covert. There were so many disparate points of view it was almost impossible to get a bead on his true nature. James acted as if he were above the law. He trampled on the rights of American citizens. While the Soviets were his adversaries, they held his skills in high esteem even adopting many of his methods. After his death the Israelis inscribed monuments in the hills west of Jerusalem and near the King David Hotel:

IN MEMORY OF
A DEAR FRIEND
JAMES J. ANGLETON
1917-1987

Despite the enduring image of Camelot in the early '60s, there was a significant undercurrent of discontent in America. JFK had his enemies: the conservative wing of the Republican Party, the bellicose General Curtis Lemay and his

Pentagon minions, the Miami Cubans, much of the CIA, critics of the botched Bay of Pigs invasion and those who believed he conceded too much during the Cuban Missile Crisis.

Meanwhile, Angleton continued his mole-hunting, and a pro Castro ex-Marine who had defected to the Soviet Union, Lee Harvey Oswald, was on the radar, but somehow was not tailed to Dallas. He had married a Russian woman named Marina and had visited the Cuban consulate and Soviet Embassy in Mexico City. The man had been on James' radar from 1959 up to the assassination on November 22, 1963. A theory exists that the CIA thought Marina and their two young children, as well as his bleak experience in the Soviet Union, had a mitigating influence on Oswald, rendering him harmless.

As lackadaisical as James had been about investigating Oswald, he shifted into high gear covering up the CIA's inattention while hindering the Warren Commission. He countered the probe with his trademark obfuscatory tools: smoke, fog and mirrors. *"No matter who fired the fatal shots in Dallas, Angleton had failed disastrously as counterintelligence chief. He could have—and should have—lost his job after November 22. Had the public, the Congress, and the Warren Commission known of his pre-assassination interest in Oswald or his post-assassination cover-up, he surely would have."*

JEFFERSON MORLEY, *The Ghost*

James Angleton was playing with fire in regard to his program CHAOS, designed to deal with leftist elements like the Students for a Democratic Society. He authorized domestic spying. He believed the core values of America left it vulnerable to infiltration. Anti-war dissidents, civil rights activists, campus radicals, journalists and a lengthy enemies list were all in his crosshairs. Countless letters were intercepted; home and office break-ins and wire taps were authorized. A wide range of people were monitored including Martin Luther King Jr., author John Steinbeck, Walter Mondale and many congressmen. It was a brazen breach of the CIA charter and an egregious, illegal abuse of power. The pressure, worry and fear were getting to Angleton. Author Morley describes the strain: *"There were so many dangers to deter, so many secrets to keep, so few who could be trusted. His family was drifting away. His colleagues were daring to question his theories. The multiple*

martinis at lunch blurred his judgment and compounded his paranoia. And his annual fishing trips…on the Brule River in Wisconsin…provided only temporary respite from the perils he battled."

★ ★ ★ ★ ★

There was no doubting Jim's cunning nature, however, and he deftly dodged interrogation by the Inspector General concerning his involvement in the Watergate break-in. He denied any connection to the burglars. At least two were ex-CIA men, E. Howard Hunt and Eugenio Martinez, both of whom he knew from the Miami office. A grand jury witness claimed James was seen visiting Hunt's office: Room 16 in the Executive Office Building next to the White House.

The Agency deflected accusations by insisting the break-in was White House initiated. Furthermore, Angleton implied direct answers to inquiries would reveal classified information. There were too many connections between Hunt and Jim to be dismissed as coincidence. They had both participated in aspects of the Bay of Pigs invasion and other anti-Castro activities out of the Miami office. Hunt and Angleton were both consumed with proving Daniel Ellsberg, the subject of the break-in, to be a Soviet spy. A frustrated Senator Howard Baker didn't buy James' story and compared CIA operatives to *"animals crashing around in the forest—you can hear them, but you can't see them."* Jim threatened to sue.

Ironically, a newspaper article brought James down, not discovery of his lack of action regarding the murder of President Kennedy or his involvement with Watergate. A front page December 21, 1975, *New York Times* piece by Seymour Hersh exposed the massive domestic spying that had taken place for 20 years under the auspices of James Angleton. Early in his Presidency, Richard Nixon, unaware of Angleton's previous domestic surveillance efforts such as CHAOS, HUNTER and LINGUAL, lifted all sanctions such as warrants for phone calls and telegram monitoring. It was called the Huston Plan and Jim was at the helm, not Hoover.

"James Jesus Angleton had seen everything: participated in practically everything; read the most intimate reports on everybody; rifled through psychiatric reports on world figures; supervised the bugging of bordellos on four countries and of individual women in twice as many."

WILLIAM F. BUCKLEY, *Spytime: The Undoing of James Jesus Angleton*

William Colby was the CIA Director and had been urged from day one to let Angleton go. James' longevity was extremely rare, and his boss gave him the option of graceful retirement but the spymaster resisted until he finally resigned. George Kalaris was Jim's successor and, when he initiated a purge of James' files, a motherlode of information, all outside the CIA's filing system, was discovered. Storerooms had been concealed and over 40 safes were drilled open. Angleton's most sensitive files, photos, memos, tapes and letters were uncovered as well as items Kalaris found too disturbing to disclose.

"He was an ingenious, vicious, mendacious, obsessive, and brilliant man who acted with impunity as he sought to expand the Anglo-American-Israeli-sphere of influence after the end of World War II…his mastery was somewhat indistinguishable from his madness. He was indeed a combination of Machiavelli, Svengali, and Iago. He was an intellectual, charming and sinister."

JEFFERSON MORLEY, *The Ghost*

The details of James' career were largely unknown to the Brule River community until his very public departure from the Agency in 1975. Neville Connolly, a member of our Noyes clan, was a Harvard Medical School friend of Chester D'Autrement, Angleton's brother-in-law, and had permission to fish his private Jack's Lake on the westernmost edge of their property. Neville certainly knew Cicely and James but if he were aware of Angleton's clandestine career, he never mentioned it. Cicely and the children didn't really know the full scope of his duties until they attended the ceremony when Jim received the Distinguished Intelligence Medal on April 25, 1975.

On occasion, a carload of Brits was delivered to the Angleton Lodge from the Duluth airport. They were introduced as "diplomats," but one wonders….

By the time Caroline Marshall visited the Angletons in 1986, James had lung cancer, had quit smoking and drank only Coca-Cola. His world had changed dramatically both in Washington and on the Brule. His favorite fishing guides, including John LaRock and Ed Dennis, were gone and rather than break in the new generation, he went it alone, paddling the river, dressed in black and wearing a miner's protective helmet which offered the dimmest of light to show the way. The bow of his canoe was weighted with rocks to keep a proper balance as he negotiated the stream at night. Broken and isolated, he died one year later.

In his way, James Angleton wrote his own epitaph while discussing the inner machinations of the Agency with Joseph Trento, author of *The Secret History of the CIA, 1946-1989:* "*I realize now that I have wasted my existence, my professional life.... There was no accountability and without accountability everything went to shit.... Fundamentality, the founding fathers of U.S. intelligence were liars. The better you lied and the more you betrayed, the more likely you were to be promoted. These people attracted and promoted each other. Outside of their duplicity, the only thing they had in common was a desire for absolute power. I did things that, in looking back on my life, I regret. But I was a part of it and loved being in it.' He referred to Dulles and his compatriots as 'grand masters' and 'if you were in a room full of people that you had to believe would deservedly end up in hell, I guess I will see them there soon.'*"

James Angleton testifying before Church Committee, 1976

Young James Angleton

[20]

THE WOMEN OF THE BRULE

"Mrs. Noyes…was in consultation, soon after the fire, with Joe Lucius, the versatile builder, and it was not long before the new lodge was started and completed under the watchful eyes and the competent direction of Mrs. Noyes, to whom it has always been to me a beautiful and fitting memorial. I keep on my wall in the lodge the cane Aunt Agnes Noyes carried on many walks with me through the woods, and I never see it without a happy memory of one who was not only a beautiful and keen-minded woman, but one who shared deeply and sincerely for over a half century our love of the Brule. She and my mother were close friends, and were a pair of admirable campers."

Dr. Arthur T. Holbrook, *From the Log of a Trout Fisherman*

★ ★ ★ ★ ★

ONE COULD ASSUME THAT Agnes Haskell Noyes, the matriarch of out Brule family, was born with a silver spoon firmly lodged in her mouth. She graduated with highest honors from the University of Wisconsin and had leadership roles in Milwaukee social, political and charitable circles. Her children were educated at the finest boarding schools and colleges in the country. That assumption, however, would be inaccurate.

   "Haskell Peak in Sierra County California, the highest mountain in the county, the elevation of which is over 8,000 feet. From the crest flow the richest gold bearing rivers the world has ever seen: the Feather River rises up on the north slope, and the Yuba upon the south. It is a superstition among old California miners that the interior of Haskell Peak is solid gold. The mountain has never been thoroughly prospected."

Haskell Family Journal

Edward Wilder Haskell Jr., a member of the Pioneers of California, travelled to the Sierra Nevada Mountains in 1849 just as the Gold Rush began. He was interested in something more permanent and established a ranch outside Sierra City in the Lost Sierra, an area isolated to this day from the rest of the planet where the three branches of the Feather River cut through the forests of ponderosa pine, cedar, birch, aspen and juniper down to valleys decorated with wildflowers and punctuated with granite rocks and redwood manzanita bushes. Edward's brother George W. Haskell, my Great-great-grandfather, married Hannah Cole in Wisconsin, caught gold fever and proceeded to California to join Edward. My Great-grandmother, Agnes Haskell Noyes, was born at the ranch in 1855.

The easy picking of gold nuggets from dry river beds was soon exhausted and the more difficult and expensive extracting of gold veins was made harder during the winter months when 15'-20' of snow covered the Sierras. Great-great-grandfather George always seemed to be a little late for the motherlode and, when gold was discovered on the eastern slope of the Sierras, he took the family to Washoe City, Nevada which made Sierra City look like paradise.

"Frame shanties pitched together as if by accident—tents of canvas, of blankets of brush, of potato-sacks, and old shirts, with empty whiskey barrels for chimneys—coyote holes in the mountain-side forcibly seized and held by men-pits and shafts with smoke issuing from every crevice-pile of goods and rubbish in the hollows, on the rocks, in the mud, in the snow everywhere, scattered broadcast in pell-mell confusion."

J. ROSS BROWNE, "A PEEP AT WASHOE,"
Harper's New Monthly Magazine, DECEMBER 1860

★ ★ ★ ★ ★

Washoe City thrived for 6 years with 21 lawyers, 11 saloons, 7 tobacco stores and no churches. The old adage claimed, *"There is no Sunday west of St. Louis—and no God west of Fort Smith."* News reports from the *Washoe Weekly News* printed typical frontier town stories as in the August 27, 1864, edition: *...certain individuals about town, who seem to have nothing in particular to engage their attention make a practice of shooting chickens if they wander a 'short distance' from home. This is wrong. It may be fine 'sport' to the individual involved in doing it, and, a nice chicken pot pie* *may agree perfectly with the stomach, but it is not very agreeable to the person raising and feeding chickens to have them disposed of in that manner…”*

The real attraction for the eastern slope was the discovery of the Comstock Lode, the largest concentration of silver found in U.S. territory. Seventeen thousand prospectors flooded the area, and a series of businesses sprang up to support the mining and lumber operations. George Haskell found a partner and started a mercantile house on 3rd Street named “Haskell and Clarke” featuring dry goods and groceries: everything from hardware, food, textiles, apparel, rugs and wagon wheels. The men frontloaded inventories in the fall as freight costs skyrocketed during the winter when roads over the Sierra Nevadas became almost impassable. Price gouging was also commonplace. Commodities such as flour would sell for as much as $40 a barrel. At times the price could reach as much as $200 a barrel. Some merchants would add a little sand to their sugar to add bulk and weight.

★ ★ ★ ★ ★

Life was uncertain in the Sierra Nevadas. Toddler Georgia Lu Haskell died, most likely from scarlet fever. Hannah took a trip east to visit relatives, possibly to assuage the death of her daughter and feel the comforts of home as she did not enjoy the scrub, tumbleweed and lack of social niceties in Washoe City. She brought Ida, their youngest, with her and left Agnes and Emily with George. Hannah’s letters to George were anxiety-filled with concerns over finances and health. They traveled by sea, which she did not enjoy. Little Ida suffered from a lingering illness the whole trip. Hannah’s correspondence revealed her homesickness and worries about money and health.

“How is your business this summer? I wish you would write me about how you are prospering. I wish I knew just now how you are doing and how you have been able to collect over in Sierra Co. If I knew you tolerably well could spare it I should be inclined to ask you to send me fifty dollars….”

Money was tight, and the Haskells lived a hand-to-mouth existence. Hannah had a reputation for being difficult but was contrite after being separated from her husband and two other daughters.

“My trip and visit so far has not been one of much pleasure to me, as you may well imagine, but if we only get back safely and find you all well and happy it is all I ask. I am sure I shall never want to leave my family so again, and it does really seem to me

now that I shall appreciate my family as I never did before and that I shall be more patient and not scold at every trifling thing as I have often done...."

The exchange of letters was bittersweet. Young Agnes, always competitive, explained that sister Emily's letter was longer because she *"double spaced."* George did not write as frequently but gave his wife cause to worry during the summer of 1862: *"You say you are nervous what is the cause of it? I am afraid you are not well, do be careful and not get sick while I am gone, for be assured if I ever live to get back I shall never leave you again for I know full well, that my own family are dearer to me than all the world...."*

Hannah was prescient. George was ill and she was still in the East. At one point he telegraphed that "all danger had passed." He relapsed and died from "a fever" in August 1863. Hannah and her daughters moved to the Midwest, leaving their Western dream and George and little Georgia Lu buried in what is now the ghost town of Washoe City in the high desert of Nevada. Georgia's stone is marked with a lamb.

Great-great-grandfather Haskell did not live to see the impact of the extraordinary women he married and fathered, but he willed them the heritage of his pioneering spirit. The three sisters took different and even opposing paths to become a significant part of the vanguard of the changing sexual politics of America. In the aftermath of George's death, Hannah Cole Haskell and her three daughters relocated to Chicago to make a fresh start. Although they needed to take in boarders to produce income, Hannah managed to raise and educate the girls while instilling a strong sense of independence.

Sisters Agnes and Emily ended up on diametrically opposite sides during the battle for a woman's right to vote.

"These women, many of them professionals, had made their way in occupations where they were belittled, scorned and rebuffed. Men ridiculed their aspirations for equal status... But a change in public perception began to be evident at the 1901 convention in Minneapolis, where reporters found suffragists to be affable, good humored, eloquent and even fashionable."

BARBARA STUHLER, *Gentle Warriors*

★ ★ ★ ★ ★

Emily Haskell Bright was a natural leader and took to the cause of suffrage with great passion. Stuhler describes her as a *"dauntless colleague....full of arrogant, saucy, and shocking feminism* [with] *several children, all original, dashing and pleasantly wild."* As a child, her mother Hannah took her to see Susan B. Anthony deliver a speech in Evanston, Illinois. Emily described it as a defining moment in her life. She became the President of the Political Equality Club of Minneapolis and head of the Minnesota Woman Suffrage Association. She served as an advisor to the national organization.

Her networking skills drew a large number of society women into the movement. The new wave of supporters contradicted the stereotype of older, dour, spinster suffragettes. Emily Bright and her compatriots were witty, attractive women who did not disguise their femininity. The MWSA believed in a more militant approach and their protesters and picketers were often treated roughly at rallies, imprisoned and force fed when they went on hunger strikes. Emily was never jailed, but she wore a "prison pin" in solidarity with those who were.

This combative strategy created publicity and is credited with helping change President Woodrow Wilson's attitude and leading him to support the 19th Amendment. Emily's husband Alfred, general counsel for the Minneapolis, St. Paul and Sault Ste. Marie Railroad, supported his wife's politics and gave legal advice in addition to attending rallies and marching in parades alongside the feminists. This was a bold stand as Emily Pennington, leader of the Minneapolis Association Opposed to Woman's Suffrage, was the wife of his boss. Alfred was proud of his wife, who was praised in a newspaper article for her *"tact, executive ability and sterling worth"* that *"distinguished her as one of the few real leaders of the suffrage movement in this country."*

Sister Agnes Haskell Noyes, my Great-grandmother, held a widely divergent view and actively campaigned against a woman's right to vote. She was the leader of many social service organizations locally, statewide and nationally and was the first female Phi Beta Kappa from the University of Wisconsin. Agnes served on the board of directors of the National Association of Collegiate Alumnae, was the President of the Social Economic Club of Milwaukee and Chairman of the General Federation of Women's Clubs. Great-grandmother was the Wisconsin Federation and anti-suffrage delegate at the annual meeting of the Massachusetts Association Opposed to the Further Extension of Suffrage for Women in April 1914.

At first blush, it seems illogical for prominent, educated, well-connected women to resist the wave of support for women's voting rights. Their point of view, however, was determined by the political clout and access to power they already possessed. They had associations with a network of male civic, business and social leaders and opposed giving lower class women the opportunity to rise up and compete with them. Agnes, in her estimation, had everything she wanted: a wonderful family and the time and means to enjoy her lofty station in Wisconsin. She also had her beautiful haven in the forested Brule River Valley.

Mrs. Noyes was no shrinking violet. She was independent and strong, but preferred the status quo and fought to preserve it. My Grandmother Margaret, Vassar educated, was cut from the same cloth and worked against a woman's right to vote in Minneapolis, contradicting her Aunt Emily Bright's efforts. Grammie proselytized the throngs at the Minnesota State Fair from the Anti-Suffrage booth. No matter their disparate political philosophies, Agnes and Emily did not let their differences interfere with their relationship. The Brights were frequent visitors to Noyes Camp.

"The new woman, in the sense of the best woman, the flower of all womanhood of past ages, has come to stay—if civilization is to endure. The sufferings of the past have but strengthened her, maternity has deepened her, education is broadening her—and she now knows that she must perfect herself if she would perfect the race, and leave her imprint upon mortality, through her offspring or her works."

WINNIFRED HARPER COOLEY, *The New Womanhood*

★ ★ ★ ★ ★

Ida Haskell, unlike her sisters, wasn't a political activist. She led by example. More women, primarily middle and upper class, were graduating from college and entering the professional arena of law, medicine, social work, science and journalism. Women were now able to remain single as "bachelor girls" without the stigma of spinsterhood.

Until the waning years of the 19th century, women were depicted by male artists as delicate, placid, chaste and decorative objects often placed in a garden serving to reinforce the metaphor of ladies as flowers. Female artists were dismissed as inferior to their male counterparts. Well trained, educated women artists emerged in the late 1800s with their own perspective and Ida Haskell was one. She studied at the Art Institute of Chicago, the Philadelphia Art Museum, the Pennsylvania Academy of Fine Arts and subsequently in Europe.

Ida and her friends formed "The Bohemian Club" as a support system for young female artists and mother Hannah accompanied her daughter and many of her colleagues to Paris as their chaperone. The young women first attended the prestigious Academie Julian, founded in 1867 with a roster of esteemed professors and students. They studied French Impressionism, often painting portraits of male nude models who were not opposed to harassing the young women who employed them.

After the dank Paris winter, the students traveled to Ritsoord, a hamlet in southern Holland. Great-great-grandmother Haskell followed the recommendation of a Chicago friend, selecting the village suited for painting landscapes in an agrarian setting with abundant summer lighting. The townspeople were also excellent subjects and their isolation from the rest of the world, and resulting curiosity, almost caused a melee when the local children, enchanted by the spectacle of American girls, encircled them in a near stampede. Ida returned to America and further honed her skills in New Orleans and California. She became an instructor at Pratt Institute in New York while continuing to paint.

Ida's painting, "Mother Love (Where Trouble Ends)," was displayed in the Women Artists Exhibit at the 1893 World's Fair. Other well-known works include "Dunes" and "Night Sky with Large Few Stars," inspired by a line from Walt Whitman's epic poem, "Song of Myself." Her paintings are still sold at auction. Ida was at the forefront of female impressionists.

Ida Haskell lived on Beaver Dam Road in Brookhaven, New York, on Long Island with famed photographer Alice Boughton in what was called a "Boston Marriage," a term coined by Henry James in his 1886 novel, The *Bostonians*, a controversial look at the New Woman Movement. Boughton was known for her portraits of literature and theatrical luminaries such as James, Maxim Gorky, William Butler Yeats and Eugene O'Neill. She also took portraits of Noyes family members.

The New Woman was a strong, independent emissary for reform through political activism, art and literature. A Boston Marriage was a long-term relationship between two cohabitating women without male financial support. Ida and Alice were companions in what the census described as a "spousal" relationship, another example of the New Woman as females took control over all facets of their lives. One of Ida's lasting legacies is the Pratt Institute Traveling Fellowship, financial aid given to deserving students for the purpose of studying abroad.

The language of C.D. O'Brien's *Brule Chronicles* from 1889, is so flowery and full of enigmatic inside jokes that it is difficult to discern fact from fiction. When women and children were invited to join the male campers from August 1-15, romance was inevitable. A man identified only as the "Major" spent the day fishing when, on his way back, he passed the Gitche Gumee site and saw Florence, or "Floy," Holbrook.

"The beautiful river had spread out before him, all of its charms, the magic of its enchantments had sunk into his heart, the added years had slipped away and once again the springs of his gallant youth welled up within his heart; the Goddess of Innocence and Fancy long banished, resumed her throne and he wholly surrendered himself to her loving whispers. In such a mood he was, when, lifting up his eyes, he first saw Florence as she stood on the bank, in front of the Gitche Gumee camp, looking up the river. How shall I describe her as the Major first saw her? Her lithe and graceful figure against the background of the dark pines, touched lightly and reverently by the softened rays of the setting sun…slender, a little above medium height, dark hair, brown eyes, broad smooth forehead, and lips so sweet, so red, so tender yet so firm, that one kiss were worth the ransom of an empire."

★ ★ ★ ★ ★

Sadly, the Major had to leave the Brule, and Florence, and *"left his heart in Gitche Gumee Camp, without guerdon, pledge, or hope of its return."* The "Author," C.D. O'Brien, also seemed impressed by Floy as he not only named a nearby pond "Lake Florence," but gifted her an Ojibwe-made birch bark canoe.

It is not known if the Major's infatuation was requited, but 100 years later, across the smoky main room of the local watering hole called the "Kro," love blossomed when Sarah Bagley, a Noyes family member, and young Matson Holbrook locked eyes. The Brule River next-door neighbors wed, fulfilling the promise, however apocryphal, of Florence and the Major.

Up until the end of the 19th century, female presence on the river was intermittent. The Paleo Indian hunting parties were male. When the glaciers receded for good, bands of Native Americans appeared and lived in the Brule River Valley on a nomadic basis. There was a distinct division of labor. Simply put, women were in charge of the camp and men masters of the forest. Women constructed the lodges, making frames and attaching rolls of birch bark to them and made rush mats for sleeping. They butchered meat, collected sap, planted, harvested and sewed birch bark to canoes. They fished with large nets fashioned with nettle stalk fiber while the men used spears, hooks and smaller dip nets.

Ojibwe females prepared hides of animals to make clothing. They were the keepers of the culture and passed the information on to succeeding generations. The women were in charge of the community when the men were away hunting and warring, although some women joined in the fighting. Older women were called *mindimooyenh* or "one who holds things together."

Women, or *ikwaywug,* arranged *wedigaywin,* unions or marriages, ensuring there were no inter-clan marriages. Love was not a factor. Sustenance and survival were the foremost considerations. Ojibwe family size was small due to a variety of factors including high infant mortality rates and sometimes, abortions. Abstinence played a part as sexual activity was discouraged until a baby was weaned.

Water was the province of women, who held it in their bodies until it flowed during child birth. It connected them with Mother Earth and Grandmother Moon. Females were in charge of water during rituals. Throughout history, Ojibwe women were valued not just for their labors but for their strength, spirituality and ability to keep the community healthy and whole. They were respected and wielded power.

"Payet, one of my Interpreters, has taken one of the Native Daughters for a Wife, and to her Parents he gave in rum & Dry Goods, etc. to the value of two hundred Dollars, and at the ceremonies attending such circumstances are that when it comes time to retire the Husband…shows his Bride where his Bed is, and they, of course, go to rest together, and they continue to do so as long as they can agree among themselves.…"

Daniel Harmon, Journal, 1801

The intrusion of the European fur trade into the interior of the continent had a seismic effect on the Ojibwe way of life, and the status and roles of native women in particular. Aboriginals in the Brule River Valley had seen little change in hundreds of years before the demand for fur in Europe forever changed the balance and symmetry of their existence. The industry could not have survived without the custom of marriage *a la facon du pays,* "according to the custom of the country." The traders would have starved or died from exposure without the expertise of Ojibwe women. They performed everyday tasks such as making moccasins and snowshoes crucial to the health of the Euros.

Despite the protestations of the Jesuit missionaries, traders took Ojibwe women as second wives. Native girls as young as 12 married and, by 14, were bearing mixed blood children known as *Metis*. In addition to their traditional roles the women became invaluable with their knowledge of geography, botany, language and cultural idiosyncrasies.

The intermarriage created a sub-culture that some scholars call "the middle ground" or "the People In Between." The Ojibwe and the French found the bonds to be mutually advantageous. The continued flow of trade items enhanced the women's standard of living. Their families not only received compensation but the added benefits of being treated fairly in exchanges of goods, and the traders would be their allies in times of tribal disputes and other hardships. The French sought wives from prominent Ojibwe families to give them leverage.

The women negotiated, interpreted, spied, guided and networked, and their diplomatic skills helped the traders navigate the subtle differences in various bands of natives who all seemed the same to the whites. The fur trade introduced some time, labor-saving and better quality objects to Ojibwe women like metal kettles, axe and hatchet heads, cooking utensils, traps and arrow tips. Glass beads and silver to decorate clothing were very desirable. Blankets and textiles were popular.

There were many negatives, however. The Euros brought disease, alcohol and firearms into their communities. The Ojibwe men spent more time away from the community, trapping fur-bearing animals, adding additional duties to the females' already heavy workloads. The introduction of metal cookware hastened the demise of ancient native craft.

The most damaging introduction was the clash between the cultural, spiritual and economic world views. The Ojibwe believed the key to the good life was balance in spirit and their environment. The idea of ownership and the acquisition of "things" was foreign to them. The European concept of commerce upset the equilibrium, and the natives became dependent on trade goods and even food as their attention largely shifted from hunting large mammals to trapping smaller animals.

The Ojibwe had once acted as trading intermediaries between the French and the Dakota. The lust for furs, alcohol, firearms and other trading goods exacerbated ill will between the various native tribes, and they battled over hunting grounds, trapping grounds and wild rice stands as the Euros crowded them and created competition between the bands who were former allies or at least at peace.

French fur traders took the time to understand the customs and rituals of the Ojibwe such as the exchange of gifts before conducting business. Women were treated as trading partners and potential customers. The English were focused on the prize and didn't spend time learning the ways of the indigenous.

The fur trade started to wane after the War of 1812 as fashions changed and pelts became scarce. There was a new normal in the Brule River Valley for Ojibwe women. Activity on the stream quieted with the occasional American explorers paddling to assess economic possibilities in mining, lumber, fishing and shipping. Mid-19th century treaties were a land grab by the U.S. government and started the process of forced assimilation.

The goal was to break down the native culture, force an agrarian way of life on the reservations and educate and Anglicize the children in boarding schools away from their traditional influences. The absence of the income from fur forced the Ojibwe to depend increasingly on the American government. Pressure mounted on native females responsible for the survival of their communities and culture.

The Finnish farm women in the Brule Valley also had exhausting lives, particularly in the winter when many of their husbands left home to supplement their incomes in logging camps. Lack of money meant many families were without firearms and ammunition. They banded together to hunt deer to sustain them for the long, hard winters just south of Lake Superior. The women dug pits on well-traveled deer runs and covered the holes with branches until a victim fell into the trap and was finished off with knives and hatchets. The carcass was drained of blood and chopped into sections of manageable size to carry home.

When the sportsmen of the Upper Midwest descended on the Brule during the latter part of the 19th century, Ojibwe or *Metis* women were employed as cooks. No distinction was made regarding their European DNA. Dr. Holbrook referred to their cook Mary Gheen as the *"squaw chef."* He was impressed by her fortitude though. While the fishermen struggled with their packs to reach the campsite, she toted a sheet-iron camp stove on her back.

While Great-grandfather George Noyes and his friends believed their male bonding time in May to be sacrosanct, he took time from Brule in 1913 to send Agnes: *"…a birthday remembrance for the 15th as I can not send you flowers or any other present only however my love and congratulations on your 58th anniversary with this hope and faith you may live to see 20 or even 30 more of them, if you be well and happy to enjoy them all...."*

★ ★ ★ ★ ★

Lodges owned by the progeny of Duluth iron ore and copper mining magnate Chester Adgate Congdon, and his wife Clara, line the upper Brule River. The homes, mostly retained by their great-grandchildren, are named Angleton, Guru Khalsa, Ott, Van Evera, D'Autremont and Ne Dodg E Won. Until recently, the six bedroom Swiftwater Farm was owned by the grandchildren of Elisabeth Congdon who purchased, refurbished and occupied the property starting in the 1940s. It is a shame that Elisabeth's murder is better chronicled than her life. She was a remarkable woman who championed the rights of children and women, in particular. Elisabeth attended Vassar College just a few years after my Grand-mother Margaret and Great aunt Helen Noyes.

Miss Congdon left Vassar early after her father's death but not before she acquired a set of values that motivated her passion for social reform including women's rights, child welfare, education and health. During World War I she was the chairman of the Minnesota branch of the Council of National Defense. Elisabeth served on the boards of Dana Hall School and Syracuse University. She was a champion of, and generous benefactor to, the arts. During World War II she rolled up her sleeves and prepared bandages for the troops at Duluth's St. Luke's Hospital.

Swiftwater Farm and the Brule River were a sanctuary for the heiress. She derived great pleasure watching her adopted daughters Marjorie and Jennifer enjoy the freedom of the woods and stream. The atmosphere there was much more casual than the formality of the family's Duluth home, the thirty-nine room, 20,000 square-foot Glensheen Mansion on the Lake Superior shore. Elisabeth suffered a debilitating stroke in 1968 which left her paralyzed, wheelchair-bound, almost totally deaf and unable to speak. Her strong spirit survived, however, and she took her physical therapy seriously. She was able to continue living at Glensheen and still derived pleasure from her visits to her precious Swiftwater Farm.

Miss Congdon spent her last day on the Brule River June 27, 1977 and was driven back to Duluth in the late afternoon. The following morning Elisabeth and her night nurse Velma Pietila were found dead: smothered with a satin pillow and bludgeoned by a brass candle holder, respectively. Suspicion was soon focused on daughter Marjorie who was often in financial trouble. Her eccentricities were evident even in childhood. She set fires and even poisoned a horse. I attended elementary school with her three oldest children, who were expelled due to sporadic attendance, delinquent tuition and Marjorie's disruptive influence. She was the quintessential figure skating stage mother. Marjorie was so consumed by her ambition for her children that she sued the august Figure Skating Club of Minneapolis, appealing her case to the Minnesota State Supreme Court where it was finally dismissed. She was good at burning bridges, as well as a few buildings along the way.

Marjorie and her second husband, Roger Caldwell, grew impatient waiting for her inheritance and Roger was convicted of the murders he tried to stage as a robbery gone wrong. Ms. Caldwell was acquitted, not so much for her innocence but through the machinations of her tenacious attorney, Ron Meshbesher. The tragic irony was that Elisabeth Congdon would not live out her final years on the banks of her beloved Brule while her ungrateful daughter was free to commit more arsons and even murders as some have suggested.

For much of its early history, Noyes Camp was a matriarchy. When his health began to fail, Great-grandfather turned over much of the management of Noyes Camp to wife Agnes. Great-grandmother was at the helm until her death in 1936. Her daughter, Katherine Noyes McLennan, was one of the early presidents of Noyes-Brule Inc. As a teen my mother Leslie had "house parties" with her girlfriends on the river. August 1939 postcards to those back in Minneapolis who couldn't attend, report *"heaps of fun"* and details concerning the heat and humidity as well as gossip about boys. Daughters Amy and Laura have had groups of friends to the Brule to enjoy canoeing and the river. When I watch my grandsons, Max and Jack, enjoy the same traditions and activities, I am reminded that without "The Women of the Brule," there would be no "Boys of the Brule." While for centuries the Brule River was largely the domain of men, strong women have been an integral part of its more recent history.

Kristin Fruen, coffee break on Noyes Camp porch

Dressed in White: Margaret Noyes and Wallis Simpson (future Duchess of Windsor) on the beach at the Hotel del Coronado, San Diego, California

[21]

DROP THE PUCK

"Here in a pungent, disease infected hockey locker-room, 20 men gather twice a week to find strange sanctuary. The motivation for this is far more elusive than carving blades into fresh ice or living out childhood hockey fantasies. There's a deeper pull: a sense of lost fraternity that is reborn in the sweaty aromatic masculinity of the locker room. Our daily lives as fathers, husbands, sons are mysteriously locked out by cinder block walls. Here in this place and this place alone, we are politically incorrect. We are profane. We are stupid. We are boys."

Robert Cribb, "Mystique of Male Bonding Lost on Women Folk,"
Toronto Star, April 15, 2010

HOCKEY HAS EVOLVED SINCE the Iroquois played a game called "Hoghee," meaning, "it hurts," on the St. Lawrence River. French explorers observed the indigenous chasing deer on the rivers and lakes wearing skates fashioned from the jawbones of hooved animals. Archeologists have found joined shoe and bone blade contrivances suggesting that skating was an ancient practice in North America. When they skated for sport, the natives used a curved stick and batted a wood ball to score. The Madeline Island Ojibwe played a sport resembling Lacrosse on the frozen surfaces of Chequamegon Bay.

The equipment has improved, and the ice may be smoother now, but hockey still is painful. Even in May, hockey is front and center for us on the river. It is, after all, Stanley Cup Playoff time after the NHL's seemingly inexorable regular season. In the mid-1970s, a core of five Boys of Brule: Dana Fitts, Rob Pearson,

Marty Schuster, Jim Hurd and I, played senior Men's Hockey on the Greenbrier team in Minneapolis. We had grown up together. All of us, with varying degrees of success, played either with or against each other in college. Chip Lindeke, our immediate Brule downstream neighbor from Winneboujou's Wendigo Lodge, was also on the team. Marty and I played against Chip in high school.

Another co-conspirator, Bill Lorntson, spent his winters playing shinny on the frozen surface of Lake Superior's North Shore, where an errant pass would sail out of sight on the immense ice sheet. Bud Chambers progressed from a wobbly Virginian into a very competent intramural goalie in college. The Melander brothers, Big T and Mike, were basketball players, but also rabid and knowledgeable Minnesota North Star fans. In high school, schedule permitting, Mike laced up the blades for some pick-up hockey.

Since television is verboten at Noyes Camp, we venture into town if our current favorite squad, the Minnesota Wild, is playing. We watch the games at the Kro-Bar, unique by virtue of the small spring that runs through the middle of the bar's basement office.

Our spiritual hockey leader was Rob's dad, the late "O.J." Pearson, a puck nut if there ever was. He had his own group of guys, Pearson's Pucksters, who attended the Minnesota State High School Tournament annually, starting after World War II. Dana's dad, Dick, and my father, Roger, were proud to wear their Pearson's Pucksters buttons around St. Paul every March.

O.J. had a lifetime love affair with hockey. At 15 he had a Minnesota-kid's dream job as a stick boy for the visiting teams when they played the Minneapolis Millers in the rough and tumble world of minor league hockey. I'm sure his vocabulary increased exponentially listening to the toothless thugs railing about the referees and the Millers.

During World War II, he played for the U.S. Army team in Chamonix, France. He continued to play in Minneapolis after the cessation of hostilities but faced combat again as a coach when he fended off the angry, drunken father of one of his players. Rob and I witnessed Miller and University of Minnesota games as far back as I can remember. We attended Golden Gopher games on campus in 7 straight decades.

Rob matured early, was a smooth skater and had a high hockey IQ. He made the Breck School Varsity hockey team as a freshman. An early highlight for him was a road game in Faribault, Minnesota, against Shattuck School. Rob scored two goals and made out with a cheerleader on the bus ride home to Minneapolis.

She would have been horrified to learn he was a 9th grader. Today we call the two goals and a bus ride make-out a "Rob Pearson Hat Trick."

Hockey, like all sports, has its humorous moments, although some are not funny at the moment they occur. Jim, Marty and I played our first Middlebury College game at Clarkson University in upstate New York. The Knights were a primarily older Canadian team and, after winning the opening faceoff, they dumped the puck into our defensive zone. Jim retrieved the puck, but the opposing left winger anticipated his breakout pass, stepped up to intercept and rifled a wicked wrist shot over my right shoulder. The crowd razzed me, a shaken rookie goalie, for giving up my first collegiate goal 8 seconds into my first game.

Dana played for Maine's Colby College and once when they visited Middlebury, Jim's parents were in attendance. Our favorite Colby Mule had the puck and was about to be blindsided by Middlebury's Dave Pierson, another rugged Minnesotan. Jim's mom Sally shouted, *"Look out, Dana!"* He narrowly avoided getting hit by the oncoming freight train.

Friends since the day I was born six months after Rob, we graduated from winter rink rats and summer pucksters in his basement to competitive players. When my Breck School team played his West High Cowboys our senior year, we lost 4-2. It really was 5-2 but I stealthily pulled the puck out of the net when West scored and the ref's view was blocked.

Sometimes egos got involved. When we played Rob's St. Lawrence University team, we lost and my friend stuck it to me verbally after the final buzzer. I responded in anger and the postgame photo of Marty, Rob and me shows hilarious body language as my oldest buddy exaggeratedly leans away from me as I sport a smoldering expression.

Freshman year in college, Marty took a high stick to the face, leaving a small cut over his left eye. I skated to him and, just when he thought I was going to commiserate, I squeezed the cut hard to draw more blood. This upped the penalty time from 2 minutes to 5. By our late 20s, we were getting a bit too mature to get into hockey fights. After all, we had to get up in the morning and go to work. We had to defend ourselves occasionally in the rough Senior Men's League games and during a particularly contentious match against Duffy's, a bar located in an area of Minneapolis dubbed "Hell's Hub" by the police, a brawl broke out.

I joined various skirmishes just to even up a mismatch. I kept running into a guy who finally said, *"Do you want to go?"* As I removed my goalie mask, he sucker punched me and another melee began. Marty tied up the initiator's arms, and I grabbed him by the scalp with my left hand and threw haymakers with my right. Soon we were wrenched apart and as Jim swung by to check on me, I showed him the clump of my opponent's hair I had thrown into the net. The next time we played Duffy's my old nemesis sported a buzz cut and gave me a wide berth.

We finally decided we were getting too old for this kind of silliness and ended our playing careers. Our families were growing and some of us turned to coaching youth hockey which was just as rewarding. Now the Boys of Brule just talk a good game of hockey.

Left to Right, Marty Schuster, Rob Pearson, Ross Fruen, Middlebury vs. St. Lawrence, January 1970 *Courtesy of Gordy Schuster*

[22]

WINDS OF CHANGE

"Something disturbed my dreams in the darkest part of that night, and I crept noiselessly in the place where the tent flaps were fastened together and peeped through them. I saw sitting upon the ground about the embers of our camp fire several Indian chiefs in their feathered bonnets, smoking their long pipes in perfect silence and gazing into the fire as though contemplating the present and the future compared with the past when the woods and stream were their very own without the invasion of the white men. Their austere and unhappy countenances frightened me in the loneliness of the woods…"

MRS. E.N. SAUNDERS, SAUNDERS FAMILY PAPERS,
Winneboujou Chronicles

★ ★ ★ ★ ★

THE OJIBWE HAD GONE through a myriad of transitions during their migration to northern Wisconsin, but nothing affected the way of life more than the arrival of the Europeans and their thirst for fur. The natives found it easier to trade if they converted to Catholicism, so many succumbed to the proselytizing of the "black robes," the French missionaries. They practiced an amalgam of Christianity and their traditional beliefs in visions, dreams and the multitude of spirits that controlled every facet of their life. The Ojibwe shifted from a philosophy of taking "just enough" from nature to one of surplus, which led to conflict with other tribes as the concept of territory evolved into a more European construct.

When the British replaced the French in the trading business in 1763, after the French and Indian War, the Ojibwe experienced another culture shock. While the French had been relatively respectful of the natives and even adopted many of their traits in the wilderness, the English brought their hierarchal idea of society to the Upper Midwest and, after a period of adjustment, treated the Ojibwe, and other tribes, with disdain.

Oral Ojibwe history details an act of treachery in 1780 that brought their society and culture to its knees and forever solidified their dependence on the white man. A trading contingent visited an English outpost on Mackinac Island on the northern end of Lake Michigan. The white men were in a vengeful mood as the natives had killed a trader a year or two previously. According to a popular version of the story, the Ojibwe were given gifts not to be opened until they returned west to the center of their civilization.

The keg of liquor and a folded British flag had been dosed with smallpox and when the Ojibwe celebrated their return to the south shore of Lake Superior, opened the keg and unfurled the flag, the disease raced through the tribe decimating as many as a few thousand. Those surviving the outbreak were driven to near starvation as their society teetered on collapse.

There were many ancillary issues beyond the calamitous loss of life. Clans were nearly destroyed leaving the few remaining members without leadership, support and protection. The elderly were particularly vulnerable to smallpox and traditions, healing and creative skills were lost as well as history and religion.

Famished, homeless and despondent, the survivors increasingly relied on the English, most of whom were not sympathetic to the plight of the Ojibwe. The natives soon begrudged their dependence on the British traders and, when the Revolutionary War started their concern was not who would win, but rather the interruption of the flow of trade goods they desired. Many bands and tribes fought on the British side in the War of 1812, but the Lake Superior and Minnesota bands of Ojibwe preferred to remain neutral as the Americans had not yet encroached on their territory. Chief Flat Mouth explained, *"When I go to war against my enemies I do not call on the whites to join my warriors. The white people have quarreled among themselves, and I do not wish to meddle in their quarrels."*

After the war ended, the United States became interested in their newly acquired territory and dispatched explorers and geologists to Northern Wisconsin to ascertain the magnitude of natural resources to be extracted from the area that was largely unknown to the young nation. Lewis Cass and Henry Schoolcraft scoured the south shore of Lake Superior, mapping the area and taking samples of minerals. Copper was of particular interest. Schoolcraft was fascinated by native culture, customs and oral history and documented them to magazine readers eager to read about the ways of the Ojibwe.

As fashions changed and supply diminished, beaver trapping gave way to muskrat and marten before the industry completely faded. Copper mining was short-lived on the Brule and the emphasis shifted to commercial fishing. In 1853, George Stuntz and his crew were hired to locate the northwest border of Wisconsin, determine township boundaries and propose potential path for railroad lines. One of the survey members dismissed the Brule region as containing *"only Indians, cruel rocks, and dense forests to the water's edge."* Change continued to accelerate as real estate and logging interests pounced on the new opportunities.

Real estate speculators known as "Yankee Land Lookers" converged on the town of Superior and began scouting the south shore of the lake for land near the rivers, which were thought to be prime investments. Col. Daniel Robertson is believed to be the first to acquire land on the Brule purchasing 160 acres just upriver from the mouth in August 1852. The Wisconsin Commission of Emigration was formed and nearly one hundred thousand pamphlets extolling the virtues of the newly minted state blanketed Europe and Scandinavia.

The largest wave of immigrants flocked to Wisconsin starting in the 1870s and Finns in particular were drawn the south shore of Lake Superior, attracted by the prospect of land and jobs. The town of Oulu was incorporated near Brule, taking the name of its sister city in Finland. Many of the immigrants wrote letters home encouraging friends and relatives to join them.

The arrival of the railroad in the Brule River Valley in 1883 was the final harbinger of change for the local Ojibwe. The trains brought numbers of visitors and soon the natives were sharing not only the land but the prime camp sites, the game and even the berries they counted on for subsistence.

The natives watched the trains arrive at the Brule station while standing in the woods, curious and perhaps wistful, as the interlopers arrived. There were some opportunities as guides, laborers and domestic help, but white expansion dealt the final blow to the territorial freedom the Ojibwe had enjoyed for many generations.

For the members of the Milwaukee Club, the window of congenial, pastoral bliss was even smaller as families grew and competition for the best sites along the river created conflict. When the Saunders of Winneboujou decided to build their lodge, the Gitche Gumee Camping Club was displaced and, in 1899, the members bought 20 acres of land from Col. John Knight for $600, just one bend upriver from their precious camping grounds.

The GGCC was incorporated in the state of Wisconsin with elaborate bylaws and an annual meeting schedule meticulously kept with a judge and an attorney involved. The land is now owned jointly by three families, making it nearly impossible to sell. Acreage is owned on the other side of the river to preserve the solitude and prevent any development. Rapid change came to the Noyes family as Great-grandfather George died in 1916 and Great-grandmother Agnes stepped in as the family leader. Neighbor Dr. Arthur T. Holbrook referred to her as a woman of *"strong character, marked ability and strong determination."* She was very intelligent, accomplished and a strong matriarch.

When Great-grandmother Agnes died in Tucson in 1936 at the age of 81, it brought a major shift to the operation of Noyes Camp, which had previously been run on an ad hoc basis. Noyes-Brule was incorporated with a president and treasurer at the helm. Each of the five children of my Grandmother Margaret's generation paid for an initial stock subscription of $500 and given equal shares with the financial obligation of $100 per year to fund the camp's expenses.

A charge of 50 cents per person per day was levied to the occupants of the Camp. The younger generation, many of whom well over the age of 21 had *"no privileges for the use of the camp unless they* [were] ...*there as guests of their parents or grandparent.* Over the years the operation of Noyes Camp has become more professional, expensive and inclusive. It is widely said that our lodge is perhaps the finest on the river. We have various committees designed to maintain the high standards such as the House Committee, for décor, and the Buildings and Grounds Committee, which looks after the physical structure of Noyes Camp. We even have a person in the charge of the boathouse, to ensure the canoes, paddles, poles and life jackets are in good shape.

We are into our seventh generation at Noyes Camp, and the number of family members grows and the length of the visits decrease, to accommodate everyone. This has the effect of short circuiting relationships between the original camps as the residents become more insular and less inclined to socialize. Jobs for townspeople have declined. Some camps are rented which further mitigates old school comradery.

★ ★ ★ ★ ★

"No man ever steps in the same river twice, for it's not the same river and he's not the same man."

Heraclitus, Greek Philosopher

Part of the Brule's distinctive nature, and the inherent challenges of paddling it, are the many changes and variety of characters as it alternately meanders and races to Lake Superior. The headwaters of the stream are adjacent to a terminal moraine where the most recent glacier dumped its debris and the accompanying sediment of glacial till outwash.

Small creeks and streamlets empty into the Upper Brule and the dry, sandy soil of the Pine Barrens absorbs precipitation which seeps into the stream, maintaining a consistent flow. Even as the river becomes navigable, the morass of tag alders slows the progress of the few canoes that travel this stretch. Numerous oxbows make it difficult to ascertain the actual length of the river as it zig zags through a series of cedar and conifer swamps. Meadows lie adjacent to the river near the source and again downstream north of the town of Brule.

Not far from Blue Springs, just upriver from Stone's Bridge, is the site known as Lone Norway, where a statuesque pine once stood. It is said to be a meeting place where bands of Ojibwe warriors prepared to defend the stands of wild rice and the river that served as the roadway to their settlements and the territory that provided sources of meat, fish and fur bearing animals.

The Brule at this point is narrow and slow until it widens near Stone's Bridge, where large boulders protrude from the water and the current slightly quickens as evidenced by the marsh grasses swaying on the surface. Spruce and tamarack line the banks as the river begins one of its many metamorphoses. The bottom also goes through many changes, now leaving the swampy bog behind in favor of sand and gravel. Cedar trees appear, then give way to red and white pines. The sloughs of Cedar Island lay hidden on the east side.

Springs continue to boil from the sandy, gravelly bottom through the clear, frigid water of deep pools. Ponds large enough to warrant names, like Hart's Lake, Rocky Lake and Sucker Lake, appear and a series of rapids spills into Big Lake, a shallow, silt-bottomed widening that marks the beginning of Trout Nirvana, which runs for a few miles past the "Club Section" including Noyes Camp and

Winneboujou. Wing dams consisting of rocks and fallen sweeper trees stiffen the current, deepen the channel and push sediment downstream.

A series of rapids transitions into a long section of dead water flanked by meadows formed by timber cutting, dam release for log drives and land cleared for farming. Agriculture along the Brule has mostly been abandoned with the few remaining dedicated to hay and pasture. Grasslands north of Highway 13 are dotted with wild roses, daisies, yellow flag, anemone and buttercup.

The slow pace continues. In one of its final personality changes, the river gradient falls 328 feet in the last 19 miles as it races to the mouth at Lake Superior through the Copper Range and fast water dominates for miles until the river widens and slows. Aspen and fir trees are prevalent. Clay banks tower over the river in this sparsely habited section.

The last ¼ mile of the stream flows slowly through open marsh. The massive Great Unsalted looms ahead as the mercurial Brule, a river of many moods and great diversity, comes to an end. Due to changing water levels the landing and driftwood-strewn beach are now submerged.

The Boys of Brule have shared life's milestones: marriage, children, career changes, divorce, deaths of parents and friends and receding hairlines that have turned gray. Every May we return to the river, take inventory and continue our traditions.

Roger and Leslie Fruen on the river

View from the Winneboujou bridge, Jess Huiras and Kyle Fruen

Heading downstream, left to right, Amy Kenner, Max Kenner, Jack Kenner, Laura Fruen

Joe Lucius rebuilding Noyes Camp, 1924

EPILOGUE

"Whether the valley can be protected from the seeds of destruction…cannot yet be answered. Probably as long as fishing remains the chief consideration, there will be no overt attempt to sell the Brule's riches to the pawnbrokers. Many hope that no human hand will be allowed to molest the mighty pines, which in their younger days gazed down on the occasional fur trader ferrying his bulky packets along the swiftly moving currents. Nor that the call of the whippoorwill of a summer's night will be rudely interrupted by man-made noises. They want this little corner of the North American continent to remain close to its natural state so as to remind people of another day and age and of the treasures and the heritage that Mother Nature has bequeathed to them!"

ALBERT MARSHALL, *Brule Country*

★ ★ ★ ★ ★

THE BRULE RIVER WATERSHED is a Cinderella story in reverse as the homely step-sisters of nature work in concert to protect the lovely jewel. Springs bubbling from the unnavigable muck of the decomposing muskeg coalesce into the meager beginnings of the stream. The stark Pine Barrens, basically unchanged for hundreds of years despite periodic thinning, filter rain water and discourage development on the east side of the upper river. Small tributaries contribute to the consistent flow as do many springs south of Noyes Camp.

It is a fragile eco-system and any small blip in the status quo has an effect. Beaver dams on the tributary streamlets slow the flow of the river and logging near the creeks removes shade and raises water temperature which invites invasive species of flora and fish. Every now and then a northern pike, probably escaped from Lake Nebagamon via the creek, cruises the Brule in search trout to eat. Panfish have been caught. Narrow-leaved and hybrid cattails have invaded the stream, finding homes in Big and Lucius Lakes. Changing political winds in Wisconsin's capital tip the balance in favor of commerce, in the form of mining and logging, and threaten the Brule and Superior's south shore.

The river valley has been a pathway for many thousands of years ever since it was carved by rushing glacial meltwater from what was to become Lake Superior. Now recreational fishermen and canoers ply its waters. The Bad River Band of Ojibwe is nearby on their mainland reservation just south of the last stop of their prophesied migration; Madeline Island near the place "where food grows on the water." *Manoomin*, or wild rice, is not only an important part of their diet and a source of income for the band, but a major icon in their spiritual activities. Their stands of wild rice are being threatened by proposed mining activity in the area. The Bad River Band's fish hatcheries are also in peril.

Stewards of the Brule River and Ojibwe activists battle increased threats of logging and open pit mining which not only gouge the land and diminish the forest but damage the fishery and pollute the air. Drilling and blasting of rock on Superior's south side will send clouds of dust skyward as well as expose the 16,000-acre wetland to acid drainage, mercury and asbestos. A *New York Times* op-ed called the issue "The Fight for Wisconsin's Soul." At this time, the mining project has been put on hold. Sixty plants and animals in the Brule River Valley have been categorized as "endangered."

The natives fear for their traditional wild ricing beds in the Kakagon Slough. There is concern regarding the farming of wild rice by big agribusiness, not only due to competition but because of the lack of understanding of the grain's sacred importance in Ojibwe culture. The prospect of genetic engineering is also very worrisome.

A proposal to increase public access to the Brule at Big Lake has been floated, including a canoe landing and another walk-in site in addition to the one graciously provided by the Winneboujou Club. Increased canoe traffic not only disturbs anglers but also harms trout habitat and water clarity in the silt-bottomed widening of the river. Additional landings, launchings and paddle strokes would have a deleterious effect on the watershed. Thankfully the outcry against this proposal was so loud, the suggestion was withdrawn.

The issue is exacerbated by the popularity of single-person kayaks, which double the number of vessels, strokes and scrapings of gravel beds and sandbars when compared to two-person canoes. Once again, the main benefit is an economic boon for the local canoe/kayak rental companies and the downside is the danger to the unique, untrammeled nature of the Brule.

The latest threat is possibly the most serious. An old railroad grade and culvert on Nebagamon Creek are collapsing with possible catastrophic effect downstream from where the creek enters the Brule River. A total collapse would dam the creek, flood its watershed, and could send a 30,000 cubic yard "sand slug" into the Brule causing massive siltation, destruction of holes and spawning beds for trout, altering the channel and blocking the path of migratory species. One hundred-thirty thousand dollars are needed to study the issue and rectify it.

"Ojibwe prophecy speaks of a time during the seventh fire when our people will have a choice between two paths. The first path is well-worn and scorched. The second is new and green. It is our choice as communities and as individuals how we will proceed."

WINONA LaDUKE, OJIBWE ACTIVIST

★ ★ ★ ★ ★

Ojibwe culture is on the rebound in the north woods as many band members are increasingly returning to the old ways, culturally, spiritually and linguistically. There is a renewal of ceremonies like the sweat lodge and activities such as the game of Lacrosse which has laid dormant for the Ojibwe since the 1950s. Gathering of food stuffs such as wild rice, berries and maple syrup signal a return to the traditional diet for Ojibwe purists.

Some Ojibwe are turning to a "Decolonizing Diet," eating from the Great Lakes region foods available before European contact such as venison, corn, fish, maple syrup, pumpkins, squash and vegetables from their gardens to battle the trend of high rates of obesity, diabetes and heart disease caused in part by government-issued processed and engineered food. This effort is believed to engender an increase in self-worth and a reconnection to place.

The natives have fought legally and even physically to pursue their ancient traditions. They won the right to resume nocturnal deer hunting in northern Wisconsin. White-tailed deer meat is an important part of the Ojibwe diet and the U.S. District Court upheld 19th century treaties ignored by the state.

The Wisconsin Walleye War of the 1990s was particularly ugly. The Lac du Flambeau Band of Ojibwe battled to preserve their tradition of spearing walleyes by torch light. Non-native sportsmen harassed the band by driving them, and the DNR agents trying to keep the peace, towards the water by throwing rocks, pipe bombs and firing shotguns. Opponents of the practice encircled the Ojibwe by recklessly racing their boats around the native anglers and ramming them.

Matters came to a head in Park Rapids, where hundreds of police officers from around the state wore riot gear and brandished shields and clubs to enforce the rights of the band.

Many of the grand old lodges on the Brule are well over one hundred years old and show signs of deterioration, requiring extensive and costly rehabilitation. Thankfully we have kept pace with the structural needs of Noyes Camp and it remains in remarkable shape. Unfortunately the same cannot be said about our version of the Boys of Brule. Knee, ankle and hip replacements, stints and a pacemaker have become part of the vernacular as our 70th birthdays approach. A hearing aid salesman could make a killing. We lost our beloved life-long friend Rob Pearson to dementia and cherished comrade Charlie Hullsiek to cancer.

We still engage in our habitual pursuits albeit at a slower pace and with the occasional grunt and groan. Our sharp edges have been sanded and buffed by time. Few photos exist of our May weekends over the decades. There is something to be said for the misty musings of nostalgia.

We turn the pages of our mental scrapbooks and choose which memories to preserve and which to jettison. I like to think we are learning the important aspects of life as we mature, in addition to the duty and loyalty fostered by our comradery. They mirror the ancient teachings of the Seven Grandfathers passed on through the generations by Ojibwe elders: the guides to achieving *bimaadiziwin*, the Healthy Way of Life. Wisdom, love, respect, bravery, honesty, humility and truth. We fall short, but are making progress.

While the Brule is an escape from life's vicissitudes, the world can intrude. My mother's cousin Emerson, and his men's group, were at Noyes Camp on September 11, 2001, when the horror of senseless terrorism penetrated even the thick boreal forest of northwestern Wisconsin. A universal panacea does not exist, but the river is as close as it gets.

There is an old saying probably first uttered by some taciturn cowboy rolling a cigarette with one hand. It is emblematic of a certain code that applies to the Boys of Brule, people in the world on whom we can depend. *"He'll do to ride the river with."*

Perhaps Marsha Anderson, our Noyes Camp caretaker, paid us the ultimate compliment. She has witnessed almost everything there is to see up and down the Brule River. She once offered, *"Ross brings real men to Brule."*

★ ★ ★ ★ ★

"So we beat on, boats against the current, borne back ceaselessly into the past."
F. SCOTT FITZGERALD, *The Great Gatsby*

Owlets in Noyes Camp window box before fledging, May 2016 *Courtesy of Tom Melander*

Bald Eagle fishing in the Brule's lake section *Courtesy of Katie Bibbs*

Noyes family portrait at wedding of Margaret McLennan and Jack Morse, Lake Forest, Illinois, July 14, 1934

EXTRO

"And one day the Gitchie Gumee camp woke up, and songs and smiles and happy laughter greeted the sun, the river and the trees from Gitchie Gumee bend on which the camp is built… There is perhaps no lovelier spot upon the river than this camp. About a quarter of a mile above it the river sings in a broad and flowing reach almost a half-circle to the east, and for that distance holds a straight course to the bank, upon which stands the camp, at just that point marked by a broadly branching white pine that leans down and seems to whisper to the bright water, again the river swings with slow and graceful curve to its northern course. And there amid the pines some twenty feet above the stream, on the summit of the terraced bank, commanding both the western and northern sweep of the river, stands the camp. The rising sun glances over it to wake the stream, who sends back to her God a thousand sparkling smiles of welcome. In the evening his last rays settle upon and mingle with the flowing waters, burnishing every ripple, wave and curve with the glory of his light. And then from the bend above the shadows steal softly out, first in hesitating lines and points, then with broadening waves and folds, till night at last, softly and soothingly, takes the river to her bosom and the evening breeze murmurs…."

C.D. O'Brien, *Brule Chronicles*

C.D. O'Brien,
Winneboujou Club founder
Photo by Truman Ingersoll

Brule River guides, John LaRock (L) and Carl Pearson (R)

ACKNOWLEDGMENTS

"We paddle in the wake of those who came before us."

Unknown

A thank you is not nearly sufficient to honor my Great-grandparents George and Agnes Haskell Noyes for their foresight, dedication and generosity in building Noyes Camp which has housed seven generations with many more to come. Also gratitude to my cousins, who keep the vision alive and running smoothly when it could easily be a contentious mess. Although I knew them for a short time, I loved my Grandparents Edward and Margaret Noyes Harrison very much and wish I could have spent many more years with them at Brule. Grandpa would have appreciated the development of golf courses in the area.

My parents, Roger and Leslie Harrison Fruen, were the keepers of the flame and passed down many stories and rituals while creating countless more. I cherish my life time friendship with Rob Pearson who shared my devotion to Noyes Camp and was instrumental in advising repairs and enhancements to the building. I also give a nod and a wink to the Boys of Brule, you know who you are. Thanks always to the honorary Boy of Brule, Kelly Griffin.

Special mention is deserved for my cousin Lucie Tingley, Family Historian, and all the friends and family who contributed photos and information, particularly cousin Katherine McLennan Bradbury, who was a key source of family lore, photos, documents and some good gossip. I received solid advice and cogent quotes from cousin Virginia Clifford Anders and her book, *Joe's War*. A special tip of the hat to Marsha Anderson for putting up with us all these years and Roger Anderson for his insights.

I was inspired as a child by our neighbor, Dr. Arthur T. Holbrook, a wonderful man who wrote *From The Log of a Trout Fisherman* which perfectly captured the magic of the river and the early days of the Gitche Gumee Camping Club. Also thanks to the other authors who described the essence of the Brule River Valley including the Marshalls, O'Brien, Jerrard, Grimsrud, Wisherd, Berube and the many explorers and traders who chronicled their journeys up and down the river.

Much appreciation goes out to Scott Wisherd and his technical photo wizardry and Nan Wisherd for her unenviable task of keeping me on the straight and narrow and her suggestions to make this a better book. I greatly appreciate the artistic skills of Jackie Pechin and Larry Verkeyn who designed the text and cover treatments respectively. The Ojibwe people have my respect for imbuing the region with so much of its soul and their efforts to keep their culture alive in the face of many obstacles.

I am indebted to my teachers at Breck School, particularly Hazel Ramsay and Beatrice Brown, who lovingly maintained high standards for the rudiments of the English language and Tom Beech, who taught me how to think. Middlebury College's Professor John Conron opened my eyes to the inextricable relationship between America's spirit, history and landscape.

Thanks and no end of love to my wife Kristin who has supported and humored me throughout this project. I am so proud of my children Amy, Kyle and Laura who share the Dream of Brule and I feel unbridled joy at the sight of my grandsons, Max and Jack, as they discover the wonders of our Pastoral Ideal.

SELECTED BIBLIOGRAPHY

Allen, Lt. James, Diary, *1832*

Anders, Virginia Clifford, *Joe's War,* CreateSpace, 2016

Armstrong, Benjamin, *Early Life Among the Indians,* Press of A.W. Bowman, 1892

Associated Press, "Chance to Guide President Came Too Late For Antoine Dennis," 1928

Bardon, John, *Papers,* 1921-37

Berube, Lawence, *The Brule River: A Guide's Story,* 1998

Boutwell, Rev. William, Journal, 1832

Bowman, Dr. Frank, "The Battle that Saved the Brule," *Wisconsin Outdoor Magazine,* February 21, 1947

Brown, Daniel, *Under a Flaming Sky,* Lyons Press, 2016

Browne, J. Ross, "A Peep at Washoe," *Harper's New Monthly Magazine,* December 1860

Carley, Rachel, *Cabin Fever,* Simon and Schuster, 1998

Chequamegon History Blog

Cooley, Winnifred Harper, *The New Womanhood,* Broadway Publishing Company, 1904

Cribb, Robert, "Mystique of Male Bonding Lost on Woman Folk," *Toronto Star,* April 15, 2010

Deliverance, Screenplay, James Dickey, 1972

The Dental Review

Dubow, Charles A., "A-fish-inados snd Angler-files," *Forbes,* 1997

Edmonds, Michael, *Out of the North Woods,* Wisconsin Historical Society Press, 2009

Eliot, T.S., "The Little Gidding," *New English Weekly,* 1942

Emery, Sarah Smith, *Reminiscences of a Nonagerian,* W.H. Huse Printers, 1879

Erdrich, Louise, "Where I Ought to Be: A Writer's Sense of Place," *Louise Erdrich's Love Medicine: A Casebook,* Oxford University Press, 2000

Erlwine, Stephen Thomas, *All Music Guide*

Feldman, James W., *A Storied Wilderness,* University of Washington Press, 2011

The Forest History Society

Frost, Robert, "The Kitchen Chimney," *The Road Not Taken,* Macmillan, 2002

Gerard, Leigh and Richard, *The Brule River of Wisconsin,* Second Edition, CreateSpace, 2011

Gess, Denise and William Lutz, *Firestorm at Peshtigo,* Holt Paprtbacks, 2003

Great Lakes Indian and Fish and Wildlife Commission, *Ojibwe Journeys*

Greif, Geoffery, *Buddy System,* Oxford University Press, 2008

Grimsrud, Jane Pearson, *Brule River Forest and Lake Superior: Cloverland Anecdotes,* 2013

Grover, J.Z., "The Brule Comes Back," *Midwest Fly Fishing,* Volume 5, Issue 1

Haas, Joanne, Wisconsin DNR

Hayrinen, Taisto, *From the Anvil of Winneboujou,* Brule Co-op Association, 1945

Harmon, Daniel, *Journal,* 1802

Hawthorne, Nathaniel, *The House of the Seven Gables,* Ticknor and Fields, 1851

Hillenbrand, Laura, *Seabiscuit: An American Legend,* Random House, 2001

Holbrook, Dr. Arthur T., *From the Log of a Trout Fisherman,* Plimpton Press, 1949

Holbrook, Morris, Time, *Space and the Market,* M.E. Sharpe, 2003

Huffington Post

The Importance of the Obvious, *A Blog on the Political Philosophy of Calvin Coolidge*

Irving, Washington, "The Legend of Sleepy Hollow," *Sketch Book,* Donohue and Benneberry, 1819

Isaksen, Susie, "Gitche Gumee on the Brule River," *American Fly Fisherman Magazine,* Vol. 3, No. 2, Spring 1976

Johnston, Basil, *Ojibwe Heritage,* University of Nebraska Press, 1987

Kinzer, Stephen, *The Brothers,* Times Books, 2013

Kirby, Dr. Elizabeth, *Neuropsychophamacology,* 2016

Komarek, Edward, *Fire in Nature,* CreateSpace, 2014

LaDuke, Winona, HuffPost, 2010

Leoso, Edith, Bad River Band of Ojibwe

Lynes, Russell, *Snobs,* Harper, 1950

Marbury, Greg, *Aussie Observer*

McQuarrie, Gordon, "When the White Throats Sing," Willow Creek Press, 1985

Marshall, Caroline, "An Afternoon with the Angletons"

Marshall, Albert M., *Brule Country,* North Central Publishing Co., 1951

Milwaukee Bar Association, 1917

Memoirs of Milwaukee County

Meerick, George, *Old Times on the Upper Mississippi,* University of Minnesota Press, 2001

Morely, Jefferson, *The Ghost,* St, Martin's Press, 2017

New York Forest Commission

New York Times, 1897

Neusil, Mark and Norman Sims, *Canoes* University of Minnesota Press, 2016

Norgaard, Chantal, *Seasons of Change,* University of North Carolina Press, 2014

O'Brien, C.C., *Brule Chronicles,* Self-Published, 1890

Pellman, Jim, *Old Brule Heritage Society*

Pessen, Edward, *Log Cabin Myth,* Yale University Press, 1984

Pierce, Henry Clay, 1893

"The Presidency: Brule," *Time Magazine,* Vol. XI, No. 24, June 11, 1928

Putnam, Robert D., *Bowling Alone,* Simon and Schuster Paperbacks, 2000

Redmond, Christopher, *Welcome to America, Mr. Sherlock Holmes*, Dundurn Press, 1987

Ritter, Luke, *Immigrant Entrepreneurship,* German Historical Institute, 2015

Roosevelt, Robert Barnwell, *Superior Fishing,* Carleton, 1868

Sandlin, Lee, *Wicked River,* Vintage, 2011

Sieur du Lhut, Daniel Greysolon, Journal

Saunders, Mrs. E.N., *Winneboujou Chronicles,* Second Edition, 2015

Shepley, Carol Fenning, *Movers, Shakers, Scalawags and Suffragettes,* Missouri History Museum Press, 2015

Sieur, du Lhut, Daniel Greysolon, *Journal,*

Slow, Edwards, "The Wiltshire Moonraker," Salisbury Edwards, 1881

Stegner, Wallace, "The Sense of Place," Random House, 1992

Stuhler, Barbara, *Gentle Warriors, Minnesota Historical Society Press,* 2015

Superior Telegram, 1893

Therrien, Steve, *Trout Shadows,* 2014

"Tips for Male Bonding," *The Dude Perfect Show,* the Onion, 2016

Trento, Joseph, *The Secret History of the CIA, 1946-1989,* Basic Books, 2005

Various, *Winneboujou Chronicles, Second Edition,* 2015

Warren William, *History of the Ojibway People,* Minnesota Historical Society, 2009

Way, Niobe, *Deep Secrets,* Harvard University Press, 2011

Weyerhaeuser, Louise W., *Frederick W, Weyerhaeuser: Pioneer Lumberman*,

Wingerd, Mary Lethert, *North Country,* University of Minnesota Press, 2010

Wisherd, Nan, *Pathways,* Waino Publishing, 2005

Wisherd, Nan, *Brule River Country,* Cable Publishing, 2017

Floy Holbrook and Susie Markham head upriver
Photo by Truman Ingersoll

INDEX